# STERN DRIVE

## SERVICE • REPAIR HANDBOOK

### OMC • MerCruiser • Volvo
### Stern-Powr • Berkeley • Jacuzzi

**ERIC JORGENSEN**
*Editor*

**JEFF ROBINSON**
*Publisher*

*Published by*

## CLYMER PUBLICATIONS

*World's largest publisher of books devoted exclusively to
automobiles and motorcycles.*

**12860 MUSCATINE STREET • P.O. BOX 20 • ARLETA, CALIFORNIA 91331**

FIRST EDITION
First Printing June, 1975

SECOND EDITION
*Revised and updated*
First Printing September, 1977
Second Printing November, 1978
Third Printing April, 1979
Fourth Printing January, 1981

THIRD EDITION
*Revised and updated by Kalton C. Lahue*
First Printing August, 1982
Second Printing June, 1983


Printed in U.S.A.


ISBN: 0-89287-186-5


*Marina Lerique, production coordinator*

# CONTENTS

# CHAPTER ONE

# GENERAL INFORMATION

The stern drive, also called inboard-outboard drive, has become very popular in recent years as a means of propelling small and medium size boats. Its main advantages are the maneuverability of an outboard engine with the reliability and power of a 4-cycle engine. The stern drive installation allows the engine to be mounted in the extreme rear of the boat. This allows more efficient use of the limited space in a small boat.

Almost all engines used with stern drives are automobile engines that have been adapted for marine use. A majority of the engines are manufactured by Chrysler, Ford, and General Motors; a great many repair parts can be obtained from their automobile dealers. A typical marine conversion consists of adding water-cooled exhaust manifold(s), removing the cooling fan and radiator, exchanging the distributor for a more water-resistant, beefed-up system. In some cases, a different carburetor is used and another water pump added. The conventional air filter is exchanged for a flame-arresting filter. Sometimes a heavier duty alternator or generator is installed.

Engine maintenance requirements are quite similar to those for automobile engines, but should be performed more frequently. The marine engine operates under more severe conditions than a car engine. Most are used only

occasionally and then stored for long periods. When in use, it is subjected to dampness and prolonged operation at set speeds. These and other factors make a program of maintenance extremely important.

## MANUAL ORGANIZATION

This handbook provides maintenance and service information for Outboard Marine Corporation (OMC), MerCruiser, Volvo, and Stern-Powr stern drive systems, and Berkeley and Jacuzzi jet drives.

Chapter Two describes preventive maintenance and the recommended intervals for all models. A lubrication summary is also provided.

Chapter Three gives instructions for tuning the engine. Required tools are described in detail, and specifications for tuning most popular engines used with stern drives are given.

Recommendations are provided in Chapter Four for preparing the boat for extended storage and for removing the boat from storage. If these instructions are followed, both engine and stern drive life will be extended.

Chapter Five gives procedures for removing and installing OMC stern drives and engine assembly and disassembly procedures are also given. This chapter pertains to the OMC 100,

120, 140, 165, 170, 190, 225, and 245 models.

The MerCruiser line of stern drives is covered in Chapters Six and Seven. These chapters apply to 9 different models of the MerCruiser and contain installation, removal, assembly, and disassembly procedures.

The Volvo 110B, 200, 250, 270, 270T, 280, and 280T models are covered in Chapter Eight. Procedures are given for installation, removal, assembly, and disassembly.

Chapter Nine covers the Stern-Powr 80, 81, and 91 stern drive units. These units also are sold under a variety of "private brand" labels, including Dieseldrive, Aqua-Flite, and many others as well as the Stern-Powr label.

Chapter Ten covers Berkeley models 12JB and 12JC and the Jacuzzi model YJ jet drives. Installation, removal, disassembly, inspection, assembly, and adjustment procedures are given.

## SERVICE HINTS

When working around a marine engine, always keep a Coast Guard approved fire extinguisher handy. Also, *never smoke* while working around the engine. Gasoline fumes are heavier than air and tend to collect in the bilges under and around the engine.

The terms NOTE, CAUTION, and WARNING have specific meanings in this manual. A NOTE provides additional or explanatory information. A CAUTION is used to emphasize areas where equipment damage could result if proper precautions are not taken. A WARNING is used to stress those areas where personal damage or death could result from negligence, in addition to equipment damage.

Most of the service procedures covered are straightforward and can be performed by anyone reasonably handy with tools. It is suggested, however, that you consider your own capabilities carefully before attempting any operation involving major disassembly.

Carefully note the position of and tag or mark all parts while dismantling assemblies. If possible, lay them out in order to help with reassembly.

Disconnect battery when working on engine electrical wiring or components. However, never run engine with battery disconnected, as damage to alternator could result.

Tight or "frozen" bolts can usually be loosened by soaking with penetrating oil and rapping bolt head sharply with a hammer.

Parts, except those requiring a press fit, usually fit together easily. If a part is hard to install or remove, find the reason before proceeding.

Clean parts thoroughly and keep opening covered to avoid introducing dirt or other contamination.

As a rule, O-rings should not be reused, but should be replaced with new ones whenever removed. The same applies to cotter pins.

When special tools are called for, a clever mechanic can usually discover an acceptable substitute. If substitutes are used, however, care should be taken to avoid damage to parts.

Once you have decided to tackle the job yourself, read the entire section in this manual which pertains to it, making sure you have identified the proper one. Study the illustrations and text until you have a good idea of what is involved in completing the job satisfactorily. If special tools are required, make arrangements to get them before you start. It is frustrating and time-consuming to get partly into a job and then be unable to complete it.

## PERIODIC SERVICE
## AND PREVENTIVE
## MAINTENANCE HINTS

1. Perform the following steps if motor is used in salt water.

   a. Tilt stern drive unit out of water when not in use.

   b. Periodically run engine in fresh water to flush out salt deposits that form in the cooling system.

   NOTE: *An adapter for flushing engine with a garden hose is available from an authorized dealer.*

   c. Clean the outside of engine with fresh water.

   d. Periodically remove propeller and apply a lubricant to the propeller shaft.

NOTE: *If paint is chipped on propeller, apply touch up paint to avoid metal corrosion.*

2. Perform the following checks and services to prolong life and performance of all engines.

   a. Use type of fuel, oil, and grease specified by the manufacturer.

   b. Never run engine with stern drive out of water or test tank.

   c. Do not overrev engines with clutch in the NEUTRAL position. Speed control should never be advanced beyond START position.

   d. Replace gear lube in gear housing at proper intervals.

   e. Properly prepare motor for off-season storage.

   f. Check propeller shaft seals after every year's use or immediately after contact with monofilament fishing line, or similar foreign objects.

   g. Never use electric starter continuously for more than 15 seconds without allowing at least 3 minutes for starter to cool.

   h. Shift gears rapidly at the proper engine speed. Do not ease gears. This causes excessive wear to the gears and clutch.

   i. Check all items subject to normal wear (water pump impeller, breaker points, spark plugs, starter ropes, starter pawls, shear pins, and items of a similar nature) at least once every season.

   j. Perform tune-up at the beginning of each season. Periodically clean, inspect, and adjust the carburetor.

   k. Never exceed recommended rpm range.

   l. Adequately protect engine against excessive spray and backwash. Spray or backwash may cause premature corrosion.

3. Perform the following steps prior to long periods of disuse or off-season storage.

   a. If engine has been used in salt water, completely flush as previously described.

   b. Run engine to operating temperature.

   c. With gearshift in NEUTRAL, run engine at fast idle. Remove fuel line from engine and quickly inject rust preventive oil in the air intakes for 10-20 seconds or until the engine dies.

   d. Drain fuel tank, lines, and carburetor.

   e. Remove spark plugs and squirt 1 or 2 ounces of engine oil into cylinders and crank engine through a few times to distribute oil. Replace spark plugs.

   f. Lubricate all miscellaneous moving parts.

   g. Remove propeller and lubricate propeller shaft. Reinstall propeller.

   h. Clean exterior of the engine.

# CHAPTER TWO

# PREVENTIVE MAINTENANCE

Almost all gasoline engines used with stern drive mechanisms are based on automobile engines. The average pleasure boat engine, however, operates under conditions which are far more severe than those encountered by the average automobile engine. This is especially true if the engine uses raw water cooling and is used in salt or polluted water. Regular preventive maintenance, if strictly followed, will pay dividends in longer engine life and safer boat operation.

This chapter offers suggestions for such a program. The maintenance intervals suggested (see **Table 1**) are a general guide only. If the engine is used regularly, the maintenance intervals can be stretched out. Inactivity permits moisture and dust to collect in and on the engine. This leads to rust, corrosion, and other damage. Active use of the boat helps prevent deterioration.

## PRE-OPERATIONAL CHECKS

Before starting the engine for the first time each day, make the following checks.

1. Remove the engine compartment cover and smell for raw gasoline fumes. If strong fumes are present, determine and correct the source before proceeding.

WARNING
*Always have a Coast Guard approved fire extinguisher close at hand when working around the engine.*

2. Check the engine oil level with the dipstick. Add oil if the level is low.

3. Check the electrolyte level in each battery cell. Add water if needed.

4. Check condition of all belts. If a belt is in doubtful condition, replace it. Spares are difficult to obtain offshore.

5. Check all water hoses for leaks, tight connections, and general condition. Repair or replace as necessary.

6. Visually check the fuel filter and/or sediment bowl. Clean or replace filter element if indicated.

7. Check oil levels in the stern drive unit. Add lubricant if required.

8. Check the fluid level in the hydraulic lift and/or trim unit reservoirs. Add fluid if needed.

9. Check bilge for excessive water. Drain or pump dry if present.

10. Turn on fuel tank valve(s).

11. Connect the battery cables to the battery (if disconnected) and replace the engine compartment cover.

Table 1 PERIODIC CHECKS

| | Every 14 Days* | After 50 Hours Operating Time** | After 100 Hours Operating Time** |
|---|---|---|---|
| Check engine oil | X | | |
| Change engine oil | | X | |
| Change filter | | | X |
| Check battery level | X | | |
| Check stern drive oil level | X | | |
| Change stern drive oil | | X | |
| Lubricate fittings in stern drive | | X | |
| Tune engine | | | X |
| Check fuel filter | X | | |
| Check spark plugs | | | X |
| Check belts and hoses | X | | |
| Check hydraulic lift oil level | X | | |
| Check anti-electrolysis devices | X | | |
| Check propeller for nicks, dents, etc. | X | | |
| Clean flame arrestor | | X | |
| Flush engine cooling system | | Each use in salt water | |

*Or each usage, whichever occurs first.
**Or once each season, whichever occurs first.

12. Check sacrificial electrolysis elements, if so equipped. Replace if more than 50 percent consumed.

13. Check propeller for nicks, dents, missing metal, etc. Repair or replace if damaged.

## STARTING CHECK LIST

After performing the pre-operational checks above, the following starting check list should be followed.

1. Operate engine compartment blower for at least 5 minutes before starting.

2. Verify that the stern drive unit is fully down, or in operating position.

3. If engine is cold, prime by operating the throttle one or two times. Set manual choke (if so equipped) to closed position.

4. Verify that gearshift lever is in neutral position.

### WARNING
*Make certain a fully charged fire extinguisher is at hand before attempting to start engine.*

5. Start engine and allow to warm up at idle speed for a few minutes.

### CAUTION
*Prolonged operation of the engine with the gearshift lever in neutral can cause damage to gears or in the stern drive unit (some models) due to improper circulation of lubricant.*

6. Observe gauges and warning lights to verify that engine is not overheating, that proper oil pressure is present, and that battery is not discharging. If any of these conditions occurs, shut

down engine at once and determine and correct cause before proceeding.

## POST-OPERATIONAL CHECKS

After each use, perform the following maintenance.

1. If the boat was used in salt or polluted water, flush the cooling system with fresh water. This minimizes corrosion and buildup of deposits in the cooling system. Many stern drive engines are equipped with flushing devices, and garden hose adapters are available for almost all models.

2. Disconnect battery cables from battery. It is a good idea to remove the battery from the boat to prevent theft.

3. Shut off fuel tank valve(s).

4. If possible, top off fuel tanks. This discourages moisture condensation in the tanks.

5. If water is present in the bilge, either drain or pump dry.

6. Wash interior and exterior surfaces of the boat with fresh water.

## PERIODIC ENGINE MAINTENANCE

The maintenance tasks discussed in this section should be performed at approximately the intervals indicated in Table 1. These intervals are guidelines; consider the frequency and extent of boat use when setting actual intervals. The following items should be performed every 50 or 100 hours of operating time, or at least once per season.

### Changing Engine Oil

Engine oil should be changed after every 50 hours of operating time, or once per season, whichever occurs first. The types and weights of oil recommended by some of the leading manufacturers are shown in **Table 2**.

Most installations do not leave enough space to permit the use of the oil drain plug in the bottom of the oil pan. A pump is the most common device used to drain oil from the crankcase. The pump has a long flexible hose which may be inserted into the oil dipstick tube and fed into the crankcase. Several makes of pumps are available at marine supply dealers. Some are hand operated, some are motorized, and others are designed to be operated by electric drill motors. The used oil should be discharged into a sealable container and disposed of properly. Used oil should never be dumped overboard. Plastic bleach and milk containers make excellent containers for used oil.

### Changing Oil Filters

The oil filter element should be changed every other oil change if the boat is used regularly, or at least once each season. Some manufacturers recommend that the filter be changed with every oil change. Filters are usually the "spin on" type. An inexpensive filter wrench is available at any auto parts or marine supply house. This wrench will come in handy in removing filters, but should not be used in installation.

When removing a filter, make certain a container is placed under the filter to catch any oil which may drain from the element. Wipe up any spills.

To install the filter, lubricate the filter gasket with a small amount of clean engine oil, and thread the element down hand-tight. Do not use a wrench or overtighten. A firm fit is all that is required; too much torque can damage the filter or cause leaks.

### Fuel Filter

Remove and clean fuel filter bowls. Filter elements should be replace at least once a year and more often if operating conditions are severe.

> NOTE: *In areas where only poor quality fuel is available, or where moisture tends to condense in fuel tanks, the addition of special fuel filters to remove moisture and other contaminants may be advisable.*

### Flame Arrestor

The flame arrestor serves as both an air filter and as a safety measure against backfiring. The flame arrestor should be removed, washed in solvent, and thoroughly dried before replacing at least every 50 hours or once per season.

### Table 2    ENGINE LUBRICANTS

| Make and Model | Capacity With Filter | Type | Weight | Oil and Filter Change Frequency |
|---|---|---|---|---|
| **MerCruiser** | | | | |
| 60 | 5.3 pt. | SE | 30W | ① |
| 80 | 5 qt. | SE | 30W | ① |
| 90 | 5 qt. | SE | 30W | ① |
| 110-120 | 4 qt. | SE | 30W | ① |
| 140 | 4 qt. | SE | 30W | ① |
| 140 | 5 qt. | SE | 30W | ① |
| 150 | 5 qt. | SE | 30W | ① |
| 160-165 | 5 qt. | SE | 30W | ① |
| 470 | 5 qt. | SE | 30W | ① |
| 200 | 6 qt. | SE | 30W | ① |
| 888 | 6 qt. | SE | 30W | ① |
| 190 | 5 qt. | SE | 30W | ① |
| 215 | 7 qt. | SE | 30W | ① |
| 225 | ** | SE | 30W | ① |
| 225II-TR | 6 qt. | SE | 30W | ① |
| 233 | 5 qt. | SE | 30W | ① |
| 250 | 7 qt. | SE | 30W | ① |
| 255 TR | 5 qt. | SE | 30W | ① |
| 255II-TR | 5 qt. | SE | 30W | ① |
| 270 | 7 qt. | SE | 30W | ① |
| 280 TRS | 5 qt. | SE | 30W | ① |
| 310 | 5 qt. | SE | 30W | ① |
| 325 | 8 qt. (approx.) | SE | 30W | ① |
| 390 | 8 qt. (approx.) | SE | 30W | ① |
| **OMC** | | | | |
| 100-120 | 4 qt. 3.5+0.5 | SE | 30W | ① |
| 140 | 4 qt. 3.5+0.5 | SE | 30W | ① |
| 165 | 4.5 qt. 4+0.5 | SE | 30W | ① |
| 175 | 6 qt. | SE | 30W | ① |
| 190 | 6 qt. | SE | 30W | ① |
| 225-245 | 6 qt. 5+1 | SE | 30W | ① |
| 235 | 6 qt. | SE | 30W | ① |
| **Volvo-Penta** | | | | |
| AQ130A, B and C | 4 qt. | SE | 10W40 | ② |
| AQ140A | 6 qt. | SE | 10W40 | ② |
| AQ165A | 6 qt. | SE | 10W40 | ② |
| AQ170A | 6 qt. | SE | 10W40 | ② |

(continued)

Table 2    ENGINE LUBRICANTS (continued)

| Make and Model | Capacity With Filter | Type | Weight | Oil and Filter Change Frequency |
|---|---|---|---|---|
| AQ190A | 5 qt. | SE | 10W40 | ② |
| AQ200A, B and C | 5 qt. | SE | 10W40 | ② |
| AQ225A, B and C | 5 qt. | SE | 10W40 | ② |
| AQ240A | 5 qt. | SE | 10W40 | ② |
| AQ255A | 5 qt. | SE | 10W40 | ② |
| **Chrysler** | | | | |
| M122B | 4 qt. | SE | 30W | ② |
| M183B | 6 qt. | SE | 30W | ② |
| M225D | 5 qt. | SE | 30W | ② |
| SB II | 5 qt. | SE | 30W | ② |
| Jet II | 5 qt. | SE | 30W | ② |
| 195 | 5 qt. | SE | 30W | ② |
| 240 | 5 qt. | SE | 30W | ② |
| SB III | 5 qt. | SE | 30W | ② |
| Jet III | 5 qt. | SE | 30W | ② |
| 265 | 5 qt. | SE | 30W | ② |
| **Waukesha** | | | | |
| 351/4 | 7 qt. | Premium | 10W30 or 10W40 | ② |
| 302/2B | 6 qt. | Premium | 10W30 or 10W40 | ② |
| 302/2A | 6 qt. | Premium | 10W30 or 10W40 | ② |
| 302/2 | 6 qt. | Premium | 10W30 or 10W40 | ② |
| 304/4 | 6 qt. | Premium | 10W30 or 10W40 | ② |
| **Chris Craft** | | | | |
| 305 GLV | 6 qt. | SE | 30W or 10W40 | ③ |
| 307 GLV | 6 qt. | SE | 30W or 10W40 | ③ |
| 307 GCLL | 6 qt. | SE | 30W or 10W40 | ③ |
| 307 QLV | 7 qt. | SE | 30W or 10W40 | ③ |
| 302 FLV | 5 qt. | SE | 30W or 10W40 | ③ |
| 350 FLV | 5 qt. | SE | 30W or 10W40 | ③ |
| 350 GLV | 6 qt. | SE | 30W or 10W40 | ③ |
| 283 FLV | 6 qt. | SE | 30W or 10W40 | ③ |
| 225 B101 | 5 qt. | SE | 30W or 10W40 | ③ |
| 307 B101 | 7 qt. | SE | 30W or 10W40 | ③ |
| 225 BVC | 5 qt. | SE | 30W or 10W40 | ③ |

(continued)

Table 2    ENGINE LUBRICANTS (continued)

| Make and Model | Capacity With Filter | Type | Weight | Oil and Filter Change Frequency |
|---|---|---|---|---|
| Berkeley Packajet | | | | |
| 455-2 | 5 qt. | SE | 20W or 10W30 | ④ |
| 455-3 | 5 qt. | SE | 20W or 10W30 | ④ |
| 455-4 | 5 qt. | SE | 20W or 10W30 | ④ |
| 455 | 5 qt. | SE | 20W or 10W30 | ④ |
| 350 | 5 qt. | SE | 20W or 10W30 | ④ |
| 350-3 | 5 qt. | SE | 20W or 10W30 | ④ |
| 351 | 5 qt. | SE | 20W or 10W30 | ④ |
| 302 | 5 qt. | SE | 20W or 10W30 | ④ |
| 460 | 5 qt. | SE | 20W or 10W30 | ④ |

*32 to 90°F. Use lighter oil for operation in colder weather and heavier oil for temperatures consistently above 90°F.

**Engines with serial No. 2278646 and below: 5 qt.; above use 7 qt.

① Change oil and filter after first 20 hours of operation; thereafter, every 50 hours or once per season (whichever occurs first).

② Change oil and filter after first 25 hours of operation; thereafter, every 50 hours or once per season (whichever occurs first).

③ Change oil and filter after first 15-20 hours of operation; thereafter, every 50 hours or once per season (whichever occurs first).

④ Change oil and filter after first 10 hours of operation; thereafter, every 50 hours or once per season (whichever occurs first).

### Tune-up

The engine should be tuned and the spark plugs cleaned, or preferably replaced, every 100 hours or at least once per season. See Chapter Three for tune-up instructions.

## PERIODIC STERN DRIVE MAINTENANCE

The following sections describe periodic maintenance recommended by the manufacturers of OMC, MerCruiser, Volvo, Stern-Powr, Berkeley, and Jacuzzi stern drives. **Table 3** lists lubricants recommended by the manufacturers; substitutions could cause damage and may void your warranty.

## OUTBOARD MARINE CORPORATION MAINTENANCE

### Changing Drive Unit Lubricant

Lubricant in the drive unit should be changed every 50 hours or at least once a season.

**Table 3    STERN DRIVE LUBRICANTS**

| Make | Component | Recommended Lubricant | Capacity | Figure | Change Frequency | Instructions |
|------|-----------|----------------------|----------|--------|------------------|--------------|
| OMC 100, 120, 140, 165 | Upper gearcase | OMC Sea-Lube gear-case lubricant (formerly type C). | 13.5 oz. | 1 and 2 | 50 hours or twice each season | Drain: Remove filler plug on top of unit and drain plug on starboard side of upper gearcase. Tilt unit slightly to aid in draining. |
| | | Note: The manufacturer warns against the use of hypoid 90 oil or any other general purpose 90W oil. This warning applies to all usage where OMC Sea-Lube is recommended. | | | | Fill: Place drive in down position. Remove oil level plug on starboard side of upper gearcase (above drain plug), fill with OMC Sea-Lube, using drain plug hole, until oil is level with oil level opening. Replace and tighten filler plug and oil level plug before removing lubricant tube. Then remove Sea-Lube tube and replace and tighten drain plug. Use filler plug on top when adding lube. |
| OMC 175, 190, 225, 235, 245 | Upper gearcase | OMC Sea-Lube gear-case lubricant | 18.25 oz. | 1 and 2 | 50 hours or twice each season | Same as above |
| OMC (all models) | Intermediate housing | OMC Sea-Lube gear case lubricant | 6.25 oz. | 1 and 2 | 50 hours or twice each season | Remove fill plug and fill through opening until lubricant is visible at top. Replace and tighten fill plug. |
| OMC (all models) | Tilt unit gearcase | OMC Premium 4-cycle engine oil | | 4 | 50 hours or twice each season | Remove oil fill and level plug. Fill until oil is visible through opening. Replace and tighten plug. |
| OMC (all models) | Lower gearcase | OMC Sea-Lube gear-case lubricant | 33.9 oz. | 3 | 1st 10 hours, then each 50 hours or twice each season | Drain and Flush: Place unit in down position and remove oil level and oil drain plugs. Tilt unit slightly to aid in draining. Fill gearcase with kerosene or fuel oil from lower hole until fluid can be seen at upper hole. Replace oil level plug securely and then remove liquid filler tube at lower hole and replace oil drain plug as rapidly as possible to prevent liquid spillage. Place boat in water or drive unit in test tank. Run engine in neutral for not more than one minute to agitate fliud. Remove boat or unit from water and remove plugs and allow to drain. Fill unit with OMC Sea-Lube, using lower hole as above. |

(continued)

Table 3   STERN DRIVE LUBRICANTS (continued)

| Make | Component | Recommended Lubricant | Capacity | Figure | Change Frequency | Instructions |
|---|---|---|---|---|---|---|
| OMC (all models) | Tilt shaft bearings | OMC Sea-Lube anti-corrosion lubricant | N/A | 1 | Every 20 hours | Use grease gun to apply lubricant at fittings shown in figure. |
| OMC (all models) | Swivel bearings | OMC Sea-Lube anti-corrosion lubricant | N/A | 5 | Every 20 hours | Remove plug and use grease gun to lubricate through fitting. Replace plug. |
| OMC (also equipped) | Tru-Course steering shaft front bearing | OMC Sea-Lube anti-corrosion lubricant | N/A | — | Every 20 hours | Use grease gun to apply lubricant at fitting. |
| Volvo 100 | Stern drive | SAE 10W 30 (alt. 20W 40) | 3¼ qt. | 34 | Every 100 hours or once each season | Remove dipstick and drain plug. Replace drain plug and fill through dipstick hole with drive unit in down position. Replace and tighten dipstick. |
| | Drive shaft bearing | Multipurpose grease | N/A | — | Every 50 hours or twice each season | Fill lubricator cup and screw it in all the way. |
| | Steering shaft | Multipurpose grease | N/A | 34 | Every 50 hours or twice each season | Use grease gun and fill through fitting shown in figure; cover outside of rod with grease. |
| | Steering rod | Multipurpose grease | N/A | 34 | Every 50 hours or twice each season | |
| Volvo 200 (to No. 219751) Volvo 200 (No. 219752 on) Volvo 250 | Stern drive | SAE 90W multipurpose, 10W30 or 10W40 | 2+ qt. | 35 and 36 | Every 100 hours or once each season | Tilt unit up and remove oil drain and filling plugs and drain unit. Replace and tighten drain plug. Fill through fill plug. Replace fill plug and lower unit. Allow oil to settle, then remove and wipe dipstick. Insert dipstick (do not screw in) and check oil level. Add as required through dipstick hole. |
| | Drive and steering shaft bearing | Multipurpose grease | N/A | 37 | Every 50 hours or twice each season | Fill lubricator cup and screw down all the way. Lubricate pivot yoke through filling with grease gun. |
| Volvo 270-280 | Stern drive | SAE 10W30 or 20W40 oil | 2¼-2½ qt. | 38, 39 and 40 | Every 100 hours or once each season | Same as for Volvo 200 |
| | Steering shaft, drive shaft bearing, steering rod | Multipurpose grease | N/A | 38 | Every 50 hours or twice each season | Same as for Volvo 100 |

(continued)

2

Table 3     STERN DRIVE LUBRICANTS (continued)

| Make | Component | Recommended Lubricant | Capacity | Figure | Change Frequency | Instructions |
|---|---|---|---|---|---|---|
| Volvo 270T-280T | Stern drive | SAE 10W30 or 20W40 oil | 2¼-2½ qt. N/A | 38, 39, and 40 | Every 100 hours or once each season | Same as for Volvo 270-280. |
| | Steering shaft, drive shaft bearing, steering rod | Multipurpose grease | | 38 | Every 50 hours or twice each season | Same as for Volvo 270-280. |
| | Hydraulic pump | ATF type F | | | Every 14 days | Check with dipstick and add as required. |
| Volvo 750 | Outboard drive | Above 68°F SAE 30W 14° to 68°F SAE 20W | 18 qt. | 41 | Every 1,000 hours | Remove drain and fill plugs and drain. Replace and tighten drain plug. Fill through fill hole. Check oil level at transparent expansion tank inside boat, top up as required, replace and tighten fill plug. |
| | Hydraulic tank | Same as for outdrive | 7 qt. | — | Every 1,000 hours | Tip up drive unit and disconnect and drain 2 hydraulic hoses. Move lever until no more oil runs out. Tip drive down and again drain hoses. Reconnect hoses. Change filter (in tank on engine). Fill with oil and turn over engine with starter. Top up as required, move lever back and forth and tip up as required. Start engine, tilt drive once or twice and top up as required. |
| Volvo 750 | Suspension pins | Water resistant grease | N/A | — | Once each season | Use grease gun to apply at fitting. |
| Dieseldrive 91 | Stern drive | SAE 90 Hypoid | 30 pt. | 42 | Once each season | Remove drain and fill plugs and drain unit. Replace drain screw and fill through filler plug hole and replace filler plug. |
| 81 | Stern drive | SAE 90 Hypoid | 26 pt. | 42 | Once each season | |
| 80 | Stern drive | SAE 90 Hypoid | 8 or 9 pt. | —* | Once each season | |
| MerCruiser 60, 80, 90 | Grease points Outside boat | Quicksilver Multipurpose Lube (C-92-49588) | N/A | 22 | Each 50 hours | Apply with grease gun through fittings shown in figure. |

(continued)

*Drain and fill plugs in same general location as Models 91 and 81.     Oil level check screw on upper rear of unit, rather than side.

**Table 3    STERN DRIVE LUBRICANTS** (continued)

| Make | Component | Recommended Lubricant | Capacity | Figure | Change Frequency | Instructions |
|---|---|---|---|---|---|---|
| | Inside boat | Quicksilver Multipurpose Lube (C-92-49588) | N/A | 20 and 21 | Each 50 hours | Apply at points shown in figures. |
| MerCruiser 0 and I | Grease points Outside boat | Quicksilver Multipurpose Lube (C-92-49588) | N/A | 23 and 24 | Each 50 hours | Apply with grease gun through fittings shown in figures. |
| | Inside boat | Quicksilver Multipurpose Lube (C-92-49588) | N/A | 20 and 21 | Each 50 hours | Apply at points shown in figures. |
| MerCruiser II 200-225 | Grease points Outside boat | Quicksilver Multipurpose Lube (C-92-49588) | N/A | 27 and 28 | Each 50 hours | Apply at points shown in figures. |
| | Inside boat | Quicksilver Multipurpose Lube (C-92-49588) | N/A | 26 | Each 50 hours | Apply at point shown in figure. |
| MerCruiser 215, II-TR and II-TRS | Grease points Outside boat | Quicksilver Multipurpose Lube (C-92-49588) | N/A | 29 | Each 50 hours | Apply at point shown in figure. |
| | Inside boat | Quicksilver Multipurpose Lube (C-92-49588) | N/A | 30 and 31 | Each 50 hours | Apply at points shown in figures. |
| MerCruiser III | Grease points Outside boat | Quicksilver Multipurpose Lube (C-92-49588) | N/A | — | Each 50 hours | Apply at points shown in figures. |
| | Inside boat | Quicksilver Multipurpose Lube (C-92-49588) | N/A | 32 and 33 | Each 50 hours | Apply at points shown in figures. |

(continued)

2

Table 3    STERN DRIVE LUBRICANTS (continued)

| Make | Component | Recommended Lubricant | Capacity | Figure | Change Frequency | Instructions |
|---|---|---|---|---|---|---|
| MerCruiser 0 60 | Stern drive* | Quicksilver Super-Duty Lubricant (C-92-52650) | 18.3 oz. | 13 and 14 | Every 100 hours | Remove oil vent (upper) and oil fill (lower) plugs and allow lubricant to drain. Fill through lower opening until fluid can be seen in upper vent opening. Replace and tighten upper oil vent plug. Remove and rapidly replace and tighten lower oil fill plug. New gaskets should be used on plugs with each lubricant change. Procedure (filling from bottom) is same, whether upper and lower chambers are connected or separated. Run unit in water for not more than one minute and recheck oil level. Add more lubricant if required. |
| MerCruiser 0 80-90 | Stern drive* | Quicksilver Super-Duty Lubricant (C-92-52650) | 22 oz. | 13 and 14 | Every 100 hours | |
| 1 | Drive shaft housing | Quicksilver Super-Duty Lubricant (C-92-52650) | 8 oz. | 15 | Every 100 hours | |
| 1 | Gear housing | Quicksilver Super-Duty Lubricant (C-92-52650) | 18 oz. | 16 | Every 100 hours | |
| MerCruiser I 1A, 1B, and 1C 1A, 1B, and 1C | Drive shaft housing Gear housing | Quicksilver Super-Duty Lubricant (C-92-52650) | 8 oz. 23 oz. | 15 16 | Every 100 hours | |
| MerCruiser I 120, 140, 160, 470, 165, 888, 200, 225S, 233 | Stern drive* | Quicksilver Super-Duty Lubricant (C-92-52650) | 28 oz. | 13 and 14 | Every 100 hours | |
| MerCruiser II 190, 200, 225, 310 | Stern drive* | Quicksilver Super-Duty Lubricant (C-92-52650) | 5¾ qt.** | 13 and 14 | Every 100 hours | |
| MerCruiser with heavy duty gear housing | Stern drive* | Quicksilver Super-Duty Lubricant (C-92-52650) | 7 qt.** | 13 and 14 | Every 100 hours | |
| MerCruiser III 250, 270, 325, 390 | Stern drive* | Quicksilver Super-Duty Lubricant (C-92-52650) | 4½ qt.** | 17 | Every 100 hours | |
| MerCruiser 215H, 215E, II-TR, II-TRS | Stern drive* | Quicksilver Super-Duty Lubricant (C-92-52650) | 4 qt.** | 17 | Every 100 hours | |

*Drive shaft and gear housing gear chambers are connected.    **Approximately

1. To change lubricant in upper gearcase, remove filler plug at top of unit (2, **Figure 1**) and the oil drain plug on the starboard side of the upper gearcase (2, **Figure 2**). Tilt the unit slightly to completely drain the unit. Return unit to down position and remove oil level plug on side of gearcase. Install filler plug.

> NOTE: *Install oil level plug before removing lubricant tube from lower drain plug. This creates an air lock and holds the oil in the gear case until the drain plug can be replaced.*

2. Insert end of gearcase lubricant tube (OMC Sea-Lube Gearcase Lubricant) into oil drain hole and fill upper gearcase until oil appears at oil level opening. Install oil level plug, then remove tube. Install filler plug. When changing or adding oil, always allow time for oil to settle and fill cavities. Then recheck level and add more lubricant if required.

3. The lower gearcase should be drained and flushed with kerosene after the first 10 hours of operation (when new). To drain, place stern drive unit in down position and remove oil level and oil drain plugs. See **Figure 3**. Tilt unit slightly to aid in draining.

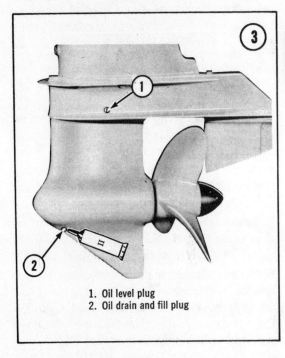

1. Oil level plug
2. Oil drain and fill plug

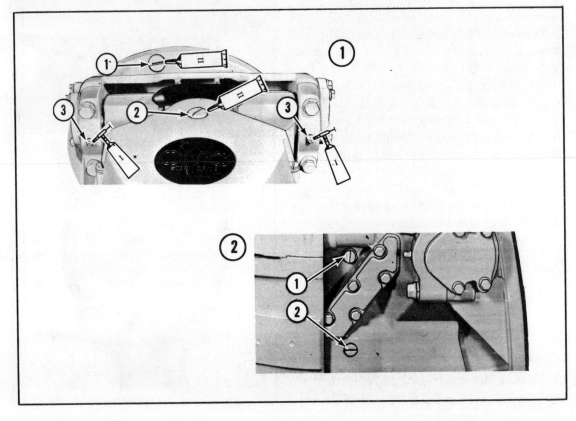

4. To flush the unit, fill it with kerosene and replace plugs securely. Place drive unit in water or test tank and run engine in neutral for not more than one minute. Drain flushing liquid.

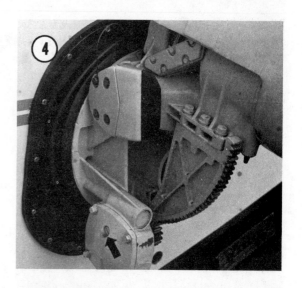

CAUTION
*Do not run unit out of water when flushing gearcase as damage to the water pump impeller may result.*

5. After flushing, fill gearcase with lubricant (OMC Sea-Lube Gearcase Lubricant) through bottom "oil drain" opening.

6. When lubricant reaches "oil level" opening, replace oil level plug and then remove lubricant tube. Quickly replace oil drain plug.

7. Allow lubricant to settle for a few minutes, then recheck level. Add more lubricant, if required. Add lubricant through oil level opening.

8. To add lubricant to the intermediate housing, remove oil fill and level plug (see Figure 1) and fill with lubricant (OMC Sea-Lube Gearcase Lubricant) until oil is level with hole. Remove tube and replace plug.

9. To change oil in intermediate housing, remove oil reservoir cover, remove oil, and flush with solvent such as kerosene, dry reservoir, and replace cover, using a new gasket and gasket compound. Add fresh lubricant (Step 8).

10. Lubricate the 2 tilt shaft fittings (see Figure 1) with a grease gun (OMC Sea-Lube Anti-Corrosion Lubricant) every 20 hours.

11. The tilt unit gearcase should be lubricated with SAE 30 premium grade motor oil (the manufacturer recommends only OMC Premium 4-cycle motor oil). Oil is added through the oil level and fill plug opening (see **Figure 4**).

12. Lubricate swivel bearings by removing plug (see **Figure 5**) and injecting grease into the swivel bearing fitting. (The manufacturer recommends OMC Sea-Lube Anti-Corrosion Lubricant.)

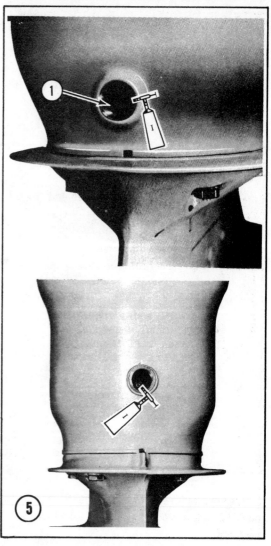

## MERCRUISER MODEL O (60, 80, 90) MAINTENANCE

### Checking Lubricant Level

1. Remove oil vent plug and gasket located on side of drive shaft housing (see **Figure 6**). Oil

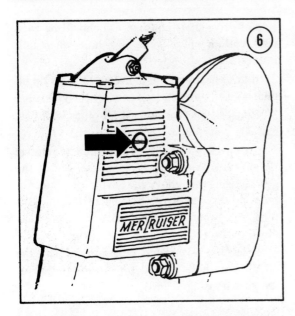

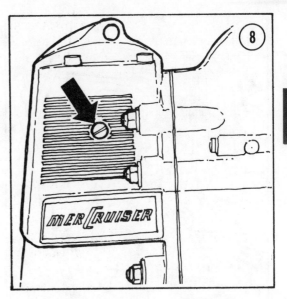

**2**

must be even with bottom of vent plug hole when unit is level.

2. If level is down, a small amount can be added through the oil fill plug hole on the opposite side of drive shaft housing.

3. Reinstall oil vent and oil fill plugs with new gaskets.

### Changing Lubricant

1. Remove drain plug from lower end of gear housing on left side (see **Figure 7**) and oil vent plug on upper gear chamber (see **Figure 8**). Tilt unit slightly to aid drainage.

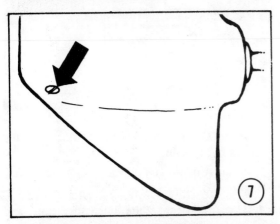

2. Insert lubricant tube into lower drain plug and fill until oil runs from upper oil vent plug hole.

3. Install oil vent plug first, then quickly remove lubricant tube and replace drain plug. Make certain new washer is under each plug to prevent water from leaking into lubricant chamber.

### Lubrication

*Inside Boat* (**Figures 9 and 10**): apply lubricant to (A) Ride-Guide steering cable end next to hand nut; (B) pivot socket of steering arm; and (C) exposed cable traversing through guide tube.

*Outside Boat* (**Figure 11**): Apply lubricant to all grease fittings, and all pivot points.

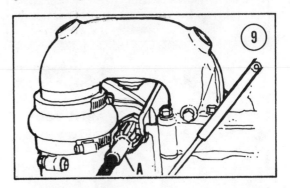

**MERCRUISER EARLY MODEL I
MAINTENANCE
(IA, IB, AND IC)**

### Checking Lubricant Level

1. To check upper gear chamber, remove oil vent plug and gasket (see **Figure 12**) located on

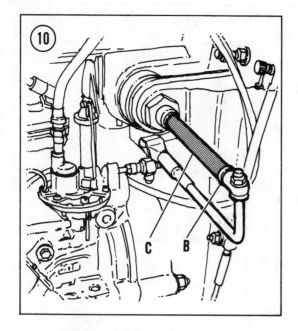

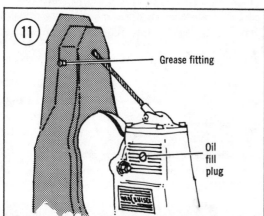

Grease fitting

Oil fill plug

Oil Vent Plug

side of drive shaft housing. Oil should be even with bottom of oil vent plug hole when unit is level.

2. If level is down, add lubricant through oil fill plug hole on opposite side of drive shaft housing.

3. Reinstall oil vent and oil fill plugs with new gaskets.

4. To check the lower gear chamber, remove the oil vent plug and gasket on the side of the gear housing just above the cavitation plate. Oil must be level with the bottom of the oil vent plug hole when the drive unit is level in the down position.

5. If level is down, add lubricant through the oil fill plug hole located on the lower side of the gear housing.

### Changing Lubricant (Upper Chamber)

1. Remove top cover (**Figure 13**). Remove old lubricant with a pump.

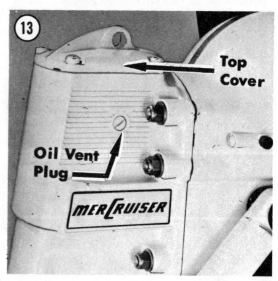

Top Cover

Oil Vent Plug

2. Reinstall top cover and O-ring. Torque screws to 20 ft.-lb.

3. Remove oil fill and oil vent plugs and gaskets (Figure 13).

4. Insert lubricant tube into filler hole and inject lubricant until it runs out of oil vent plug hole.

5. Reinstall oil fill and oil vent plugs with new washers.

### Changing Lubricant (Lower Chamber)

1. Remove filler plug (**Figure 14**) from lower end of gear housing on left side and oil vent plug just above cavitation plate to drain unit.

2. Insert lubricantion tube into filler plug hole and inject oil until it starts to flow from oil vent plug hole.

3. Install oil vent plug with new gasket first, then remove lubricant tube and quickly install filler plug with new gasket.

### Lubrication

*Inside Boat* (Figures 9 and 10): apply lubricant to (A) Ride-Guide steering cable end next to hand nut; (B) socket of pivot of steering arm; and (C) exposed shaft of cable traversing through cable guide tube.

*Outside Boat* (**Figures 15 and 16**): apply lubricant to grease fittings at gimbal housing upper and lower pivot pins; tilt pins on both sides of gimbal ring; and the gimbal bearing.

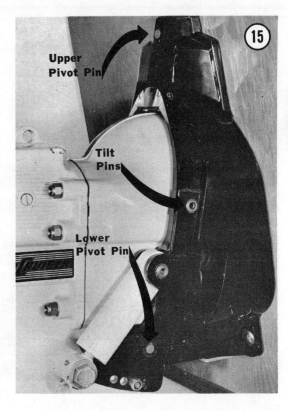

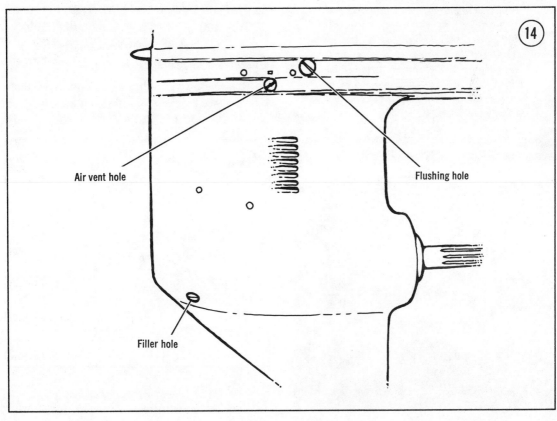

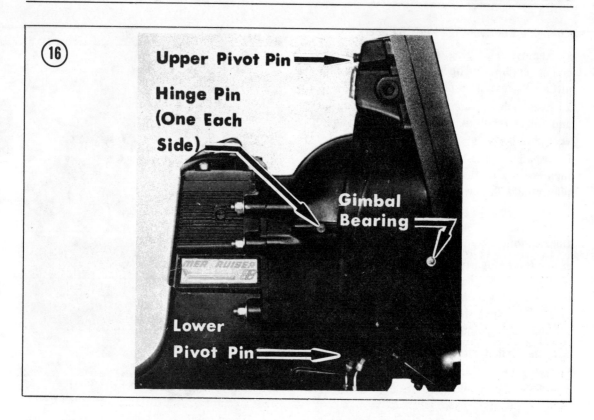

NOTE: *On early models, tapered end of lubricant gun fits counterhose (no fitting is used). If difficulty is encountered in forcing grease into tilt pin (Figure 17), a special fitting (Part No. B-22-37668) should be installed in tilt pin. Grease fitting must be removed after lubrication.*

Lubricate universal joint bearings with Universal Joint Lubricant (C-92-58229-1).

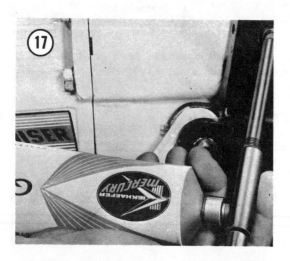

## MERCRUISER LATE MODEL I (110, 120, 140, 150, 160, 165, 470, 888, 200, 225S, 233) MAINTENANCE

### Checking Lubricant Level

1. Remove oil vent plug on side of drive shaft housing (see **Figure 18**). Lubricant must be even with bottom of threaded hole.

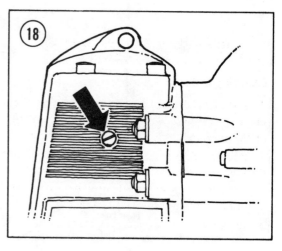

NOTE: *On older models, oil vent plug is on opposite side.*

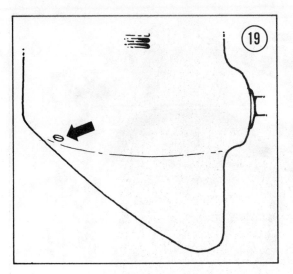

2. If level is down, remove oil filler plug on lower side of gear housing (see **Figure 19**) and quickly insert oil tube. Add oil until proper level is reached.

3. Reinstall oil vent plug and new gasket before removing lubricant tube. Quickly replace oil filler plug and new gasket.

**Changing Lubricant**

Follow the procedure for the MerCruiser Model O.

**Lubrication**

Follow the procedure for the MerCruiser Model O.

## MERCRUISER II (190, 225, 310) MAINTENANCE

**Checking Lubricant Level**

1. Remove filler plug and gasket (see **Figure 20**). Oil must be level with the bottom edge of the threaded hole.

2. If level is down, a small amount can be added through the filler plug hole. If unit is empty or an appreciable amount of oil must be added, see draining and filling instructions below.

3. Install filler plug with new gasket.

**Changing Lubricant**

Follow procedure for MerCruiser Model O.

**Lubrication**

*Inside Boat* (**Figure 21**): Lubricate Ride-Guide steering cable end next to hand nut; inner transom mounting plate on left side at base of crank unit and right side top for crank gear ring; and inside steering lever housing for steering lever shaft.

*Outside Boat* (**Figures 22 and 23**): Lubricate gimbal housing upper and lower pivot pins; and tilt pins on both sides of gimbal housing.

## MERCRUISER 215, II-TR, II-TRS, AND III (215, 225II-TR, 250, 270, 255TR, 255II-TR, 280TRS, 325, 390) MAINTENANCE

**Checking Lubricant Level**

1. Check oil level with dipstick (**Figure 24**) or sight glass (**Figure 25**) located on the inner transom plate.

2. Add oil as required through dipstick tube or oil filler hole.

**Changing Lubricant**

1. Remove oil filler and oil vent plugs and allow oil to drain (see **Figure 26**).

2. Install oil vent plug with new gasket.

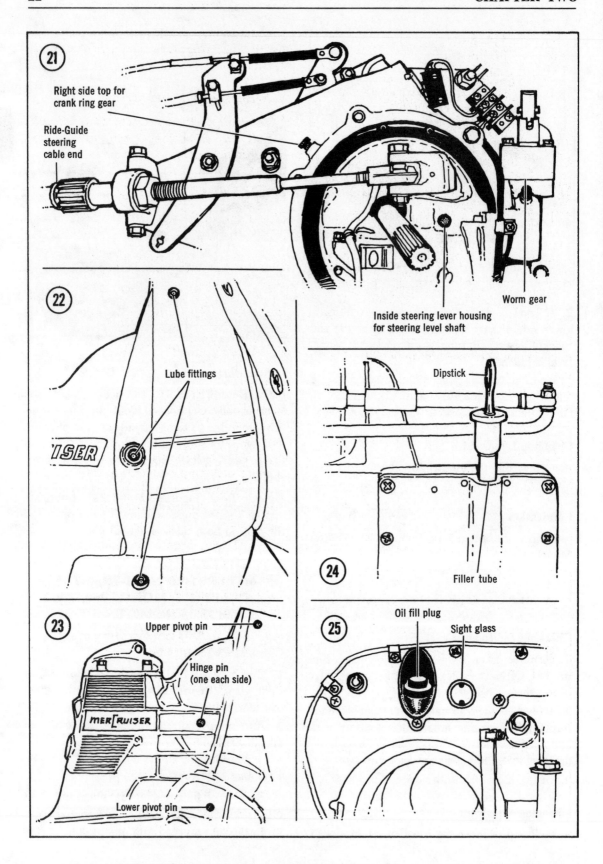

㉑

Right side top for
crank ring gear

Ride-Guide
steering
cable end

Worm gear

Inside steering lever housing
for steering level shaft

㉒

Lube fittings

RUISER

Dipstick

㉔ Filler tube

㉓

Upper pivot pin

Hinge pin
(one each side)

MERCRUISER

Lower pivot pin

㉕

Oil fill plug

Sight glass

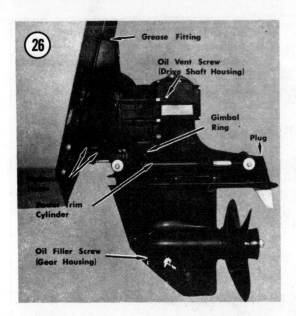

3. Using hand-type lubricant pump, fill drive unit through filler plug hole until oil level meets line on sight glass (**Figure 27**) on MerCruiser III, or dipstick (**Figure 28**) on 215, II-TR, and II-TRS.

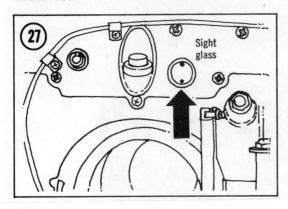

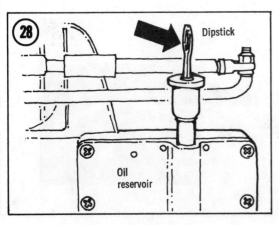

4. After filling, quickly remove pump and install filler plug with new gasket. Tighten securely.

### Lubrication (215, II-TR, II-TRS)

Lubricate drive unit upper and lower pivot pins (**Figure 29**) through grease fittings with anti-corrosion grease.

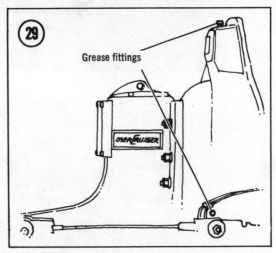

*Manual Steering* (**Figure 30**)—Lubricate steering cable through grease fitting with small amount multipurpose lubricant, apply a light coat of grease to exposed steering cable and to steering lever pivot points. Do not overlubricate the cable.

*Power Steering* (**Figure 31**)—Lubricate steering cable through grease fitting with small amount of multipurpose lubricant. Apply light coat of same lubricant to exposed cable and to extension rod. Do not overlubricate.

NOTE: *Lubricate pivot points of dual tie bar, if installed.*

### Lubrication (Model III)

Lubricate drive unit upper and lower pivot pin grease fittings with multipurpose lubricant.

*Manual Steering* (**Figure 32**)—Lubricate steering cable through grease fitting with multipurpose lubricant. Apply coating of grease to exposed cable. Do not overlubricate.

*Power Steering* (**Figure 33**)—Lubricate steering cable through grease fitting with small amount

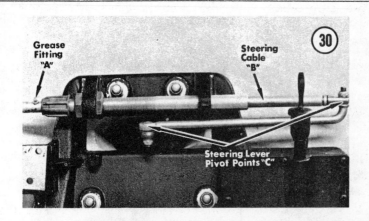

Grease Fitting "A"

Steering Cable "B"

Steering Lever Pivot Points "C"

Grease Fitting "A"

Steering Cable "B"

Extension Rod "D"

Steering Cable Pivot Points "C"

Grease Fitting

Steering Cable

Coupler Nut

Pin

Cotter Pin

of multipurpose lubricant. Also apply small amount of grease to exposed cable and to steering lever pivot points. Do not overlubricate.

NOTE: *Lubricate pivot points of dual tie bar, if installed.*

## VOLVO MAINTENANCE

### Volvo 100B

1. Place drive unit in down position.

2. Drain unit by removing drain hole plug and dipstick (see **Figure 34**). Replace the drain hole plug.

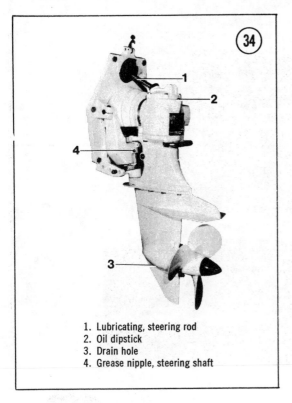

1. Lubricating, steering rod
2. Oil dipstick
3. Drain hole
4. Grease nipple, steering shaft

3. Fill with oil through dipstick hole, using oil scavenging pump if available.

4. Check oil level by inserting dipstick.

NOTE: *Do not screw dipstick down when measuring oil level.*

5. If required, add oil until level is between the 2 marks on the dipstick.

### CAUTION
*Never allow oil level to go above top mark on dipstick, as oil pressure built*

*up during operation could cause damage to the unit.*

6. Replace and screw in dipstick.

7. Fill lubricator cup on flywheel housing with multipurpose grease and screw down tightly.

8. Lubricate steering shaft bearing through grease fitting, using grease gun.

9. Grease outside of steering rod with multipurpose or anti-corrosion grease.

### Volvo 200-250

1. Drain oil by removing oil drainage plug (see **Figure 35**) and air hole plug.

NOTE: *To properly drain and fill stern drive, unit must be placed in tipped up position.*

2. Replace oil drainage plug.

3. Fill unit through oil filling hole. A pump (see **Figure 36**) will greatly help in filling unit.

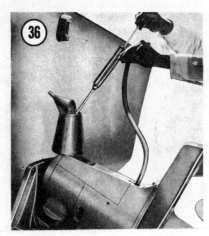

4. Replace oil filling plug and air hole plug and return stern drive unit to down position.

5. Wait a few minutes for oil to settle and fill cavities, then check dipstick. Any additional oil needed can be added through dipstick hole.

NOTE: *Do not screw dipstick down when measuring oil level. Just unscrew and remove dipstick, wipe it clean, then insert it in hole as far as it will go. Remove dipstick and take reading.*

6. Replace and screw in dipstick and plug in the cover on the upper drive housing.

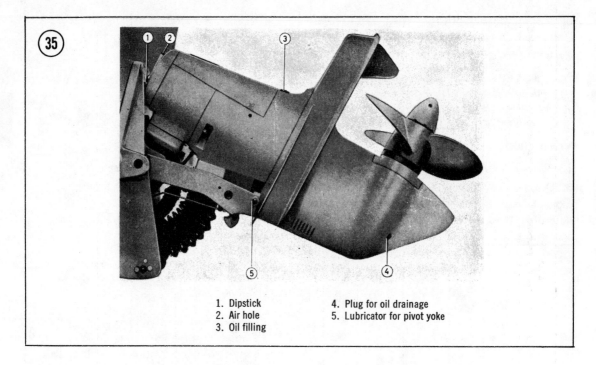

35

1. Dipstick                    4. Plug for oil drainage
2. Air hole                    5. Lubricator for pivot yoke
3. Oil filling

7. Lubricate drive shaft bearing (on flywheel housing) by filling grease cup (see **Figure 37**) with multipurpose grease and screwing it down tightly.

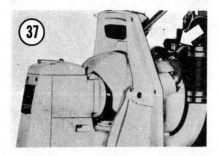

37

8. Using grease gun, lubricate the lower bearing on pivot yoke (see Figure 35).

### Volvo 270-270T

1. Tilt stern drive unit to tipped-up position.

2. Remove drain hole plug and dipstick (see **Figure 38**) and allow oil to drain.

3. Replace drain hole plug.

4. Fill unit with oil through oil filler hole, using oil scavenging pump if avaliable.

5. Replace oil filler plug and return drive unit to down position.

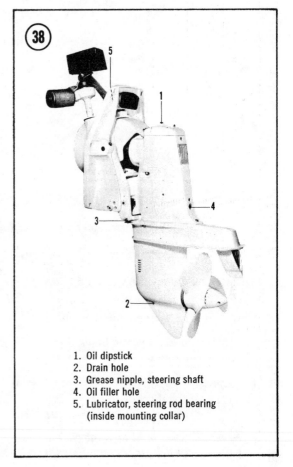

38

1. Oil dipstick
2. Drain hole
3. Grease nipple, steering shaft
4. Oil filler hole
5. Lubricator, steering rod bearing
   (inside mounting collar)

6. Using dipstick, measure oil level.

NOTE: *When measuring oil level, do not screw dipstick down.*

7. Add oil as required through dipstick hole to bring oil level within field on the lower flat part of dipstick.

### CAUTION
*Never allow oil level to be above* MAX *mark on the dipstick, as damage to the drive unit could result.*

8. Replace and screw in dipstick.

9. Fill grease cup on flywheel housing with multipurpose grease and screw cup in all the way.

10. Use grease gun to lubricate fitting on steering shaft bearing (see Figure 38).

11. Lubricate steering rod bearing through grease fitting on inside of mounting collar (see Figure 38).

### Volvo 280-280T

1. Tilt unit to tipped-up position and remove oil drain plug (**Figure 39**) and oil filling plug (**Figure 40**), allowing drive unit to drain.

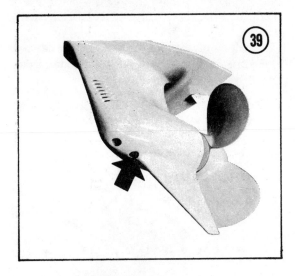

2. Replace oil drain plug.

3. Fill unit with oil through filling hole, using pump if available.

4. Replace oil filling plug and tilt drive unit to down position.

5. Allow oil to settle a few minutes, then unscrew and wipe dipstick and measure oil level.

NOTE: *Do not screw dipstick in when measuring oil level.*

6. Add oil as required, to bring level within the field on the lower flat part of dipstick.

### CAUTION
*Never allow oil level to be above* MAX *mark on dipstick, as damage to the unit could result.*

7. Replace and screw in dipstick.

8. Fill grease cup on flywheel housing with multipurpose grease and screw all the way down.

9. Using grease gun, lubricate steering rod bearing through grease fitting on inside of mounting collar.

10. Lubricate steering shaft bearing through grease fitting, using a grease gun.

### Volvo 750

1. Remove oil drain and oil filler plugs (see **Figure 41**) and allow oil to drain. Replace the drain plug.

2. Fill with new oil through oil filler hole.

3. Replace filler plug and check oil level in transparent expansion tank inside mounting collar.

4. Add oil, if required, through expansion tank opening to bring level between MIN and MAX marks on dipstick.

5. Lubricate suspension pins through grease fittings with grease gun.

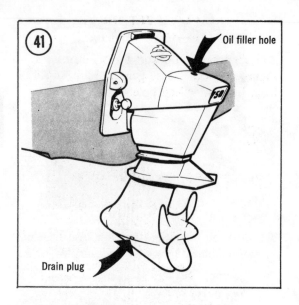

Oil filler hole

Drain plug

## STERN-POWR MAINTENANCE
## (MODELS 80, 81, AND 91)

1. Place unit in vertical (down) position, remove drain screw and filler plug (see **Figure 42**), and allow unit to drain.

NOTE: *Drain screw has a self-locking feature and must be replaced after being removed 7 or 8 times.*

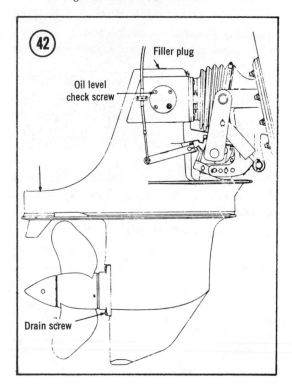

Filler plug

Oil level check screw

Drain screw

2. Replace drain screw securely, remove oil level check screw and fill until oil runs from level check hole.

3. Allow oil to stop running, then replace oil filler plug and oil level check screw.

NOTE: *Remove air pockets by cranking unit and rechecking one hour after filling.*

## BERKELEY-PACKAJET
## MAINTENANCE

1. Apply a light coat of engine oil to the starter gear and shaft (see **Figure 43**).

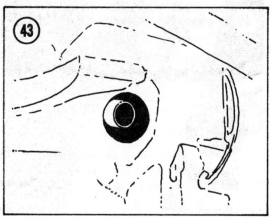

2. Remove inspection panel (see **Figure 44**) and lubricate each of 2 universal joint fittings, using hand grease gun (**Figure 45**).

CAUTION
*Do not use high pressure grease gun.*

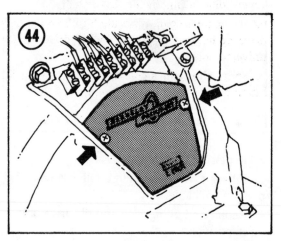

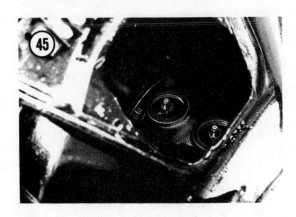

3. Using hand grease gun, lubricate fitting on front of jet drive suction piece (see **Figure 46**).

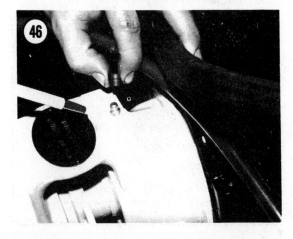

4. Remove 2 plugs from top of bowl assembly and using oil can or squeeze bottle, fill with oil (Chevron 45X or equivalent). Replace plugs tightly.

5. Using hand grease gun, lubricate the universal joint fitting on the drive shaft.

6. Using grease gun, lubricate fitting on flanged drive coupling (connected to aft drive shaft) universal joint).

7. Spray all bright metal surfaces with rust inhibiting lubricant (WD-40 or equivalent).

## JACUZZI JET DRIVE MAINTENANCE

1. Lubricate fitting for thrust bearing (see **Figure 47**) with grease gun until grease bleeds from lubricant bleed hole.

Thrust Bearing Fitting

2. Apply grease at bowl fitting inside discharge nozzle deflector (see **Figure 48**).

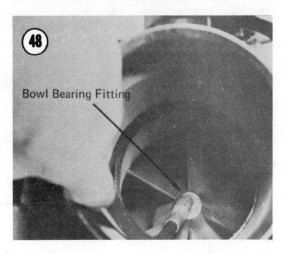

Bowl Bearing Fitting

3. Using a hand-operated grease gun, lubricate fittings on each drive shaft universal joint.

# CHAPTER THREE

# TUNE-UP AND TROUBLESHOOTING

A smooth running, dependable marine engine is more than a convenience. At sea, it can mean your life. To keep your engine running right, you must have a regular program of preventive maintenance.

Part of any engine maintenance program is a thorough engine tune-up. A tune-up is a series of accurate adjustments to restore maximum power and performance. In addition, some ignition parts which deteriorate with use must be replaced.

Most manufacturers recommend engine tune-up every 50 hours. If the engine is used infrequently, a tune-up should be performed at least annually.

## RECOMMENDED TUNE-UP EQUIPMENT

Three items of special equipment are essential to properly tune a modern gasoline engine. These are:

a. Dwell meter

b. Tachometer

c. Timing light

An optional, but convenient, item of equipment is a remote starter button. This permits cranking the engine while you are near it.

Additional equipment needed for troubleshooting an engine includes the following.

a. Compression tester

b. Vacuum gauge

c. Fuel pressure gauge

d. Multimeter (voltmeter, ammeter, and ohmmeter)

e. Hydrometer

Quality and price vary considerably. Adequate light duty equipment can be purchased for the cost of 3 or 4 tune-ups. Professional tune-up and troubleshooting equipment can cost several hundred dollars. As with most tools, cost is usually a fair indicator of quality.

### Dwell Meter

A dwell meter (**Figure 1**) measures the distance in degrees of cam rotation that the breaker points remain closed while the engine is running. Since this angle is determined by breaker point gap, dwell angle is an accurate indication of breaker point gap.

Many tachometers intended for tuning and testing incorporate a dwell meter as well. Follow the manufacturer's instructions to measure dwell angle.

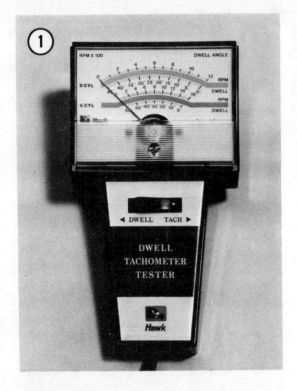

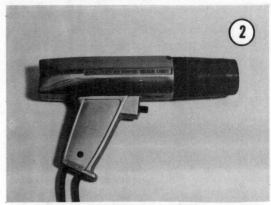

## Tachometer

A tachometer is necessary for tuning. Ignition timing and carburetor adjustments must be performed at the specified idle speed. The best instrument for this purpose is one with a low range of 0-1,000 or 0-2,000 rpm for setting idle, and a high range of 0-4,000 or more for setting ignition timing at 3,000 rpm. Extended range (0-6,000 or 0-8,000) instruments lack accuracy at lower speeds. The instrument should be capable of detecting changes of 25 rpm on the low range.

## Timing Light

This instrument is required for accurate engine timing adjustment. The light flashes each time the number one cylinder fires, making the position of the timing marks visible at that instant. When the engine is properly timed, the timing marks will be aligned.

Suitable timing lights range from inexpensive neon bulb types ($2-3) to powerful xenon strobe lights ($20-40). See **Figure 2**. Neon timing lights are difficult to see and must be used in dimly lit areas. Xenon strobe timing lights can be outside in bright sunlight.

Xenon strobe lights are available for either AC or DC operation. Since access to AC might be a problem on a small boat, the more expensive DC operated xenon strobe timing light is probably the best choice; it operates from the boat's 12-volt battery.

## Compression Tester

The compression tester measures the compression pressure built up in each cylinder. The results, when properly interpreted, can indicate general cylinder and valve condition.

Most compression testers have long flexible extensions as accessories. See **Figure 3**. Such an extension is not necessary since the spark plug holes are easily accessible.

Many service manuals describe a "dry" compression test and a "wet" compression test. Usually these tests must be interpreted together to isolate the trouble in cylinders or valves.

### Dry Test

1. Warm the engine to normal operating temperature. Ensure that the choke valve and throttle valve are completely open.

2. Remove the spark plugs.

3. Connect the compression tester to one cylinder following the manufacturer's instructions.

4. Have an assistant crank the engine over until there is no further rise in pressure.

5. Remove the tester and record the reading.

6. Repeat Steps 3-5 for each cylinder.

When interpreting the results, actual readings are not as important as the difference between readings. All readings should be from about

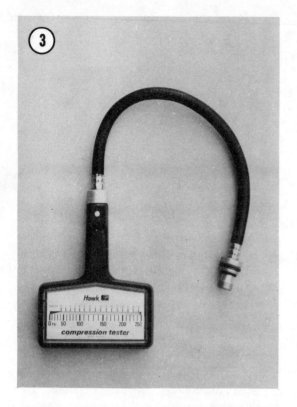

132-162 psi (9-11 kg/cm²). Reading below 100 psi (7 kg/cm²) indicate that an engine overhaul is due. A maximum difference of 20 psi (1.5 kg/cm²) between any 2 cylinders is acceptable. Greater differences indicate worn or broken rings, leaky or stick valves, or a combination of all. Compare with vacuum gauge reading to isolate the trouble more closely.

*Wet Test*

Add one tablespoon of heavy oil (at least SAE 30) to any cylinder which checks low. Repeat the procedure above. If compression increases noticeably, the rings are probably worn. If adding oil produces no change, the low reading may be caused by a broken ring or valve trouble.

**Vacuum Gauge**

The vacuum gauge (see **Figure 4**) is one of the easiest instruments to use, but one of the most difficult for the inexperienced mechanic to interpret. The results, when interpreted with other findings, can provide valuable clues to possible trouble.

**Figure 5** shows numerous typical readings with interpretations. Results are not conclusive without comparing to to other tests such as compression.

**Fuel Pressure Gauge**

This instrument is invaluable for evaluating fuel pump performance. Fuel system trouble-shooting procedures in this chapter use a fuel pressure gauge. Usually a vacuum gauge and fuel pressure gauge are combined.

**Voltmeter, Ammeter, and Ohmmeter**

For testing the ignition or electrical system, a good voltmeter is required. An instrument covering 0-20 volts is satisfactory. One which also has a 0-2 volt scale is necessary for testing relays, points, or individual contacts where voltage drops are much smaller. Accuracy should be ±½ volt.

An ohmmeter measures electrical resistance. This instrument is useful for checking continuity (open- and short-circuits), and testing fuses and lights.

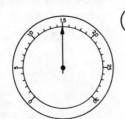
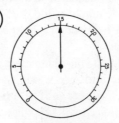
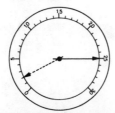

**1. NORMAL READING**
18-22" at idle.

**2. NORMAL READING**
High lift cam with large overlap.

**3. LATE IGNITION TIMING**
14-17" at idle. Normal cam.

**4. LATE VALVE TIMING**
8-15" at idle.

**5**

**3**

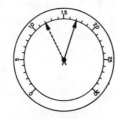
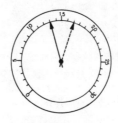
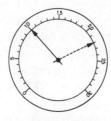

**5. INTAKE LEAK**
Low steady reading.

**6. NORMAL READING**
Drops to 2, then rises to 25 when accelerator is rapidly depressed and released.

**7. WORN RINGS, DILUTED OIL**
Drops to 0, then rises to 22 when accelerator is rapidly depressed and released.

**8. STICKING VALVE(S)**
Normally steady. Intermittently flicks downward about 4".

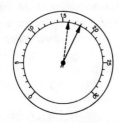

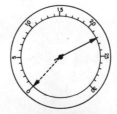

**9. LEAKY VALVE**
Regular drop about 2".

**10. BURNED OR WARPED VALVE**
Regular, evenly spaced down-scale flick about 4".

**11. WORN VALVE GUIDES**
Oscillates about 4".

**12. WEAK VALVE SPRINGS**
Violent oscillation (about 10") as rpm increases. Often steady at idle.

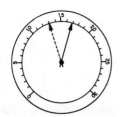

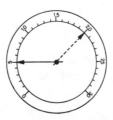
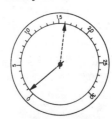

**13. IMPROPER IDLE MIXTURE**
Floats slowly between 13-17".

**14. SMALL SPARK GAP or DEFECTIVE POINTS**
Slight float between 14-16".

**15. HEAD GASKET LEAK**
Floats between 5-19".

**16. RESTRICTED EXHAUST SYSTEM**
Normal when first started. Drops to 0 as rpm increases. May eventually rise to about 16.

The ammeter measures electrical current. Ammeters should cover 0-50 amperes and 0-250 amperes. These are useful for checking battery charging and starting current.

Several inexpensive VOM's (volt-ohmmeters) combine all 3 instruments into one which fits easily in any tool box. See **Figure 6**. The ammeter ranges are usually too small for engine work, though. Combination instruments designed especially for engine diagnostic work are available, however, and they are not excessively expensive.

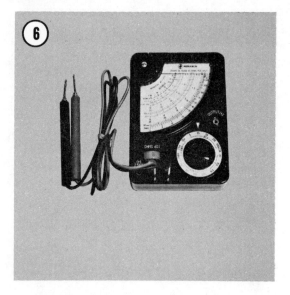

### Hydrometer

Hydrometer testing is the best way to check battery condition. Use a hydrometer with numbered graduations from 1.100 to 1.300 rather than one with color coded bands. To use the hydrometer, squeeze the rubber ball, insert the tip in the cell and release the ball (see **Figure 7**). Draw enough electrolyte to float the weighted float inside the hydrometer. Note the number in line with the surface of the electrolyte; this is the specific gravity for this cell. Return the electrolyte to the cell from which it came.

The specific gravity of the electrolyte in each battery cell is an excellent indication of that cell's condition. A fully charged cell will read 1.275-1.380, while a cell in good condition may read from 1.250-1.280. A cell in fair condition reads from 1.225-1.250, and anything below 1.225 is practically dead.

If the cells test in the poor range, the battery requires recharging. The hydrometer is useful for checking the progress of the charging opera-

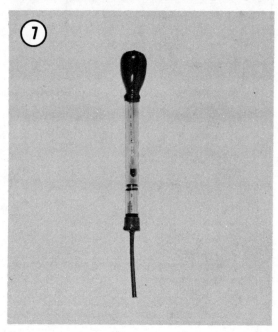

tion. A reading from 1.200 to about 1.225 indicates a half charge; 1.275-1.380 indicates a full charge.

CAUTION
*Always disconnect both battery connections before connecting charging equipment.*

### ENGINE TUNE-UP

Careful and accurate adjustment is crucial to a successful engine tune-up. Each procedure in this section must be performed exactly as described and in the order presented. **Tables 1-7** at the end of the chapter provide specifications.

### Compression Test

Before attempting a tune-up, check the compression of each cylinder. Use the procedures outlined earlier with the compression tester description. If more than a 20 pound difference exists between the highest and lowest cylinders, the engine cannot be tuned to develop maximum power.

**Table 1     BERKELEY TUNE-UP SPECIFICATIONS**

| Engine Cyl. | Carb. | Disp. | Model | Idle Speed | Compression (in psi) | Point Gap | Distributor Dwell Angle | At Eng. rpm | Spark Plugs Type | Gap (Inch) | Timing (° BTDC) | Firing Order | Horsepower | Remarks |
|---|---|---|---|---|---|---|---|---|---|---|---|---|---|---|
| 8 | 4 bbl | 455 | 455-2 | 1,100 | 140 | 0.020 | 26° | 1,100 | AC-R44S | 0.030 | 12 | 18436572 | 330 | Mallory ignition |
| 8 | 4 bbl | 455 | 455-3 | 1,100 | 140 | 0.020 | 26° | 1,100 | AC-R46S | 0.040 | 14 | 18436572 | 295 | Mallory ignition |
| 8 | 4 bbl | 455 | 455-2 | 1,100 | 140 | 0.015 | 30° | 1,100 | AC-R44S | 0.030 | 12 | 18436572 | 330 | Delco ignition |
| 8 | 4 bbl | 455 | 455-3 | 1,100 | 140 | 0.015 | 30° | 1,100 | AC-R46S | 0.040 | 8 | 18436572 | 270 | Delco ignition |
| 8 | 4 bbl | 455 | 455 | 850 | 140 | 0.015 | 30° | 850 | AC-R43S | 0.030 | 8 | 18436572 | 290 | |
| 8 | 4 bbl | 455 | 455-4 | 1,100 | 140 | 0.020 | 30° | 1,100 | AC-R46S | 0.040 | 10 | 18436572 | 320 | |
| 8 | 4 bbl | 350 | 350 | 850 | 140 | 0.015 | 30° | 30° | AC-R43S | 0.030 | 8 | 18436572 | 220 | |
| 8 | 4 bbl | 350 | 350-3 | 1,100 | 140 | 0.015 | 30° | 1,100 | AC-R46S | 0.040 | 12 | 18436572 | 230 | |
| 8 | 4 bbl | 351 | 351 | 850 | ① | 0.017 | 31° | 850 | Autolite BRE-3M | 0.035 | 10 | 13726548 | 230 | Prestolite ignition |
| 8 | 4 bbl | 351 | 351 | 850 | ① | 0.020 | 26° | 850 | Autolite BRE-3M | 0.035 | 10 | 13726548 | 230 | Mallory ignition |
| 8 | 2 bbl | 302 | 302 | 850 | ① | 0.017 | 31° | 850 | Autolite BRE-3M | 0.035 | 10 | 13726548 | 180 | Prestolite ignition |
| 8 | 2 bbl | 302 | 302 | 850 | ① | 0.020 | 26° | 850 | Autolite BRE-3M | 0.035 | 10 | 13726548 | 180 | Mallory ignition |
| 8 | 4 bbl | 460 | 460 | 850 | ① | 0.017 | 31° | 850 | Autolite ARF-32 | 0.035 | 10 | 15426378 | 320 | |

① Look for balance rather than a specific number. Lowest cylinder must be no less than 75% of highest reading.

3

Table 2    CHRIS-CRAFT AND MARINE POWER TUNE-UP SPECIFICATIONS

| Engine | | | Model | Idle Speed | | Compression (in psi) | Point Gap | Distributor | | Spark Plugs | | Timing (° BTDC) | Firing Order | Horsepower | Remarks |
|---|---|---|---|---|---|---|---|---|---|---|---|---|---|---|---|
| Cyl. | Carb. | Disp. | | In Gear | In Neutral | | | Dwell Angle | At Eng. rpm | Type | Gap (Inch) | | | | |
| 8 | 4 bbl | 305 | 305GLV | 600 | 650 | 150 | 0.018① | 28-30°② | 650 | AC-MR43T | 0.035 | 4③ | 18436572 | 225 | |
| 8 | 4 bbl | 307 | 307GLV | 600 | 650 | 150 | 0.018① | 28-30°② | 650 | AC-MR43T | 0.035 | 4③ | 18436572 | 215 | |
| 8 | 2 bbl | 307 | 307GCLL | 600 | 650 | 150 | 0.018 | 28-30° | 650 | Champion RBL9Y | 0.028 | 4 | 18436572 | 200 | |
| 8 | 2 bbl | 307 | 307QLV | 500 | 550 | 160 | 0.020 | 28° | 550 | Champion UJ6 | 0.028 | Align marks | 18436572 | 200 | |
| 8 | 2 bbl | 307 | 307GCLV | 600 | 650 | 150 | 0.018① | 28-30°② | 650 | AC-MR43T | 0.035 | 4③ | 18436572 | 200 | |
| 8 | 4 bbl | 302 | 302FVL | 700 | 800 | 170 | 0.019 | 29-31° | 800 | AC-CR43K | 0.035 | 10 | 18436572 | 310 | |
| 8 | 4 bbl | 350 | 350FLV | 700 | 800 | 170 | 0.019 | 29-31° | 800 | AC-CR43K | 0.035 | 10 | 18436572 | 350 | Before S/N 611027 |
| 8 | 4 bbl | 350 | 350FLV | 600 | 650 | 160 | 0.019 | 29-31° | 650 | AC-MR43T | 0.030 | 8④ 12⑤ | 18436572 | 320 | S/N 611027 to 620000 |
| 8 | 4 bbl | 350 | 350FLV | 600 | 650 | 150 | 0.019 | 29-31° | 650 | AC-MR43T | 0.035 | 12 | 18436572 | 300 | S/N 620001 to 620184 |
| 8 | 4 bbl | 350 | 350FLV | 600 | 650 | 150 | 0.018 | 28-30° | 650 | AC-MR43T | 0.035 | 4 | 18436572 | 300 | S/N 620185 to 620606 |
| 8 | 4 bbl | 350 | 350FLV | 600 | 650 | 150 | 0.020 | 28-30°② | 650 | AC-MR43T | 0.035 | 8 | 18436572 | 300 | S/N 620607 on |
| 8 | 4 bbl | 350 | 350GLV | 600 | 650 | 150 | 0.018① | 28-30°② | 650 | AC-MR43T | 0.035 | 4③ | 18436572 | 250 | |
| 8 | 2 bbl | 283 | 283FLV | 500 | 550 | 150 | 0.017 | 27-31° | 550 | Champion UJ6 | 0.025 | Align marks | 18436572 | 185 | |
| 6 | 1 bbl | 225 | 225B-101 | 500 | 550 | 160 | 0.016 | 30° | 550 | AC-43S | 0.035 | 5 | 153624 | 150 | |
| 8 | 2 bbl | 307 | 307B | 500 | 550 | 160 | 0.020⑥ 0.016⑦ | 26°⑥ 30°⑦ | 550 | AC-MR43T | 0.028 | 4 | 18436572 | 200 | |
| 6 | 1 bbl | 225 | 225BVC | 500 | 550 | 160 | 0.016 | 30° | 550 | AC-43S | 0.035 | 5 | 153624 | 150 | |

① 0.020 if equipped with Mallory Dual Point distributor.
② If equipped with Mallory Dual Point distributor, dwell is 26° for one set and 31-35° for both sets of points.
③ 8° BTDC if equipped with Dual Point distributor.
④ Engines with Delco 1111267 or 1112049 distributor.
⑤ Engines with Delco 1112074 distributor.
⑥ Mallory distributor.
⑦ Prestolite distributor.

**Table 3    CHRYSLER TUNE-UP SPECIFICATIONS**

| Engine | | | | Idle Speed | Compression (in psi) | Distributor | | | Spark Plugs | | Timing (° BTDC) | Firing Order | Horsepower |
| Cyl. | Carb. | Disp. | Model | | | Point Gap | Dwell Angle | At Eng. rpm | Type | Gap (Inch) | | | |
|---|---|---|---|---|---|---|---|---|---|---|---|---|---|
| 4 | 2-1bbl | 122 | M122B | 900 | 170 | 0.018 | 59-65° | 900 | Bosch W225T-35 | 0.028 | 12 | 1342 | 130 |
| 6 | 3-1bbl | 183 | M183B | 900 | 145 | 0.012 | 37-43° | 900 | Bosch W225T-35 | 0.028 | 12 | 153624 | 170 |
| 6 | 1 bbl | 225 | M225D | 750 | ① | 0.018 | 40-45° | 750 | Champion XN6 | 0.035 | 2½ | 153624 | 155 |
| 8 | 4 bbl | 318 | SB II | 750 | ① | 0.018 | 28-32° | 750 | Champion XN9Y | 0.035 | 5 | 18436572 | 225 |
| 8 | 4 bbl | 318 | Jet II | 750 | ① | — | — | — | Champion XN9Y | 0.035 | 5 | 18436572 | 225 |
| 8 | 4 bbl | 318 | 195 | 750 | ① | 0.018 | 28-32° | 750 | Champion N13Y | 0.035 | TDC | 18436572 | 195 |
| 8 | 2 bbl | 318 | 240 | 750 | ① | — | — | — | Champion RN12Y | 0.035 | 2 | 18436572 | 240 |
| 8 | 4 bbl | 360 | SB III | 750 | ① | 0.018 | 28-32° | 750 | Champion XN9Y | 0.035 | 2½ | 18436572 | 250 |
| 8 | 4 bbl | 360 | Jet III | 750 | ① | — | — | — | Champion XN9Y | 0.035 | 2½ | 18436572 | 250 |
| 8 | 4 bbl | 360 | 265 | 750 | ① | — | — | — | Champion RN12Y | 0.035 | 6 | 18436572 | 265 |

① Lowest reading must be within 80% of highest reading.

3

Table 4    MERCRUISER TUNE-UP SPECIFICATIONS

| Engine | | | | Idle Speed | Compression (in psi) | Distributor | | | Spark Plugs | | Timing (° BTDC) | Firing Order | Horsepower | Remarks |
| --- | --- | --- | --- | --- | --- | --- | --- | --- | --- | --- | --- | --- | --- | --- |
| Cyl. | Carb. | Disp. | Model | | | Point Gap | Dwell Angle | At Eng. rpm | Type | Gap (Inch) | | | | |
| 4 | 1 bbl | 67.58 | 60 | 650 | 135 | 0.016 | 56-60° | 650 | AC-44F | 0.025 | TDC | 1342 | 60 | |
| 4 | 1 bbl | 89.70 | 80 | 650 | 140 | 0.019 | 49-55° | 650 | AC-44XL | 0.025 | 2 ATDC | 1342 | 80 | |
| 4 | 2 bbl | 95.5 | 90 | 650 | 170 | 0.017 | 53-57° | 650 | AC-R42XL | 0.032 | 2 | 1342 | 90 | |
| 4 | 2 bbl | 153 | 110-120 | 500-600 | 140 | 0.022 | 31-34° | 550 | AC-CR44N ① | 0.035 | 8 | 1342 | 110-120 | |
| 4 | 2 bbl | 181 | 140 | 500-600 | 140 | 0.022 | 31-34° | 550 | AC-R44N ② | 0.035 | 6 | 1342 | 140 | |
| 4 | 2 bbl | 224 | 470 | 650-700 ⑨ | 165-180 | 0.022 | 28-34° | 650 | Champion RBL-9Y | 0.035 | 8 | 1342 | 170 | |
| 6 | 2 bbl | 194 | 140 | 500-600 | 140 | 0.016 | 31-34° | 550 | AC-CR44N | 0.035 | 10 | ③ | | |
| 6 | 2 bbl | 230 | 150 | 500-600 | 140 | 0.016 | 31-34° | 550 | AC-R44N | 0.035 | 6 | ③ | 150 | |
| 6 | 2 bbl | 250 | 160-165 | 500-600 | 140 | 0.016 | 31-34° | 550 | AC-R44N | 0.035 | 6 | ③ | 160-165 | |
| 6 | 2 bbl | 292 | 200 | 500-600 | 140 | 0.016 | 31-34° | 550 | AC-R44N | 0.035 | 8 | ③ | 200 | |
| 8 | 4 bbl | 302 | 888 | 550-600 ⑨ | 125 | 0.019 | 26-31° | 550 | AC-C83T ④ | 0.030 | 10 | ⑤ | 188 | |
| 8 | 4 bbl | 302 | 225S | 550-600 | 140 | 0.019 | 26-31° | 550 | AC-C83T ④ | 0.030 | 10 | ⑤ | 225 | |
| 8 | All | 283 | 190 | 550-600 | 140 | 0.016 | 28-32° | 550 | AC-CR43K | 0.025 | ⑥ | ⑦ | 190 | |
| 8 | 4 bbl | 302 | 215 | 550-600 | 150 | 0.017 | 26-31° | 550 | AC-C83T | 0.030 | ⑧ | ⑤ | 215 | |
| 8 | 4 bbl | 327 | 225 | 550-600 | 140 | 0.016 | 28-32° | 550 | AC-CR43K | 0.035 | ⑥ | ⑦ | 225 | |

(continued)

**Table 4　MERCRUISER TUNE-UP SPECIFICATIONS** (continued)

| Engine Cyl. | Carb. | Disp. | Model | Idle Speed | Compression (in psi) | Distributor Point Gap | Dwell Angle | At Eng. rpm | Spark Plugs Type | Gap (Inch) | Timing (° BTDC) | Firing Order | Horse-power | Remarks |
|---|---|---|---|---|---|---|---|---|---|---|---|---|---|---|
| 8 | 4 bbl | 302 | 225II-TR | 550-600 | 150 | 0.017 | 26-31° | 550 | AC-C83T | 0.030 | 10 | ⑤ | 225 | |
| 8 | 4 bbl | 327 | 250 | 550-600 | 150 | N.A. | N.A. | N.A. | AC-V40K | Polar Plug | 10 | ⑦ | 250 | Thunderbolt ignition |
| 8 | 4 bbl | 350 | 270 | 550-600 | 150 | N.A. | N.A. | N.A. | AC-V40K | Polar Plug | 10 | ⑦ | 270 | Thunderbolt ignition |
| 8 | 4 bbl | 350 | 255TR | 550-600 ⑨ | 150 | 0.019 | 26-31° | 550 | AC-R43T | 0.035 | 6 | ⑦ | 255 | S/N 4175500 and up |
| 8 | 4 bbl | 351 | 255II-TR | 550-600 | 150 | 0.017 | 26-31° | 550 | AC-C83T | 0.030 | 10 | ⑤ | 255 | S/N 4175499 and earlier |
| 8 | 4 bbl | 351 | 233 | 550-600 ⑨ | 125 | 0.019 | 26-31° | 550 | AC-CR83T ④ | 0.030 | 10 | ⑤ | 233 | |
| 8 | 4 bbl | 350 | 280TRS | 850-900 ⑨ | 150 | 0.019 | 26-31° | 850 | AC-R43T | 0.035 | 6 | ⑦ | 280 | |
| 8 | 4 bbl | 409 | 310 | 550-600 | 140 | 0.016 | 28-32° | 550 | AC-43N | 0.035 | 12 | ⑦ | 310 | |
| 8 | 4 bbl | 427 | 325 | 550-600 | 150 | N.A. | N.A. | N.A. | AC-V40NK | Polar Gap | 10 | ⑦ | 325 | Thunderbolt ignition |
| 8 | 4 bbl | 482 | 390 | 550-600 | 170 | N.A. | N.A. | N.A. | AC-WR41N | 0.035 | 10 | ⑦ | 390 | Thunderbolt ignition |

① AC-R43T on S/N 3825579 and later
② AC-R43T on S/N 3826282 and later
③ 153624
④ If 14mm plug is required, use AC-MR43T
⑤ 13726548
⑥ Engines with distributor No. 1111076 and 1111249 — 8° BTDC; No. 1111297 — 5° BTDC; all others—12° BTDC
⑦ 18436572
⑧ Distributor No. C9JF-12127 B or A — 12° BTDC; No. D1JF-12127 JA or KA — 10° BTDC
⑨ In forward gear

3

**Table 5     OMC TUNE-UP SPECIFICATIONS**

| Engine | | | | Idle Speed | Compression (in psi) | Distributor | | | Spark Plugs | | Timing (° BTDC) | Firing Order | Horse-power |
| Cyl. | Carb. | Disp. | Model | | | Point Gap | Dwell Angle | At Eng. rpm | Type | Gap (Inch) | | | |
|---|---|---|---|---|---|---|---|---|---|---|---|---|---|
| 4 | 1 bbl | 153 | 100 | 550 | 130 | 0.019 | 31-34° | 550 | AC C44N | 0.035 | 4 | 1342 | 100 |
| 4 | 2 bbl | 153 | 120 | 550 | 130 | 0.019 | 31-34° | 550 | AC-M43T | 0.035 | 4 | 1342 | 120 |
| 4 | 2 bbl | 181 | 140 | 550 | 130 | 0.019 | 31-34° | 550 | AC-M43T | 0.035 | 4 | 1342 | 140 |
| 6 | 2 bbl | 250 | 165 | 550 | 130 | 0.019 | 31-34° | 550 | AC-MR43T | 0.035 | 6 | 153624 | 165 |
| 8 | 2 bbl | 302 | 175 | 550 | ① | 0.017 | 31° | 550 | Champion RBL8 | 0.030 | 10 | 15426378 | 175 |
| 8 | 2 bbl | 302 | 190 | 550 | ① | 0.017 | 31° | 550 | Champion RBL8 | 0.030 | 10 | 13726548 | 190 |
| 8 | 4 bbl | 307 | 225 | 550 | 165 | 0.018 | 30° | 550 | AC-MR43T | 0.035 | 10 | 18436572 | 225 |
| 8 | 4 bbl | 351 | 235 | 550 | ① | 0.017 | 31° | 550 | Champion RBL8 | 0.030 | 10 | 13726548 | 235 |
| 8 | 4 bbl | 307 | 245 | 600 | 165 | 0.018 | 30° | 600 | AC-MR43T | 0.035 | 10 | 18436572 | 245 |

① Minimum reading must be within 75% of maximum reading.

**Table 6   VOLVO-PENTA TUNE-UP SPECIFICATIONS**

| Engine Cyl. | Carb. | Disp. | Model | Idle Speed | Compression (in psi) | Point Gap | Dwell Angle | At Eng. rpm | Spark Plugs Type | Gap (Inch) | Timing (° BTDC) | Firing Order | Horsepower |
|---|---|---|---|---|---|---|---|---|---|---|---|---|---|
| 4 | 2-1bbl | 121 | AQ130A, B, and C | 900-1,000 | 170 | 0.018 | 59-65° | 900 | Bosch W225T-35 | 0.028 | 12 | 1342 | 130 |
| 4 | 2-1bbl | 130 | AQ140A | 750 | 145 | 0.016 | 59-65° | 750 | Bosch W225T-30 | 0.028 | 6 ① | 1342 | 140 |
| 6 | 3-1bbl | 182 | AQ165A | 800-900 | 145 | 0.012 | 37-43° | 800 | Bosch W225T-35 | 0.028 | 12 | 153624 | 165 |
| 6 | 3-1bbl | 182 | AQ170A | 900-1,000 | 145 | 0.012 | 37-43° | 900 | Bosch W225T-35 | 0.028 | 12 | 153624 | 170 |
| 8 | 2 bbl | 302 | AQ190A | 750 | 150 | — | — | — | AFR-42 | 0.044 | 4 | 15426378 | 182 |
| 8 | 2 bbl | 307 | AQ200A and B | 900 | 150 | 0.019 (new) | 29-31° | 900 | R44T | 0.035 | 4 | 18436572 | 190 |
| 8 | 2 bbl | 305 | AQ200C | 800 | 150 | — | — | — | R45TS | 0.045 | 6 | 18436572 | 190 |
| 8 | 4 bbl | 307 | AQ225A and B | 900 | 150 | 0.019 (new) | 29-31° | 900 | R44T | 0.035 | 4 | 18436572 | 225 |
| 8 | 4 bbl | 305 | AQ225C | 800 | 150 | — | — | — | R45TS | 0.045 | 6 | 18436572 | 220 |
| 8 | 4 bbl | 351 | AQ240A | 900 | 150 | — | — | — | ARF-42 | 0.034 | 16 | 13726548 | 240 |
| 8 | 4 bbl | 350 | AQ255A | 1,000 | 150 | — | — | — | R45TS | 0.045 | 8 | 18436572 | 250 |

① 10° BTDC on later production units.

3

Table 7  WAUKESHA AND PLEASURECRAFT TUNE-UP SPECIFICATIONS

| Engine | | | | Idle Speed | Compression (in psi) | Distributor | | | Spark Plugs | | | Timing (° BTDC) | Firing Order | Horse-power |
| Cyl. | Carb. | Disp. | Model | | | Point Gap | Dwell Angle | At Eng. rpm | Type | Gap (Inch) | | | | |
|---|---|---|---|---|---|---|---|---|---|---|---|---|---|---|
| 8 | — | 302 | 302/2 | 600 | ① | 0.018 | 24-29° | 600 | Autolite BTF3M | 0.035 | | 10 | 15426378 | 185 |
| 8 | — | 302 | 302/2A | 600 | ① | 0.018 | 24-29° | 600 | Autolite BTF3M | 0.035 | | 10 | 15426378 | 165 |
| 8 | — | 302 | 302/2B | 600 | ① | 0.018 | 24-29° | 600 | Autolite BTF3M | 0.035 | | 10 | 15426378 | 155 |
| 8 | — | 302 | 302/4 | 600 | ① | 0.018 | 24-29° | 600 | Autolite BTF3M | 0.035 | | 10 | 15426378 | 215 |
| 8 | — | 351 | 351/4 | 600 | ① | 0.018 | 24-29° | 600 | Autolite BTF3M | 0.035 | | 10 | 13726548 | 255 |

① Lowest reading must be within 75% of highest reading.

**3**

## Spark Plug Replacement

Remove plugs in order. That way you'll know which cylinder is malfunctioning should such be the case. Examine the spark plugs and compare their appearance with **Figure 8**. Electrode appearance is a good indication of performance in each cylinder and permits early recognition of trouble. Gap new plugs to clearance specification in **Tables 1-7** (end of chapter). See **Figure 9**. Use a wire type feeler gauge. Bend negative electrode as necessary to adjust gap. Apply a drop of engine oil to the threads of each spark plug. Install the plugs and torque to 22 ft.-lb. (3 mkg).

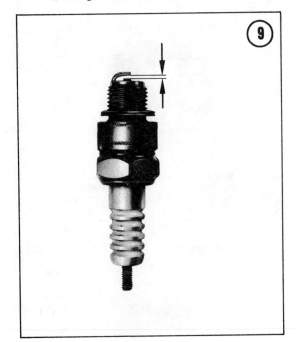

## Breaker Point Replacement

1. Remove distributor cap and rotor.

2. Remove and examine breaker point. If contacts are badly worn, pitted, or burnt, replace them with new ones. Note carefully how they are installed so that new ones can be installed in exactly the same way.

> NOTE: *If the contact points are light gray in color and show no signs of pitting, erosion, mounding, burning, etc., they may be reused. However, in view of the low cost of replacements and the importance of reliability to safe*

*boat operation, it is advisable to replace both points and condenser at each tune-up.*

3. Remove and replace condenser.

4. Clean the breaker plate, cam, and exposed distributor shaft with a clean, lint-free cloth. Place fresh cam lubricant (about the size of a match head) on the cam at a point where it will contact the rubbing block of the points.

> CAUTION
> *Do not use an excessive amount of lubricant, as it may tend to spread and may eventually cause damage to the breaker points.*

5. Install points, but do not tighten locking screw. Connect lead wires from points and condenser to terminal (typical) as shown in **Figure 10**.

6. With the points closed, make certain the contact surfaces are properly aligned with each other (see **Figure 11**). Make adjustments as required, bending the stationary arm of the points only. If reusing old points, they should not be realigned.

7. Adjust breaker point gap as described below.

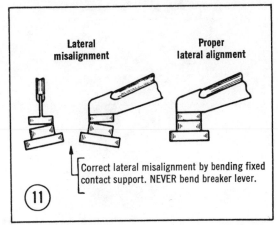

## Breaker Point Gap Adjustment

There are 2 ways to adjust breaker point gap.

a. Feeler gauge

b. Dwell meter

The dwell meter method is the most accurate.

To set the gap with a feeler gauge:

1. Ground high tension lead from ignition coil.

Normal plug appearance noted by the brown to grayish-tan deposits and slight electrode wear. This plug indicates the correct plug heat range and proper air fuel ratio.

Red, brown, yellow and white coatings caused by fuel and oil additives. These deposits are not harmful if they remain in a powdery form.

Carbon fouling distinguished by dry, fluffy black carbon deposits which may be caused by an over-rich air/fuel mixture, excessive hand choking, clogged air filter or excessive idling.

Shiny yellow glaze on insulator cone is caused when the powdery deposits from fuel and oil additives melt. Melting occurs during hard acceleration after prolonged idling. This glaze conducts electricity and shorts out the plug.

Oil fouling indicated by wet, oily deposits caused by oil pumping past worn rings or down the intake valve guides. A hotter plug temporarily reduces oil deposits, but a plug that is too hot leads to pre-ignition and possible engine damage.

Overheated plug indicated by burned or blistered insulator tip and badly worn electrodes. This condition may be caused by pre-ignition, cooling system defects, lean air/fuel ratios, low octane fuel or over-advanced ignition timing.

Spark plug condition photos courtesy of AC Spark Plug Division, General Motors Corporation.

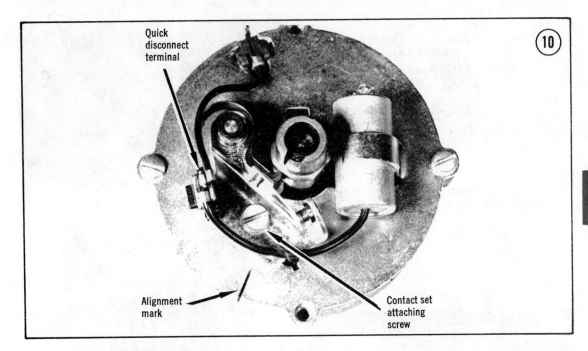

Quick disconnect terminal

Alignment mark

Contact set attaching screw

3

2. Crank engine until breaker point rubbing block rests on a distributor cam lobe. At this location, the points are open to their fullest.

3. Insert feeler gauge (see Tables 1-7, at end of chapter) between contacts, and adjust points with either the adjusting screw or with a screwdriver inserted in the slotted hole. When a slight drag is felt on the gauge blade, tighten the locking screw. Recheck gap to make certain that the points did not move during tightening.

To adjust point gap with a dwell meter:

1. Remove distributor cap and rotor.

2. Connect dwell meter following manufacturer's instructions.

3. Crank engine with starter and read dwell angle on meter.

4. Adjust dwell by varying breaker point gap.

5. Tighten the point locking screw.

6. Recheck dwell as in Step 3.

7. Install distributor cap and rotor.

8. Start engine and check dwell while engine is idling.

To adjust Delco-Remy distributor point gap:

1. Connect dwell meter following manufacturer's instructions.

2. Start engine and run at idle.

3. Read dwell angle on meter.

4. Adjust dwell angle as necessary with an Allen wrench through the distributor window.

**Ignition Timing**

1. Locate cylinder No. 1. This is the cylinder nearest to the front of the engine. Note that on V-8 engines, one bank (left or right) of cylinders is slightly offset from the other.

2. Connect timing light to spark plug No. 1 following light manufacturer's instructions.

3. Disconnect vacuum hose from distributor vacuum advance unit and plug vacuum hose with blunt pencil, golf tee, or tape.

4. Locate timing marks on block and crankshaft vibration damper or flywheel. Determine timing specification for your engine from Tables 1-7, end of chapter.

NOTE: *The timing marks usually consist of a notch or pointer, and a calibrated scale. On some engines the notch or pointer is located on the engine block or a stationary housing, and on others it is on the crankshaft pulley or flywheel. After determining the proper timing specification, a bit of white paint applied to the notch or pointer and to the proper place on the calibrated scale will provide better visability. See* **Figures 12-16** *for timing mark locations on MerCruiser engines, and* **Figures 17 and 18** *for OMC engines.*

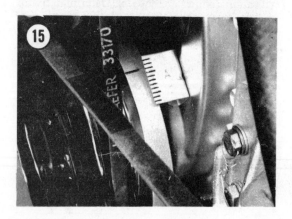

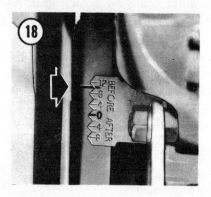

5. Operate the engine at slow idle and aim the timing light at the timing marks. If the engine is in time, the moving mark will appear to stand still opposite the stationary mark.

6. If timing marks are not properly aligned, loosen the hold-down bolt at the base of the distributor and rotate the distributor body until the marks come into alignment.

7. Tighten the hold-down bolt and recheck timing. Repeat Step 6 if timing was disturbed while tightening the bolt.

8. With vacuum hose still disconnected and engine operating at slow idle, note the position of the timing marks with timing light.

9. Gradually increase the engine speed to about 1,800 rpm while observing the timing marks. The moving timing mark should move steadily in the direction opposite of engine rotation.

10. Decrease engine speed to slow idle while observing timing marks. Timing mark should move back smoothly as speed decreases.

> NOTE: *If timing mark moves with jerking motion, or does not start to move within 50 to 100 rpm of the specified speeds, distributor must be cleaned or repaired.*

11. Operate the engine at about 1,500 rpm.

12. Reconnect vacuum hose and observe timing change. Timing mark should move in direction opposite to engine rotation to advance spark. Timing mark should be beyond the range of the calibrated indicator.

> NOTE: *If timing mark does not move as described above, check vacuum hose for breaks, leaks, or obstructions. If vacuum is present at distributor, cleaning or repair of distributor is indicated.*

**Carburetor Idle Adjustments**

1. Determine proper engine idle speed from Tables 1-7 (end of chapter) or manufacturer's literature.

2. Attach tachometer to engine, following the manufacturer's instructions. Usually, the red lead is attached to the distributor terminal on the coil (usually marked "—", "D", or "Dist." and black lead grounded on engine block).

3. Locate the idle mixture screw(s) on your engine (usually a spring-loaded screw near the base of the carburetor). **Figure 19** is typical.

4. Start engine and let run until normal operating temperature is reached.

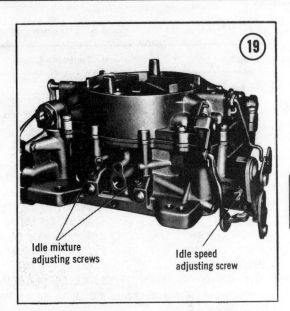

Idle mixture adjusting screws

Idle speed adjusting screw

5. Kill engine.

6. Turn idle mixture screw(s) in (clockwise) as far as possible, allowing it (them) to bottom *lightly*. Back screw(s) out three turns or until a stop is felt, whichever occurs first.

7. Start engine again and let it idle for one minute.

8. Turn idle mixture screw(s) in either direction until the highest steady rpm is indicated on tachometer.

9. Readjust idle to specified rpm, using idle speed screw in accelerator linkage. Figure 19 is typical.

**TROUBLESHOOTING**

Any engine requires an uninterrupted fuel supply, air, unfailing ignition (gasoline engine) and adequate compression. If any one of these is lacking, the engine will not run. Troubleshooting must first localize the trouble to one of these areas, then concentrate on finding the specific cause. **Tables 8 and 9** will help you to localize specific troubles with a minimum of effort.

Table 8        TROUBLESHOOTING DIESEL ENGINES

| Trouble | Probable Cause |
|---|---|
| Low cranking speed | 1, 2, 3, 4 |
| Will not start | 5, 6, 7, 8, 9, 10, 12, 13, 14, 15, 16, 17, 18, 19, 20, 22, 31, 32, 33 |
| Difficult starting | 5, 7, 8, 9, 10, 11, 12, 13, 14, 15, 16, 18, 19, 20, 21, 22, 24, 29, 31, 32, 33 |
| Lack of power | 8, 9, 10, 11, 12, 13, 14, 18, 19, 20, 21, 22, 23, 24, 25, 26, 27, 31, 32,33 |
| Misfiring | 8, 9, 10, 12, 13, 14, 16, 18, 19, 20, 25, 26, 28, 29, 30, 32 |
| Excessive fuel consumption | 11, 13, 14, 16, 18, 19, 20, 22, 23, 24, 25, 27, 28, 29, 31, 32, 33 |
| Black exhaust | 11, 13, 14, 16, 18, 19, 20, 22, 24, 25, 27, 28, 29, 31, 32, 33 |
| Blue/white exhaust | 4, 16, 18, 19, 20, 25, 27, 31, 33, 34, 35, 45, 56 |
| Low oil pressure | 4, 36, 37, 38, 39, 40, 42, 43, 44, 58 |
| Knocking | 9, 14, 16, 18, 19, 22, 26, 28, 29, 31, 33, 35, 36, 45, 46, 59 |
| Erratic running | 7, 8, 9, 10, 11, 12, 13, 14, 16, 20, 21, 23, 26, 28, 29, 30, 33, 35, 45, 59 |
| Vibration | 13, 14, 20, 23, 25, 26, 29, 30, 33, 45, 47, 48, 49 |
| High oil pressure | 4, 38, 41 |
| Overheating | 11, 13, 14, 16, 18, 19, 24, 25, 45, 50, 51, 52, 53, 54, 57 |
| Excessive crankcase pressure | 25, 31, 33, 34, 45, 55 |
| Poor compression | 11, 19, 25, 28, 29, 31, 32, 33, 34, 46, 59 |
| Starts and stops | 10, 11, 12 |

**Key to Troubleshooting Chart**

1. Battery capacity low
2. Bad electrical connections
3. Faulty starter motor
4. Incorrect grade of lubricating oil
5. Low cranking speed
6. Fuel tank empty
7. Faulty stop control operation
8. Blocked fuel feed pipe
9. Faulty fuel lift pump
10. Choked fuel filter
11. Restriction in air cleaner
12. Air in fuel system
13. Faulty fuel injection pump
14. Faulty atomisers or incorrect type
15. Incorrect use of cold start equipment
16. Faulty cold starting equipment
17. Broken fuel injection pump drive
18. Incorrect fuel pump timing
19. Incorrect valve timing
20. Poor compression
21. Blocked fuel tank vent
22. Incorrect type or grade of fuel
23. Sticking throttle or restricted movement
24. Exhaust pipe restriction
25. Cylinder head gasket leaking
26. Overheating
27. Cold running
28. Incorrect tappet adjustment
29. Sticking valves
30. Incorrect high pressure pipes
31. Worn cylinder bores
32. Pitted valves and seats
33. Broken, worn, or sticking piston ring(s)
34. Worn valve stems and guides
35. Overfull air cleaner or use of incorrect grade of oil
36. Worn or damaged bearings
37. Insufficient oil in sump
38. Inaccurate gauge
39. Oil pump worn
40. Pressure relief valve sticking open
41. Pressure relief valve sticking closed
42. Broken relief valve spring
43. Faulty suction pipe
44. Choked oil filter
45. Piston seizure/pick up
46. Incorrect piston height
47. Damaged fan
48. Faulty engine mounting (housing)
49. Incorrectly aligned flywheel housing or flywheel
50. Faulty thermostat
51. Restriction in water jacket
52. Loose fan belt
53. Choked radiator
54. Faulty water pump
55. Choked breather pipe
56. Damaged valve stem oil deflectors (if fitted)
57. Coolant level too low
58. Blocked sump strainer
59. Broken valve spring

Table 9    TROUBLESHOOTING GASOLINE ENGINES

| Trouble | Probable Cause | Correction |
|---|---|---|
| Starter will not crank engine | Discharged battery | Charge or replace battery |
| | Corroded battery terminals | Clean terminals |
| | Loose connection in starting circuit | Check and tighten all connections |
| | Defective starting switch | Replace switch |
| | Starter motor brushes dirty | Clean or replace brushes |
| | Jammed bendix gear | Loosen starter motor to free gear |
| | Defective starter motor | Replace motor |
| Starter motor turns but does not crank engine | Partially discharged battery | Charge or replace battery |
| | Defective wiring or wiring of too low capacity | Check wiring for worn acid spots. |
| | Broken bendix drive | Remove starter motor and repair drive |
| Engine will not start | Empty fuel tank | Fill tank with proper fuel |
| | Flooded engine | Remove spark plugs and crank engine several times. Replace plugs |
| | Water in fuel system | If water is found, clean tank, fuel lines, and carburetor. Refill with proper fuel |
| | Inoperative or sticking choke valve | Check valve, linkage, and choke rod or cable for proper operation |
| | Improperly adjusted carburetor | Adjust carburetor |
| | Clogged fuel lines or defective fuel pump | Disconnect fuel line at carburetor. If fuel does not flow freely when engine is cranked, clean fuel line and sediment bowl. If fuel still does not flow freely after cleaning, repair or replace pump |
| Engine will not start. (Poor compression and other causes) | Air leak around intake manifold | Check for leak by squirting oil around intake connections. If leak is found, tighten manifold and if necessary replace gaskets |
| | Loose spark plugs | Check oil plugs for proper seating, gasket, and tightness. Replace all damaged plugs and gaskets |
| | Loosely seating valves | Check for broken or weak valve springs, warped stems, carbon and gum deposits, and insufficient tappet clearance |
| | Damaged cylinder head gasket | Check for leaks around gasket when engine is cranked. If a leak is found, replace gasket |
| | Worn or broken piston rings | Replace broken and worn rings. Check cylinders for "out-of-round" and "taper" |

(continued)

3

Table 9     TROUBLESHOOTING GASOLINE ENGINES (continued)

| Trouble | Probable Cause | Correction |
|---|---|---|
| Engine will not start (ignition system) | Ignition switch "off" or defective | Turn on switch or replace |
| | Fouled or broken spark plugs | Remove plugs and inspect for cracked poreclain, dirty points, or improper gap |
| | Improperly set, worn or pitted distributor points. Defective ignition coil | Remove center wire from distributor cap and hold within ⅜ in. of motor block. Crank engine. Clean, sharp spark should jump between wire and block when points open. Clean and adjust points. If spark is weak or yellow after adjustment of points, replace condenser. If spark still is weak or not present, replace ignition coil |
| | Wet, cracked, or broken distributor | Wipe inside surfaces of distributor dry with clean cloth. Inspect for cracked or broken parts. Replace parts where necessary |
| | Improperly set, worn, or pitted magneto breaker points (magneto models only) | Remove spark plug wire and hold within ⅜ in. of engine block. Clean, sharp spark should jump between wire and block when engine is cranked. If spark is weak or not present, clean and adjust breaker points |
| | Improperly set, worn, or pitted timer points. Defective coil or defective condenser | Remove spark plug wire and hold within ⅛ in. of engine block. A clean, sharp spark should jump between wire and block when engine is cranked. Clean and set timer points. If spark still is not present when engine is cranked, replace coil |
| | Improper timing | Set timing |
| Excessive coolant temperatures | No water circulation | Check for clogged water lines and restricted inlets and outlets. Check for broken or stuck thermostat. Look for worn or damaged water pump or water pump drive |
| | Broken or stuck thermostat | Replace thermostat |
| No oil pressure | Defective gauge or tube | Replace gauge or tube |
| | No oil in engine | Refill with proper grade oil |
| | Dirt in pressure relief valve | Clean valve |
| | Defective oli pump, leak in oil lines, or broken oil pump drive | Check oil pump and oil pump drive for worn or broken parts. Tighten all oil line connections |
| Low oil pressure | Too light body oil | Replace with proper weight oil |
| | Oil leak in pressure line | Inspect all oil lines. Tighten all connections |
| | Weak or broken pressure relief valve spring | Replace spring |
| | Worn oil pump | Replace pump |
| | Worn or loose bearings | Replace bearings |

(continued)

**Table 9     TROUBLESHOOTING GASOLINE ENGINES** (continued)

| Trouble | Probable Cause | Correction |
|---|---|---|
| Oil pressure too high | Too heavy body oil | Drain oil and replace with oil of proper weight |
| | Stuck pressure relief valve | Clean or replace valve |
| | Dirt or obstruction in lines | Drain and clean oil system. Check for bent or flattened oil lines and replace where necessary |
| Loss of rpm | Damaged propeller | Repair propeller |
| | Bent rudder | Repair |
| | Misalignment | Realign engine to shaft |
| | Too tight stuffing box packing gland | Adjust |
| | Dirty boat bottom | Clean |
| Vibration | Misfiring or preignition | See correction under preignition |
| | Loose foundation or foundation bolts | Tighten |
| | Propeller shaft out of line or bent | Repair |
| | Propeller bent or pitch out of true | Repair |
| Preignition | Defective spark plugs | Check all spark plugs for broken porcelain, burned electrodes, or electrodes out of adjustment. Replace all defective plugs or clean and reset |
| | Improper timing | Retime ignition |
| | Engine carbon | Remove cylinder head and clean out carbon |
| | Engine overheating | See correction under "Excessive coolant temperature" portion of this table |
| Backfiring | Insufficient fuel reaching engine due to dirty lines, strainer, or blocked fuel tank vent. Water in fuel | See correction under "Engine will not start" portion of this table |
| | Poorly adjusted distributor | See correction under "Engine will not start" portion of this table |
| Sludge in oil | Infrequent oil changes | Drain and refill with proper weight oil |
| | Water in oil | Drain and refill. If trouble persists, check for cracked block, defective head gasket, and cracked head |
| | Dirty oil filter | Replace filter |

**3**

# CHAPTER FOUR

# LAY-UP AND FITTING OUT

## LAY-UP

Boats that are to be stored for more than four or five weeks should be prepared carefully. This is necessary to prevent damage to the engine and the stern drive unit from freezing, corrosion and/or fuel system contamination. Preparation for lay-up should begin, if possible, while the boat is still in the water. If the boat has been removed from the water, a supply of coolant water must be made available to the engine. This can be accomplished in two ways. The stern drive unit can be submerged in a test tank, or a garden hose may be attached to the cooling system using an adapter (available for most stern drive models).

The suggestions for lay-up preparation which follow are based on recommendations made by a number of leading engine and stern drive manufacturers.

### In-The-Water Preparation

1. Operate the engine for 15-20 minutes, or until normal operating temperature is reached. Kill engine, then drain the engine oil and replace oil filter element.
2. Refill crankcase with oil (see Chapter Two, *Preventive Maintenance*, for proper type and amount of oil for make and model of engine).

Restart engine and run for several minutes to allow oil to circulate to all lubricated areas.

3. Fog engine by one of the following methods:

   a. Add a fuel conditioner (such as Chris-Craft Fuel Conditioner and Valve Lubricant) to the fuel supply, following manufacturer's instructions. Run engine for about 15 minutes to disperse conditioner throughout engine. Close fuel valve at tank and allow engine to die of starvation.

### WARNING
*The following step requires the removal of the flame arrestor from the carburetor. A fire extinguisher should be close at hand and the engine observed at all times.*

   b. Remove flame arrestor (**Figure 1**) from carburetor intake and start engine. Fog engine by slowly pouring six or eight ounces of fogging oil (OMC Rust Preventive Oil, Chris-Craft Fogging Oil, Shell VSI, or equivalent) into the carburetor intake while running engine at fast idle. Then decrease engine speed to normal idle and rapidly pour several more ounces of fogging oil into carburetor. This should stall engine. If not, turn off ignition im-

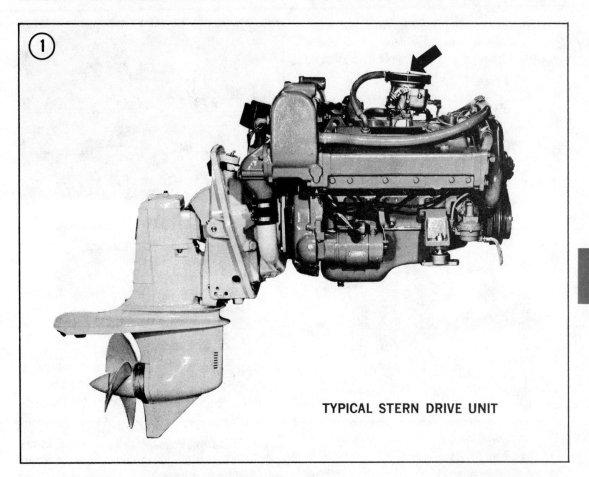

TYPICAL STERN DRIVE UNIT

4

mediately. Clean flame arrestor with solvent, dry, and replace on carburetor.

FUEL PUMP

FUEL FILTER

YOKE SCREW

### WARNING
*Before performing next step, turn off fuel switch at tank to avoid spilling fuel into bilges. When removing filter bowl, or fuel filter element, use a plastic bag or other container to catch spillage.*

4. Remove and clean or replace fuel filter element (depending upon type) and/or fuel filter sediment bowl (see **Figure 2** for typical filter).

5. Remove boat from water, keeping bow higher than stern if possible to assist in draining the exhaust system.

### Out-of-Water Preparation

1. Adjust trailer or cradle so that engine is in a level position. Lower stern drive unit to DOWN position.

2. Flush cooling system with fresh water. This is especially important if boat has been operated in salt or contaminated water. For more thorough drainage, open drain valves and/or plugs

on exhaust manifold(s) (see **Figures 3 and 4** for typical locations) and on side(s) of cylinder block (see **Figures 5 and 6** for typical locations).

> NOTE: *Marine engines usually employ 2 water pumps. The raw water pump, which may be located either in the stern drive unit or on the engine as an attachment, provides the water source for engine and exhaust cooling. The circulating pump performs the same function and is similar in appearance to an automotive water pump, but is usually a heavy-duty marine pump.*

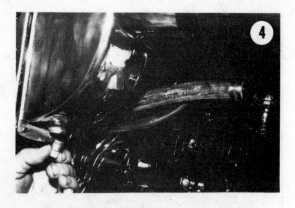

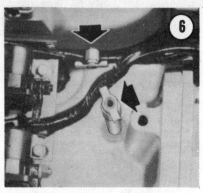

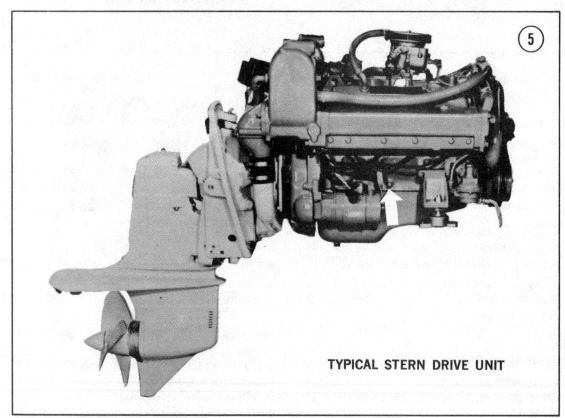

TYPICAL STERN DRIVE UNIT

3. Disconnect the intake and discharge hoses to the circulating pump (and also the raw water pump, if located on engine). Disconnect and ground coil lead to distributor. Crank engine over a few times to discharge any water present. Replace hoses, tighten clamps, and reconnect coil lead to distributor.

4. Some engines have readily removable access plates or plugs on the intake manifold. If present, remove these plates or plugs and, using a pump (an oil suction pump is ideal) remove any water present. Replace plates or plugs.

> NOTE: *The following step is optional, but is one which should be considered if the boat is to be stored for an extended period or subjected to extreme temperatures during storage period.*

5. Make certain all valves, plugs, plates and hoses opened or removed in the steps above are closed and replaced. Using the hose attached to the circulating pump intake as a funnel, fill the engine with a 50 percent solution of permanent anti-freeze. This helps prevent scale formation, freezing damage, and drying out of seals and gaskets. Reconnect and tighten water hose.

6. Cover flame arrestor and carburetor with a plastic bag and tape tightly into place. This will help prevent moisture from entering the carburetor and intake manifold.

7. Either completely drain the fuel system, or add a fuel conditioner (such as OMC 2+4) and top off fuel tank. The latter will help prevent moisture condensation and scale formation in the fuel tank.

8. Tape the exhaust outlets to prevent moisture from entering the exhaust manifolds and the valve chambers.

9. Cover through-hull fuel tank ventilators with tape to help keep moisture from the fuel tank.

10. Clean engine exterior thoroughly and retouch any blemishes with engine touch-up paint.

11. Apply a film of rust preventative oil to all exposed engine surfaces.

12. Remove battery from boat. Wash exterior with baking soda solution to remove corrosion and acid traces. Cover terminals with light coat of petroleum jelly. Store battery in area not subject to freezing temperatures. Either hook battery to trickle charger, or arrange to have battery recharged periodically (once a month is typical).

13. Remove distributor cap and apply light film of oil to points and cam. Replace distributor cap.

## Stern Drive Units

1. Drain oil from the stern drive unit and fill with preservative oil (Shell Ensis Oil 20 or equivalent).

2. Remove all marine growths and deposits from the stern drive unit.

3. Clean the stern drive unit with fresh water, and then with kerosene, mineral spirits, or similar solvent.

4. Touch up any paint blemishes.

CAUTION
*Do not paint sacrificial zinc rings, plugs, or bars, if present. These must be left unpainted in order for them to prevent electrolysis damage.*

5. Apply a protective coating of rust preventive oil to all exterior surfaces.

## Jet Drive Units

1. Wash out jet unit with fresh water, especially if used in salt water.

2. If jet is equipped with intake strainer system, remove both hoses and allow to drain. Reconnect hoses. Remove strainer bowl, empty water, and replace.

3. Lubricate thrust bearing, bowl bearing, drive shaft, and other lubrication points (see Chapter Two, *Preventive Maintenance*).

4. Perform Steps 2 through 5 of *Stern Drive Unit* instructions above.

## FITTING OUT

Preparing the boat engine and stern drive unit for use after storage is relatively easy if the boat was properly prepared before storage. The following suggestions for fitting out are based on the recommendations of several engine and stern drive manufacturers.

1. Clean engine and stern drive unit with a solvent such as kerosene to remove accumulated

dirt and preservative oil. Retouch any paint blemishes.

> NOTE: *If the boat is to be left in the water for an extended period of time, it may be advisable to cover the underwater surfaces, including the stern drive unit, with antifouling paint. Many manufacturers strongly advise against using a paint containing copper or mercury, as these elements may hasten electrolysis damage.*

2. Remove protective covers installed on flame arrestor, carburetor, exhaust outlets, and fuel tank ventilators.

3. Make sure that all drain valves and plugs are tightly closed, and that all water hoses are securely clamped in place.

4. Inspect all hoses for cracks, weak walls, and leaks, and replace any which are questionable.

5. Check all through-hull fittings for leaks and proper valve operation.

6. Remove, clean, and install flame arrestor.

7. Check fuel system. If tanks were drained, refill. Turn on fuel shut-off valve(s), and check all fuel lines for leaks.

8. Check battery water level and fill if necessary. Make certain battery has a full charge. Install battery, making certain cables are installed with proper polarity. Cover battery terminals with light coat of petroleum jelly.

9. Drain preservative oil from stern drive unit. Refill with oil of the proper weight and quantity (see Chapter Two, *Preventive Maintenance*).

10. Check oil level in crankcase. Add oil if necessary.

> NOTE: *If oil was not changed at time of lay-up, or if engine has been in storage for an extended period, change oil and oil filter.*

11. Make a thorough check of the boat, engine, and stern drive unit for loose or missing nuts, bolts and screws. Pay particular attention to the stern drive transom connection and, in the case of jet drives, water intake adapters. Tighten, replace, or make other repairs, as necessary.

12. Examine sacrificial zinc elements, if present, and replace if more than 50 percent eaten away.

13. Remove distributor cap and examine distributor points. Replace points if any wear is evident. If old points are to be reused, clean thoroughly with alcohol or acetone to remove all traces of oil. Install and set points, using a dwell meter (see Chapter Three, *Tune-ups*). Clean and replace distributor cap.

14. Provide a source of water for engine cooling. Make certain a fire extinguisher is handy, and start engine. Allow engine to warm up, making certain that water is circulating properly and engine does not overheat.

15. Proceed with engine tune-up. See Chapter Three for instructions and specifications.

# CHAPTER FIVE

# OMC STERN DRIVES

## GENERAL INFORMATION

The OMC stern drive system consists of 3 interacting components:

a. Intermediate housing group
b. Upper gearcase group
c. Lower gearcase group

The intermediate housing group connects the engine drive shaft to the vertical drive shaft of the upper and lower gearcases, and provides watertight passage of its own drive shaft through the transom.

The upper gearcase has a ball gear and shaft assembly which meshes with the ball gear at the end of the intermediate housing drive shaft. This group has pivot points for tilting the drive system and for steering.

The maintenance and repair instructions in this chapter are limited to those that a skilled amateur mechanic with a well-equipped toolbox could reasonably be expected to accomplish.

Disassembly of the drive train itself is not recommended because special tools and skills not possessed by most amateur mechanics are required. Tools required include an arbor press, special gear and bearing pullers, special holding devices, special wrenches, and special bearing gear and seal insertion tools. Improvised substitutes for these tools could result in destruction or serious damage to parts of the unit. The cost of acquiring all the special tools for one time or even occasional use would be prohibitive.

Procedures are given, however, for removing the intermediate housing group, the upper gearcase group, and the lower gearcase group from the boat and for replacing these components.

The intermediate housing is attached to the engine by an adapter housing. The ball gear shaft and bearing can be serviced without removing the housing from the engine. Should it be necessary to replace the intermediate housing, the vertical drive unit must be removed. Then the housing and engine must be removed from the boat as an assembly before separating the two. The intermediate housing is secured to the adapter by 14 nuts.

**Table 1** contains torgue tightening specifications. This table is located at the end of this chapter.

## TILT SYSTEM

The tilt system consists of an electric motor (DC) driving a worm which rotates a worm wheel and clutch assembly. The tilt motor is activated and controlled by tilt solenoids, tilt switch, the battery, and associated wiring. The system operates only when the ignition switch is in the ON position.

**Troubleshooting the Tilt System**

Before suspecting the tilt system, first check the battery. If the battery has a full charge, proceed as follows.

1. Operate tilt motor. If it runs, then stalls, check for obstruction or mechanical binding. If present, remove or correct. If not, proceed to Step 2.

2. Using a voltmeter, check for 12V DC at tilt motor connections with switch in UP and DOWN positions. If 12V is present, remove tilt motor (see below) and repair or replace.

3. If either the UP or DOWN circuit registers less than 12V at tilt motor, trace circuits back to battery positive (+) terminal to determine faulty component. Make voltage checks at each component (tilt solenoids, tilt switch, ignition switch, ammeter, starter solenoid) and at each connector. Remove and repair or replace any faulty component.

**Bench Checking Tilt Motor**

1. Remove tilt motor from intermediate assembly by unthreading 2 thru-bolts and disconnecting convertor. Remove coupling, key, spring, 2 washers, and gasket from shaft.

2. Install two ¼-20 nuts on thru-bolts to hold motor together and clamp motor in vise.

3. Connect positive pole of a fully charged battery and ammeter in series to green lead on tilt motor. Connect voltmeter between green lead and ground. Connect another lead to negative battery pole.

4. Attach a screwdriver socket to an inch-pounds torque wrench. Install the screwdriver socket in slot in end of motor armature shaft.

5. Momentarily ground the lead from the battery negative pole while firmly grasping torque wrench. Take readings from torque wrench, ammeter, and voltmeter.

> NOTE: *Motor stall torque must be not less than 27 in.-lb. Voltmeter readings should be approximately 11 volts, and the ammeter reading should be about 120 amps.*

6. Change battery positive lead and ammeter lead to motor green terminal, reverse torque

wrench-screwdriver setup, and repeat test. Readings should be approximately the same.

> CAUTION
> *Do not operate motor any longer than required to take readings. Allow motor to cool several minutes between tests. Heat generated during successive tests could damage motor or result in lower than normal torque readings.*

Low current and torque readings indicate high resistance in internal connections or in brush contacts. High current with low torque indicates faulty armature or field windings. To check for faulty armature, repeat stall-torque test above and turn torque wrench in opposite direction of tilt motor. If torque changes materially or dead spots with no torque reading are encountered, armature is probably at fault.

**Tilt Motor Cleaning and Inspection**

1. Using wire brush, remove sealing compound from tilt motor exterior. Any clinging particles can be removed with a clean cloth dipped in solvent.

> CAUTION
> *Use solvent sparingly and do not allow it to penetrate into motor winding, as this could result in damage to motor. Use only a clean cloth to clean armature and other motor internal parts.*

2. Remove thru-bolts, then remove motor end heads and examine brushes. If brushes are worn unevenly (ends should be evenly concave to match curvature of commutator), or if they are less than ¼ in. long, they must be replaced as follows.

  a. Cut off old brushes so that about ⅜ in. of each lead remains on end head.

  b. Splice new brush leads to remains of old leads attached to end head. Splice may be wrapped with fine wire to hold it together while soldering.

  c. Solder lead connections, allowing solder to flow freely into splice. Trim ends of wrapping wire when solder joint cools.

3. Check armature for short circuits, using milliammeter between commutator segments. Work

from segment to segment. Readings all should be approximately the same. A significantly lower reading indicates a shorted armature.

> NOTE: *If test indicates shorted armature, turn commutator on a lathe, undercut insulation between segments, and recheck. If this does not remedy the defect, armature must be replaced. Turning and undercutting should be performed by a qualified mechanic.*

4. Rotate one lead of a continuity checker around the commutator while holding the other lead to the armature core. An indication of continuity means a grounded armature that must be replaced.

5. Check end head bearings on the armature shaft for wear (side-play). If wear is present, replace end heads (bearings cannot be replaced separately). Cut lead to field coil as close as possible to end head. Solder field coil lead directly to brush holder of new end head.

6. To check field coils for short circuit, connect one lead of a test light to either the blue or green tilt motor lead and ground the other test light lead to motor frame (with armature removed from motor). If test light goes on, field coil is grounded and must be replaced.

### Tilt Motor Reassembly

After parts have been cleaned and worn or damaged parts replaced, reassemble tilt motor in reverse order of disassembly, observing the following.

1. Apply a few drops of engine oil to felt at end head bearings.

2. Apply a light coat of rust preventative oil to armature shaft at drive end only.

3. Before securing thru-bolts, make certain end heads are properly aligned. Scribe marks on drive end head should match scribe marks on motor frame. Tab on commutator end head fits notch in frame.

4. During final assembly pull out blue and green leads to remove excess wire from interior of the motor.

5. After assembly is completed, coat both end head seams, pole shoe screws, and thru-bolt heads, and area where leads enter motor, with waterproof sealer.

### Testing Tilt Solenoids

Solenoids seldom cause trouble, and are not repairable. To test a solenoid:

1. Connect a continuity light or a test meter to the 2 large solenoid terminals.

2. Connect a 12V DC battery (or power supply) to the 2 small solenoid terminals. If the meter shows continuity, the solenoid will operate at the voltage supplied by the battery or power supply.

> NOTE: *If a carbon pile or other variable voltage control is available, connect it in series with the battery, and reduce voltage input to solenoid to less than 6 volts. Then gradually increase voltage until continuity checker or meter gives an indication. If voltage reading is between 6 and 8 volts, solenoid is OK. If reading is above 8 volts, solenoid should be replaced to assure consistent performance.*

### Tilt Unit Worm Gear and Shaft Removal/Installation

1. Remove retaining ring (see **Figure 1**).

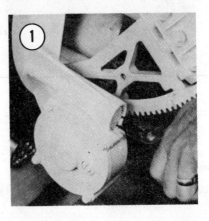

2. Grasp outdrive unit and tilt it upward by hand. This will push out the retainer bearing and O-ring seal, worm gear, and shaft (see **Figure 2**).

CAUTION
*Do not use power tilt to raise drive unit.*

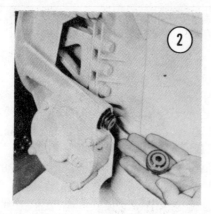

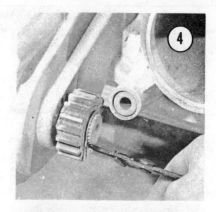

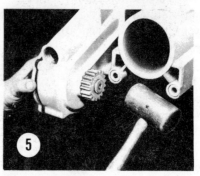

NOTE: *If vertical drive has been removed, a special spanner wrench (OMC No. 907700) can be used on the tilt gear to perform the operation described in Step 2.*

3. Remove worm and shaft.

4. Installation is the reverse of these steps.

### Clutch Cover Removal/Installation

1. Remove the worm gear and the shaft as described previously.

2. Loosen 4 clutch cover retaining screws (see **Figure 3**) and drain oil.

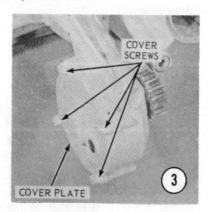

3. Remove retaining ring securing tilt gear to clutch shaft (see **Figure 4**).

4. Hold clutch cover so that it does not fall and gently tap end of clutch shaft with rawhide mallet. Tap until clutch cover is loosened, but do not remove cover (see **Figure 5**).

5. Hold tilt gear and pull clutch cover and clutch assembly from housing (see **Figure 6**).

6. Remove worm wheel from clutch assembly. Separate cover and clutch assembly. Remove cover gasket and O-ring (see **Figure 7**).

7. Installation is the reverse of these steps.

### Tilt Unit and Clutch Assembly Removal/Installation

1. Remove thrust washer from splined end of clutch shaft (or from inside clutch housing). See **Figures 8 and 9**.

2. If oil seal at rear of tilt clutch cavity appears to be damaged, remove seal with a punch or other tool.

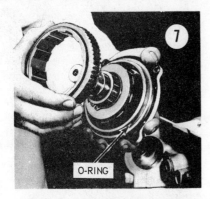

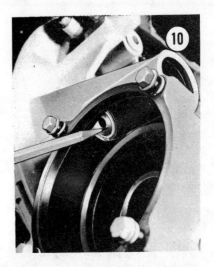

**Figure 11.** *If care is taken, a large vise or C-clamp (or some models of drill press) could be substituted for an arbor press.*

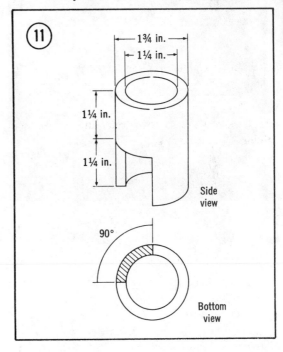

NOTE: *Once removed, old seal cannot be reused. Make certain replacement is available before removing it. Also note direction of seal lip to aid in assembly.*

3. If worn, remove tilt worm shaft by removing tilt motor and driving out bushing with a drift (see **Figure 10**).

4. Place clutch and shaft in an arbor press, depress the belleville springs, and release the retaining ring.

> NOTE: *A suitable tool for depressing clutch can be made from a piece of pipe, using dimensions shown in*

5. Remove and inspect clutch discs. If damage, excessive wear, and/or corrosion are present, the entire clutch pack with shim(s) should be replaced.

> NOTE: *Use all shims that come with replacement kit, as width of clutch disc assembly is held to close tolerances.*

6. Installation is the reverse of these steps.

## OIL RESERVOIR COVER

### Removal/Installation

1. Remove 6 screws from oil reservoir cover. Remove cover and discard gasket.

2. Remove oil, flush reservoir with solvent and dry thoroughly.

3. Clean gasket surfaces on cover plate and intermediate housing.

4. Reassemble using new gasket and gasket sealing compound (see **Figure 12**).

## VERTICAL DRIVE ASSEMBLY

### Removal

The vertical drive assembly, consisting of the upper and lower gearcase assemblies, must be removed before the intermediate assembly and engine can be removed from the boat. The instructions below are for removal of the vertical drive and separation into upper and lower gearcase assemblies.

#### CAUTION

*The lower gearcase assembly contains the electramatic gear shifting arrangement. This arrangement uses a switch and electromagnetic coils, rather than mechanical linkage, to shift the stern drive into forward, neutral, and re-*

*verse. Use care when removing or installing wiring to these coils to prevent loosening connections and/or breaks in insulation. Either could cause malfunctioning of the shifting system and possibly damage to the gears.*

As noted above, removal of the drive train shafts, bearings, gears, shims, etc., from the gearcase is not within the scope of this book as highly specialized skills and special tools are required. To remove the vertical drive assembly, proceed as follows.

1. Drain oil by placing drive unit in down position and removing oil drain and oil level plugs. Tilt unit slightly to alow oil to drain completely.

2. Disconnect shift wires at back of power head on port side of engine, above tilt motor. Slide back rubber covers and disconnect the blue and green wires (see **Figure 13**).

SHIFT WIRE TERMINALS

3. Turn the drive unit to the full starboard turn position and pull wires through hole in intermediate housing.

4. Remove retaining clip from shift wires (see **Figure 14**). Then remove wires from spring and clamp assembly (see **Figure 15**).

CABLE CLAMP

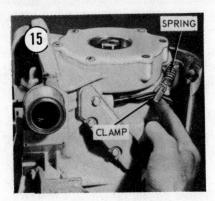

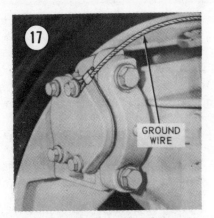

5. Remove propeller by removing cotter pin, propeller nut, and drive pin.

6. Mark ball gear teeth for correct engagement upon reassembly (see **Figure 16**).

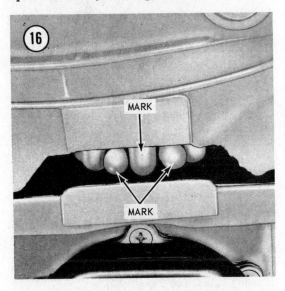

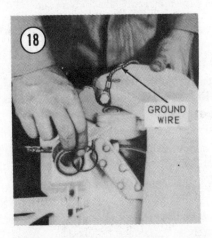

7. Loosen 4 capscrews, port and starboard, holding end cover plates to intermediate housing (see **Figure 17**). Remove ground wire from port end cover plate screw.

### CAUTION
*If end cover plates are not loosened, O-ring seal (**Figure 18A**) will be damaged, causing a water leak.*

8. Pry off rubber bumpers, if so equipped, and loosen 2 cap screws (port and starboard) that hold the pivot cap assemblies. See **Figure 18B**.

9. Support the drive unit securely. Remove cap screws and pivot cap assemblies. Remove the drive unit.

NOTE: *The manufacturer recommends special holding fixtures to support the drive unit after removal. However, it may be possible to support the unit by clamping the skeg in a large, strong vise (firmly attached to a stable work bench) with padded jaws. The drive unit should also be supported from above, using a chain fall or other suitable device.*

### CAUTION
*Leave pivot liners on pivot arms to protect their machined surface from damage. Keep pivot caps in a safe place. Also, pivot caps are marked "R" and "L" for right and left, and should not be interchanged when reinstalled.*

### Installation

To install the upper and lower gearcase assemblies to the intermediate housing, proceed as follows.

5

1. Install new O-rings on pivot arms. Lubricate liners with anti-corrosion lubricant (see Figure 18) and install liners with split 180 degrees from grease filling cap.

2. Align boat steering wheel to center of travel and install upper and lower gear case assembly on intermediate housing.

### CAUTION
*Make certain that ball gear teeth marked during disassembly are intermeshed properly when reassembling the stern drive (see Figure 16). Otherwise damage to gears may result.*

3. Install pivot caps in their proper port and starboard positions, but do not tighten at this time (see Figure 17).

4. Install cover plates, gaskets, and end caps (see Figure 17). Be sure gaskets and plates have flat edges at top. Reinstall ground wire under upper port rear end cap screw.

5. Tighten end cap screws to 5-7 ft.-lb. of torque. This will position liners. Now torque pivot cap screws to 18-20 ft.-lb.

6. Pull shift cable through intermediate housing to cable clamp and connect spring and clip assembly to cable (see Figure 15).

7. Connect shift cable blue and green leads to leads of matching colors (see Figure 13). Attach retaining clamp (see Figure 14).

8. Use grease gun and lubricate fittings on pivot caps. Fill upper and lower gearcases with OMC gearcase lubricant (see Chapter Two).

9. Replace propeller, using propeller nut, drive pin, and cotter pin.

## UPPER AND LOWER GEARCASES

1. Remove bumper and ground wire leg (see **Figure 19**).

2. Remove exhaust housing cover by removing 5 screws (see **Figure 20**). Place 2 medium sized screwdrivers under front of cover (see **Figure 21**). Lift up gently to loosen cover, then remove cover.

### CAUTION
*A splined embossment on the bottom of the exhaust housing cover engages a worm wheel (Tru-Course Steering Models) in the top of the upper gearcase. Lift cover straight up to avoid damage to the spline.*

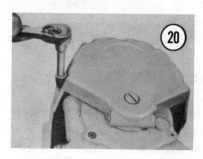

3. Remove O-ring from top of spline on exhaust housing cover (see **Figure 22**).

4. Remove washers and spring from top of upper gearcase (see **Figure 23**).

NOTE: *Washers and spring removed in Step 4 provide the ground for the shifting system.*

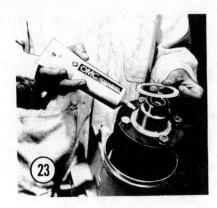

5. Remove upper gearcase by lifting straight up, then out.

### Joining

1. Liberally coat nylon swivel housing washer with anti-corrosion lubricant, then position washer, concave side first, on bottom of swivel housing (see Figure 23).

2. Position upper gearcase on lower gearcase. Make sure spline is properly seated by turning upper gearcase back and forth.

3. Align the flat on front of exhaust housing cover spline with flat at front of worm wheel spline (Tru-Course Steer models) and install exhaust housing cover.

4. Secure cover to exhaust housing with 5 mounting screws.

5. With upper gearcase resting naturally in lower gearcase, measure gap between exhaust housing cover and gear housing cover, using a feeler gauge (see **Figure 24**).

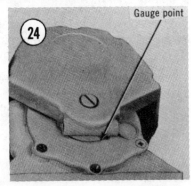
Gauge point

6. Raise upper gearcase as far as it will go and recheck gap.

NOTE: *Difference between the measurements taken in Steps 5 and 6 should not exceed 0.005 to 0.015 in.*

7. Remove exhaust housing cover (and worm wheel on Tru-Course Steer models) and install new O-ring in groove above spline. Select number of shims (each is 0.010 in.) required to bring gap into tolerance and install them over boss in center of upper gearcase (see **Figure 25**). Reinstall worm wheel (Truc-Course Steer models) making sure flat of internal spline is still toward front of gearcase.

8. Reinstall ground spring and washers on boss at top of upper gearcase (see **Figure 26**).

WASHER
SPRING

9. Reroute and fasten shift cable with guide and spring (rear of gearcase) and clip (front of gearcase). See Figures 14 and 15.

10. Lightly coat exhaust housing cover O-ring with anti-corrosion lubricant. Make certain that flat on exhaust housing cover spline matches flat on worm wheel spline. Press exhaust housing cover into place and fasten with 5 screws.

11. Recheck gap between exhaust housing cover and gearcase cover to make certain it is between 0.005 and 0.015 in. Repeat shimming procedure (Step 7) if necessary to bring into tolerance.

12. Reinstall bumper assembly and ground wire assembly on front of exhaust housing cover, using 2 mounting screws and lockwashers. Torque to 5-7 ft.-lb.

> NOTE: *Check assembly of vertical drive by using an inch-pound torque wrench and a 1-1/16 in., 12 point socket on the spur gear. Turn gear clockwise and then counterclockwise (full port to full starboard and back). Torque should not exceed 10 in.-lb. at any point.*

## INTERMEDIATE HOUSING

### Removal

To remove the intermediate housing group, the intermediate housing, adapter housing, and engine must be removed from the boat as a unit and then separated. Because of the weight of the units involved, a hoist with at least 1,000 pounds capacity is required.

1. Using the procedure found above, remove vertical drive unit from boat.

2. Remove engine mount bolts.

3. Remove transom seal assembly clamp.

4. Attach lifting harness to engine (lifting eyes or cylinder head studs), and harness to lifting device.

5. Raise engine slightly and check balance of lifting harness. Adjust as required.

6. Lift engine assembly just clear of engine mounts, then move lifting device ahead to clear transom seal with intermediate adapter.

7. Lift engine assembly clear of boat.

8. Remove 14 attaching screws to remove intermediate housing from adapter.

### Installation

Installing the intermediate housing is the reverse of removal. Care should be taken to carefully mate the drive shaft spline with the drive shaft adapter on the engine.

## SERVICING REMOTE CONTROLS

The manufacturer supplies 3 different types of remote control devices. All 3 perform the same functions: gear shifting and engine speed control.

### Troubleshooting Shift Malfunction

1. Turn ignition switch ON and observe boat ammeter reading.

2. Operate remote control lever to forward, then to reverse, and note ammeter readings for each position. Additional current at each position should not exceed 2.5 amperes. If current draw exceeds this amount in either gear, disconnect shift leads at intermediate housing and repeat test. If draw is still excessive, a short in the remote control switch or wiring is indicated (see remote control switches check procedure below). If no change is noted, trouble is in gearcase coils or wiring.

### CAUTION

*If coil leads are shorted to each other, both shift coils will operate at the same time. This will result in stalled engine or broken drive shaft.*

3. Connect ohmmeter alternately between each coil lead and ground. Resistance should be between 4.5 and 6.5 ohms for each coil. No reading indicates an open circuit. Higher reading indicates shorted wiring or shorted coil. If short is indicated, vertical drive unit should be removed and checked by a qualified mechanic.

### Troubleshooting—Starting Malfunction

Remote controls are wired to prevent starting of engine when gearshift is in either forward or reverse.

1. Place remote control lever in neutral position.

2. If starter fails to operate, check 20 A fuse between ignition switch BAT terminal and ammeter GEN terminal. Replace if blown.

3. If fuse is OK, check for continuity at white leads between remote control and ignition switch starter ST terminal and starter solenoid.

4. If starter operates in either gear, and neutral, check for short between the 2 white leads in control box wiring.

## Checking Remote Control Switches

1. Disconnect remote control switch cable at connector.

2. Connect test light or continuity meter between ignition (purple) lead terminal and forward (green) lead terminal. Operate control lever from forward to neutral and reverse positions. Circuit must indicate closed in forward and open in both neutral and reverse.

3. Connect test light or meter between ignition (purple) lead terminal and reverse (blue) lead terminal. Again operate control to all 3 positions. Circuit must be closed in reverse and open in neutral and forward.

4. Connect test light or meter between 2 neutral (white) lead terminals and operate control lever to all 3 positions. Circuit must indicate closed in neutral and open in forward and reverse.

NOTE: *If malfunction is indicated in any of the above 3 tests, replace the switch and cable assembly.*

## Single Lever Remote Control Disassembly

1. Remove 3 screws attaching control to boat and disconnect switch cable at connector.

2. Remove 3 screws holding control unit front and rear housings together.

3. Remove 2 screws retaining switch to front housing, then remove switch and cable.

4. Test switch and cable assembly, using procedure above.

NOTE: *Switch and cable cannot be repaired. Replace if defective.*

5. Examine interior of control unit for evidence of dirt, corrosion, and broken parts. Clean parts, if required, and wipe parts with oiled cloth.

CAUTION
*Do not immerse switch in cleaning solvent.*

## Single Lever Remote Control Assembly

1. Reassemble control unit components as shown in **Figure 27**. Make certain large chamfered side of hole in cam lever washer is facing out so that screw head turns down flush with the washer.

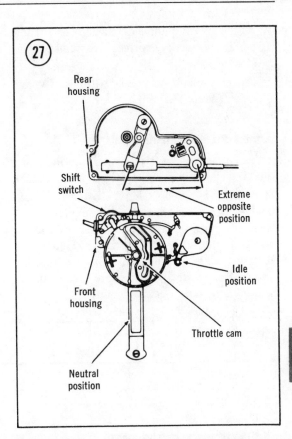

Rear housing

Shift switch

Extreme opposite position

Idle position

Front housing

Throttle cam

Neutral position

2. Place control lever in neutral position and auxiliary throttle in extreme idle position (see Figure 27).

3. Remove levers in rear housing to extreme opposite direction (see Figure 27).

4. Lubricate control mechanisms with anti-corrosion lubricant, particularly the throttle cam and cam roller.

5. Install switch and cable assembly in front housing, making certain grommet is properly seated in housing and switch toggle is centered in slot in control lever drum. Secure switch with 2 screws.

6. With control lever in neutral and rear housing levers in extreme opposite positions( see Figure 27), reassemble front and rear housings and secure with 3 screws.

NOTE: *Housings must be reassembled with levers in positions specified in Step 6 to allow cam roller to engage slot in throttle cam without disengaging switch toggle from slot in control lever drum.*

7. Recheck continuity of switch and cable assembly to verify correct reassembly (see procedure above).

8. Attach control unit to boat with 3 screws and reconnect cable assembly.

### Auxiliary Throttle Adjustment

1. Place control lever in neutral position and auxiliary throttle in full start position. Crank engine with key switch.

2. If starter doesn't crank, place auxiliary throttle in idle position and adjust set screw counter clockwise (CCW) a half turn (see **Figure 28**). Return auxiliary throttle to full start position and try starter. Repeat procedure (a half turn at a time) until starter cranks engine.

3. If starter does crank engine in Step 1 with auxiliary throttle fully advanced, back off on auxiliary throttle to determine point at which starter will not operate. Readjust set screw clockwise until starter operates with auxiliary throttle in full start position only.

Table 1    TORQUE SPECIFICATIONS

| Location | Ft.-Lb. | In.-Lb. |
|---|---|---|
| Lower gear case-to-exhaust housing bolts | 16-18 | |
| Fill and drain oil plugs | 4-5 | |
| Setscrews on clutch springs | | 60 |
| | | 30-35 |
| Elastic locknut on pinion gear | 70-80 | |
| Gear case head screws | 5-7 | |
| Tilt motor stall torque | | 27 |
| End cap screws | 5-7 | |
| Pivot cap screws | 18-20 | |
| Bumper assembly screws | 5-7 | |

# CHAPTER SIX

## MERCRUISER STERN DRIVES MODELS O AND I

This chapter describes the removal, installation, and repair of the Model O and I stern drives.

The procedures in this chapter can be performed by anyone with average mechanical skill and a well-equipped tool chest. This chapter does not include complete disassembly of the drive train as this requires special skills and tools that only an experienced MerCruiser mechanic and repair shop are likely to have.

Tightening torques are given in **Tables 1 and 2** at the end of this chapter.

### MERCRUISER MODEL O STERN DRIVE

#### Engine Removal (MerCruiser 60)

1. Unplug instrument panel harness plug from engine connector.
2. Disconnect cables from battery.
3. Disconnect throttle and shift cables.
4. Remove steering rod from steering clevis.
5. Remove clevis pin and clevis from steering arm, after removing cotter pin and washer.
6. Disconnect Ride-Guide steering cable from steering rod.
7. Disconnect tilt switch leads from condenser mounting bracket and ignition coil (**Figure 1**).

8. Remove hydraulic shift unit from mounting bracket and shift lever (see **Figure 2**).

CAUTION
*Do not remove hydraulic lines from hydraulic shift unit.*

9. Secure engine to overhead hoist, using suitable lifting sling or chains installed to engine

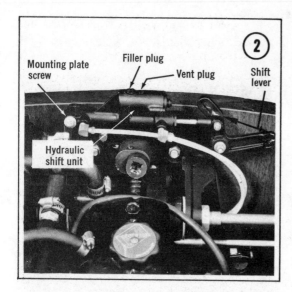

Mounting plate screw — Filler plug — Vent plug — Shift lever — Hydraulic shift unit — ②

lifting eyes. Take up all slack so that hoist will support engine when transom bolts are removed.

10. Remove nuts and washers from lower transom plate mounting bolts. Remove bolts (see **Figure 3**).

Elastic Nuts & Washers — ③

11. Remove tilt-up cable from top cover of stern drive unit.

12. Remove nuts and washers from upper transom mounting bolts (see **Figure 4**). Remove bolts and manual tilt-up unit from transom.

13. Disconnect the fuel line at the fuel pump connection.

### CAUTION
*Before disconnecting fuel line, make certain fuel valve at tank is closed. Use a suitable container to catch gasoline*

Hydraulic Shift Mounting Plate — Manual Tilt-Up — Elastic Nuts & Washers — ④

*when fuel line is disconnected. Do not allow smoking in or near the boat and keep a Coast Guard approved fire extinguisher at hand.*

14. Make a final check to assure that no wires, lines, etc., remain attached between the engine and the boat.

15. Pull engine forward approximately 4 in. to permit inner transom plate to disengage from stern drive unit.

16. Lift engine straight up and out of boat.

> NOTE: *Cooling system and crankcase may be drained at this time, if work is to be done on engine. Oil filter, ignition coil and fuel pump may also be removed if required.*

17. If engine is to be overhauled, mount it on suitable work stand.

### Engine Removal (MerCruiser 80 and 90)

1. Disconnect battery cables and unplug instrument panel wiring harness.

2. Close fuel tank valve and disconnect fuel line and throttle and shift control cables.

### CAUTION
*Use a suitable container to catch gasoline when disconnecting fuel line. Also, keep a Coast Guard approved fire extinguisher close at hand.*

3. Disconnect Ride-Guide steering cable from steering rod.

4. Loosen locknut, then remove steering rod from steering clevis.

5. Remove cotter pin and washer, then remove clevis pin and clevis from steering arm.

6. Disconnect tilt switch leads from engine harness and at starter solenoid (see **Figure 5**).

7. Remove hydraulic shift unit from mounting bracket (see **Figure 6**).

**CAUTION**
*Do not remove hydraulic lines from hydraulic shift unit.*

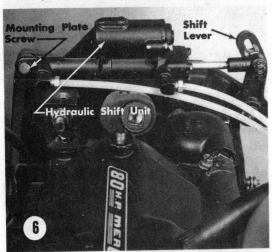

8. Attach engine to overhead hoist, using suitable sling or chains through engine lifting eyes. Take up all slack in hoist so that engine will be supported when transom bolts are removed.

9. Remove nuts and washers from lower transom plate mounting bolts, then remove bolts (see **Figure 7**).

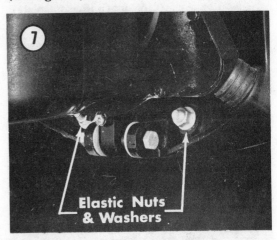

10. Remove tilt-up cable from top cover of stern drive unit.

11. Remove nuts and washers from upper transom mounting bolts (see **Figure 8**). Remove bolts and manual tilt-up unit from transom.

12. Make final check to see that no wires or lines are attached between engine and boat.

13. Pull engine forward approximately 4 in. to disengage inner transom plate from stern drive unit.

14. Lift engine straight up, then out of boat.

**Engine Installation**
**(MerCruiser 60, 80, and 90)**

NOTE: *Gimbal housing must be installed prior to engine installation.*

6

1. Apply a liberal coat of multipurpose lubricant (Mercury Part No. C-92-49588) to water tube (located on gimbal housing), guide bar, and exhaust tube (located on inner transom plate). See **Figure 9** for locations.

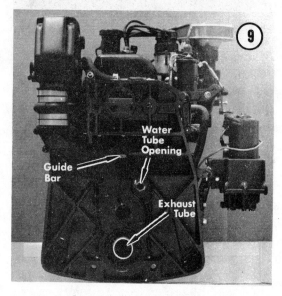

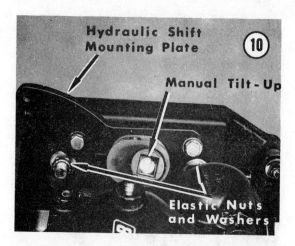

2. Attach engine to overhead hoist, using suitable lifting sling or chains attached to engine lifting eyes.

3. Lift engine up and into boat. Align exhaust tube and guide bar groove and exhaust opening on gimbal housing.

4. Carefully guide engine into position, watching water tube on gimbal housing to assure proper mating with hole in inner transom plate.

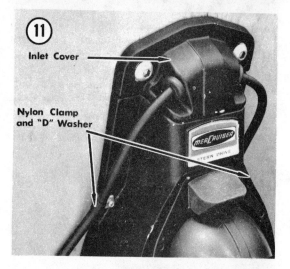

### CAUTION
*Be careful in aligning engine, as rocking engine from side to side may damage water tube seal located in transom plate. If seal is damaged, water leakage will result and engine will have to be removed to replace seal.*

5. Insert manual tilt unit (**Figure 10**) or hydraulic inlet cover (see **Figure 11**) and hoses through transom opening from outside boat and position on transom. If necessary, move hydraulic shift unit mounting plate up or down to povide clearance for tilt unit (see **Figure 12**).

NOTE: *Route MerCruiser 60 and 80 power tilt hoses to port side.*

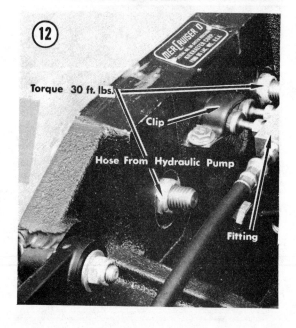

6. Place washers on 2 bolts, as shown in **Figures 13 and 14**, and insert bolts through upper hole in tilt unit, transom, and inner plate from outside bolt.

> NOTE: *Sealing washers are required on bolts on earlier models only. Take care to keep transom seal in position while tightening bolts.*

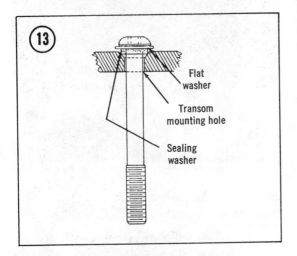

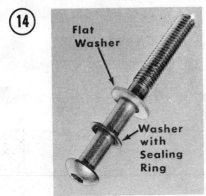

7. Install flat washer and elastic stop nut on each bolt. Tighten to 20-25 ft.-lb. Use a 5/16 in. Allen wrench to hold bolt heads during torquing.

8. Place washers on 2 bolts, as shown in Figures 13 and 14, and insert bolts in bottom holes of gimbal housing (from outside boat), transom, and inner transom plate.

9. Install flat washer and elastic stop nut on each bolt (see **Figure 15**) and torque to 20-25 ft.-lb., using 5/16 in. Allen wrench to hold bolt head.

10. Relieve tension on hoist and remove sling or chains from engine lifting eyes.

11. Tighten bolts holding hydraulic shift unit to transom plate (60 and 80 models only).

12. Place hydraulic shift unit piston on shift lever stud and position shift unit to mounting (or transom) plate with cap screw, spacer, washers, and nut (see **Figure 16 or 17**).

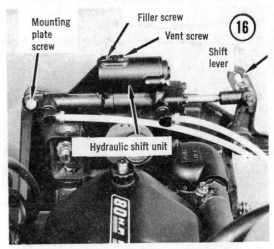

13. Fasten hydraulic shift unit piston to shift lever mounting stud with spacer, washer, and elastic stop nut.

> NOTE: *Do not tighten nut securely, as piston must pivot freely on stud.*

14. Mount hydraulic tilt hose to transom plate with metal clip, screw, and washer (Figure 12).

15. Remove cap from pump hydraulic hose and felting and quickly connect to prevent loss of fluid.

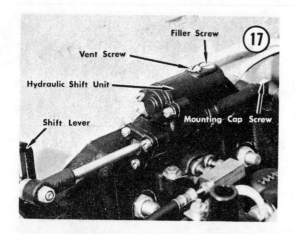

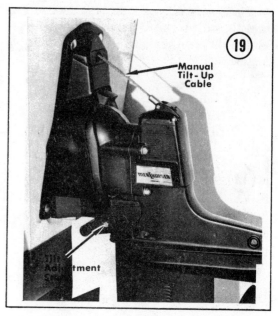

NOTE: *Further engine alignment is not a requirement for this type of installation.*

16. Reconnect fuel lines and battery cables. Plug instrument panel harness plug into engine receptacle.

17. Connect Ride-Guide, shift cable, and throttle cable as described in later procedures.

**Stern Drive Removal
(MerCruiser Model O)**

1. Remove tilt adjustment stud from gimbal ring. Then remove tilt cylinders, if so equipped (see **Figure 18**).

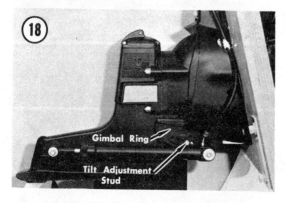

2. Remove manual tilt-up cable from top cover of stern drive unit, if so equipped (**Figure 19**).

3. Remove 4 elastic stop nuts and washers from studs attaching stern drive unit to bell housing.

4. Attach stern drive unit to overhead hoist using suitable sling. Support unit with hoist.

5. Carefully guide stern drive unit straight back and remove from boat.

**Stern Drive Installation
(MerCruiser Model O)**

1. Lubricate drive shaft housing pilot and drive shaft splines with multipurpose lubricant (Mercury Part No. C-92-49588). See **Figure 20**.

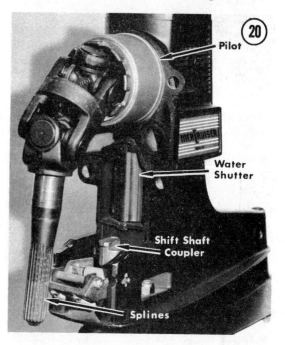

2. Position intermediate shift shaft coupler (located in drive unit) straight ahead as shown in Figure 20.

NOTE: *Position coupler by rotating propeller shaft.*

3. Check position of water shutter (see Figure 20). Make certain tabs on shutter are in recesses in drive shaft housing.

4. Lubricate inside of bell housing bore and shift shaft coupler (see **Figure 21**) with multi-purpose lubricant.

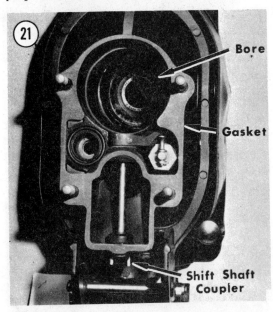

5. Place gasket in position on bell housing (see Figure 21).

6. Operate shift lever (inside boat) as far left as it will go to position upper shift shaft coupler as shown in Figure 21.

### CAUTION
*If upper and intermediate shift shaft couplers are not positioned as shown in Figures 20 and 21, bell housing and couplers will be damaged while attempting to install stern drive unit.*

7. Insert stern drive unit into bell housing guiding drive shaft through gimbal housing bearing into engine coupling.

NOTE: *If drive shaft splines do not engage with engine coupling splines, rotate propeller shaft counterclockwise until unit can be pushed into position.*

8. Install 4 flat washers and elastic stop nuts on studs connecting shaft housing to bell housing. Tighten nuts evenly, then torque to 40±3 ft.-lb.

9. Attach manual tilt-up cable (if so equipped) to top cover of stern drive unit (see Figure 19).

10. Install tilt adjustment stud in gimbal ring and tilt cylinders, if so equipped (see Figure 18).

### Gimbal Housing Removal

1. Remove stern drive as described elsewhere.

2. Remove bolts securing gimbal housing to transom. See **Figure 22**.

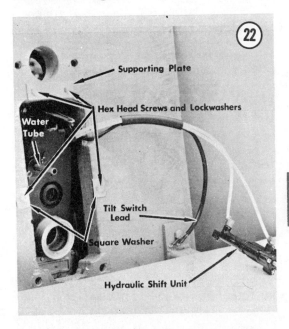

3. Remove gimbal housing and inside supporting plate.

### Gimbal Housing Installation

1. Insert hydraulic shift unit and tilt switch leads through large opening in boat's transom (see Figure 22).

2. Position gimbal housing on outside of transom. Hold housing in this position and position supporting plate on inside of transom.

3. Insert hex head bolts with lockwasher through supporting plate and transom and thread into holes for gimbal housing (see Figure 22).

4. Thread hex head bolts with lockwashers and flat washers through transom into gimbal housing (see Figure 22).

*CAUTION*
*Do not drive bolts through transom as threads in gimbal housing will be damaged.*

5. Tighten hex head bolts evenly and torque to 20 ft.-lb.

**Ride-Guide Attachment**

1. Lubricate cable guide tube with multipurpose lubricant.

2. Insert cable end through tube and thread fastening nut securely into tube.

3. Position steering rod clevis on steering arm (see **Figure 23**) and install clevis pin, washer, and cotter pin.

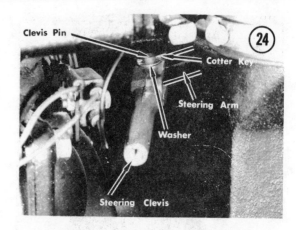

4. Thread steering rod into clevis and assemble cable on steering rod (see **Figure 24**). Tighten nut securely, then back off ¼ turn.

5. Center gimbal ring in gimbal housing by turning steering wheel.

> NOTE: *If steering wheel is not centered when gimbal ring is centered, remove steering rod from cable and adjust steering rod in clevis to center steering wheel. Then reinstall steering rod (see Step 4 above) and tighten locknut securely against clevis.*

**Shift Cable Attachment**

1. Place remote control handle in full forward position.

2. Pull shift lever out as far as possible (this shifts stern drive unit into forward gear). While shifting, turn propeller shaft counterclockwise

as far as it will go to ensure that the clutch is fully engaged.

3. Loosen hydraulic shift unit piston anchor stud, move anchor stud to bottom of shift lever slot, and tighten nut. Place remote control shift cable end guide on shift lever (see **Figure 25 or 26** as appropriate).

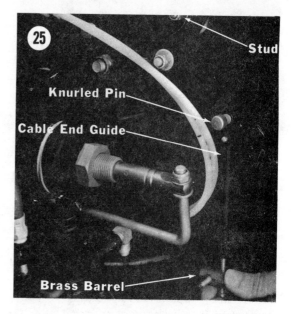

4. Pull outer shift cable as far as possible away from cable guide and adjust brass barrel on remote control shift cable to align with mounting stud on transom plate anchor point (Figure 25).

5. Fasten brass barrel with washers, spacer, and nut—tightening nut securely.

> NOTE: *If equipped with power tilt, secure hydraulic hose with Nygrip clamp and "D" washer.*

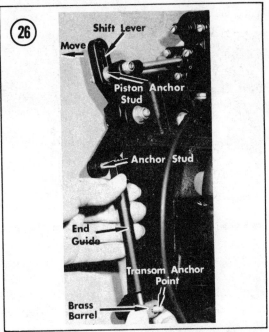

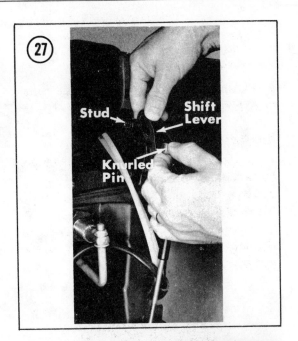

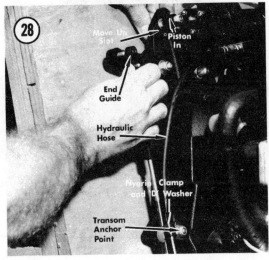

6. Disconnect remote control shift cable end guide from shift lever and move remote control handle to full reverse position.

7. Push shift lever as far in as it will go. This shifts stern drive unit into reverse. While shifting, rotate propeller shaft clockwise until shaft stops to assure full clutch engagement.

8. Loosen hydraulic shift unit piston anchor stud and move up slot in shaft lever until cable end guide can be reinstalled (see **Figure 27 or 28** as appropriate).

9. Tighten nut on stud fastening hydraulic shift unit piston to shift lever.

10. Install the hydraulic shift tube on MerCruiser 60 shift sender unit (mounted on inner transom plate assembly) by attaching long hydraulic tube to left inlet (looking aft from inside boat). Attach short tube to right inlet.

11. Attach short tube to upper inlet of shift receiver (located in bell housing) and long tube to lower inlet of shift receiver.

**Throttle Cable Attachment**

1. Make certain there are no sharp bends in throttle cable.

2. If required, attach cable to side and transom of boat, using cable clips.

3. Grasp cable behind brass barrel and push in on cable end guide. Adjust brass barrel to align with attaching points. Place flat washer sleeve and brass barrel on attaching stud. Then place flat washer and stop nut on stud. Tighten nut securely. See **Figures 29 through 33**.

4. Verify that throttle valve in carburetors are fully open when remote control lever is fully forward. Return control handle to neutral and verify that throttle valves are fully closed.

CAUTION
*Do not operate engine unless a source
of cooling water is flowing through*

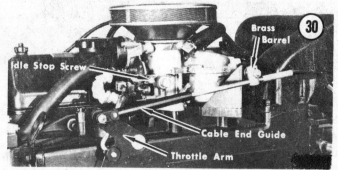

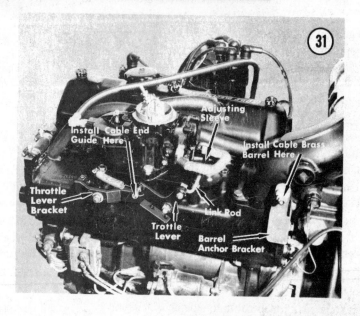

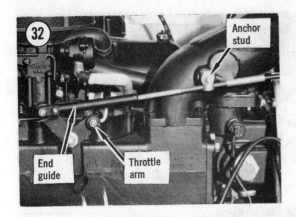

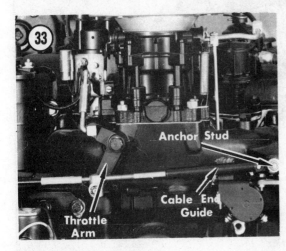

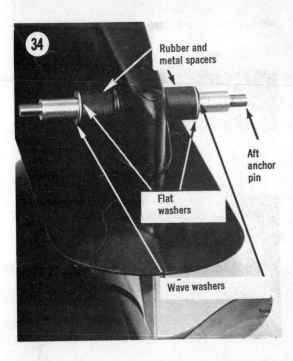

*water pump. Damage to neoprene water pump impeller will result if engine is operated without water.*

5. Start the engine and set the idle speed by adjusting the idle stop screw on the carburetor. See Chapter Three.

**Tilt and Shock Cylinder Installation**

1. Insert aft anchor pin in drive shaft housing and assemble parts on anchor pin as shown in **Figure 34 or 35**.

2. Insert forward anchor pin in gimbal ring and place parts, as required, on each end of anchor pin as shown in **Figure 36 or 37**.

3. Place cylinders, with filler plug up, in position on forward and aft anchor pins as shown in **Figure 38 or 39**.

4. Place parts on forward and aft anchor pins as shown in Figure 38 or 39.

5. Install and securely tighten the nuts on the anchor pins.

**Gear Housing Removal**

This procedure applies to MerCruiser 60, 80, 90, 110, 120, 140, 150, 160, 165, 470, 888, 200, 225S and 233.

1. Drain lubricant from stern drive unit (see Chapter Two, *Preventive Maintenance*).

2. Place wood block between propeller and anti-cavitation plate (to prevent propeller from turning). Bend tabs on tab washer and remove propeller nut (right-hand thread). Remove tab washer, cupped thrust washer, propeller, thrust hub, and washer assembly.

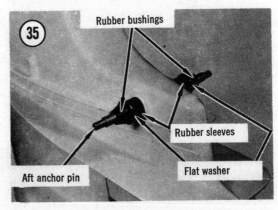

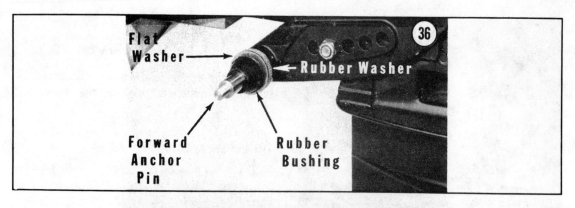

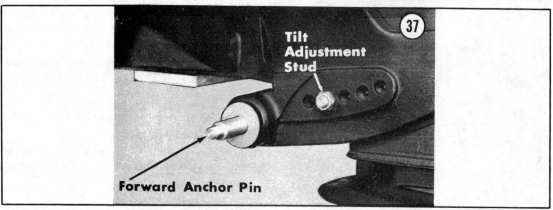

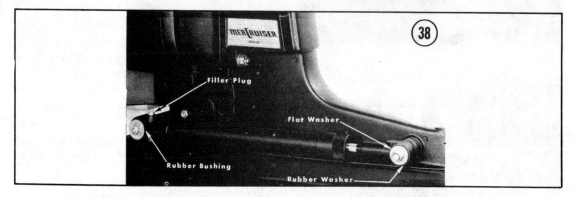

3. Remove three ⅝ in. locknuts which hold drive shaft housing (leading edge) to gear housing.

4. Remove two ⅝ in. locknuts located in center of bottom side of anti-cavitation plate.

5. Mark position of trim tab on anti-cavitation plate (see **Figure 40A**). Remove plastic plug. Remove Allen head bolt from inside rear of drive shaft housing. Remove trim tab.

6. Remove Allen head bolt from inside trim tab cavity (b, **Figure 40B**). Models 60, 80, and 90 have a 9/16 in. nut instead of a bolt.

*NOTE*
*Steps 7-9 are required only on late models. If the gear housing does not have the additional fasteners shown in* **Figure 40B** *and* **Figure 40C**, *separate the gear housing from the drive shaft housing.*

7. On late models, it will be necessary to remove the 2 locknuts (c, **Figure 40B**) from the bottom center of the anti-cavitation plate.

8. Remove the locknut from the front of the gear housing mounting stud.

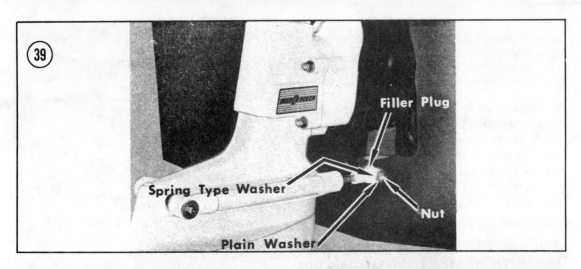

**39**

Filler Plug

Spring Type Washer

Nut

Plain Washer

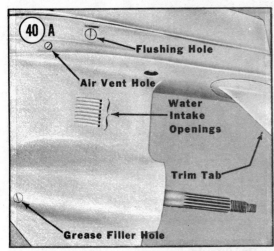

**40** A

Flushing Hole

Air Vent Hole

Water Intake Openings

Trim Tab

Grease Filler Hole

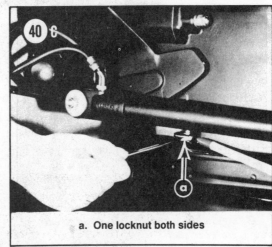

**40** C

a. One locknut both sides

6

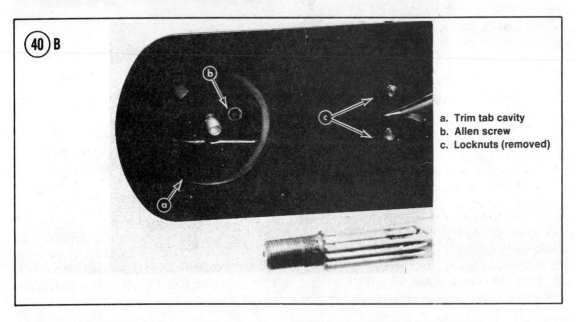

**40** B

a. Trim tab cavity
b. Allen screw
c. Locknuts (removed)

*CAUTION*
*Do not remove one of the nuts in Step 9 before loosening the other nut sufficiently or damage to the drive shaft housing may result.*

9. Loosen but do not remove the side mounting locknuts (**Figure 40C**).

10. Separate the gear housing from the drive shaft housing as far as the loosened nuts will permit. Support the gear housing and remove the loosened nuts. Remove the gear housing from the drive shaft housing.

**Gear Housing Installation**

1. If water inlet tube was pulled out during removal of gear housing, coat upper end of tube with multipurpose lubricant and slip it into rubber seal in drive shaft housing.

2. Place light coat of multipurpose lubricant on lower end of water tube.

3. Apply heavy coat of multipurpose lubricant on drive shaft splines.

4. Insert socket head into its place on top of gear housing.

5. Verify that shift control lever and lower unit are in forward gear before installing gear housing.

> NOTE: *Hold in forward gear by applying slight counterclockwise pressure to propeller shaft.*

6. Insert drive shaft into drive shaft housing, aligning water tube with water tube guide and drive shaft splines with upper drive shaft. Slide into place while joining the gear housing with the drive shaft housing.

*CAUTION*
*Make certain water inlet tube enters plastic water tube guide in water pump body recess and that rubber seal is in water pump covers. Oil passage O-ring must be in position on gear housing with inter-connected oil chambers.*

7. Rotate propeller shaft, if necessary, to align drive shaft splines with upper drive shaft splines. Upper and lower shift shaft splines must also be aligned.

8. When gear housing and drive shaft housing are joined, install and tighten locknuts removed

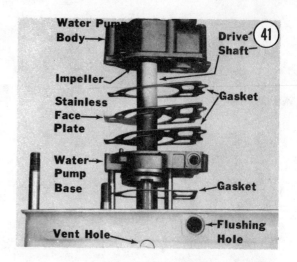

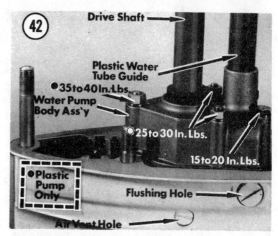

during disassembly. Replace Allen-head bolt inside trim tab cavity (or 9/16 in. nut on 60, 80, and 90 models).

9. Install trim tab and torque socket head bolt to 180 in.-lb. Replace plastic plug.

> NOTE: *When replacing trim tab, be sure to position it as marked in the removal procedure. However, if boat does not steer to right and left with equal ease, adjust tab as required to equalize steering. If steering wheel turns more easily to right, position trailing edge of trim tab to right. If wheel turns more easily to left, position trailing edge to left.*

**Water Pump Disassembly**

This procedure applies to MerCruiser 110, 120, 140, 150, 160, 165, 470, 888, 200, 225S, and 233.

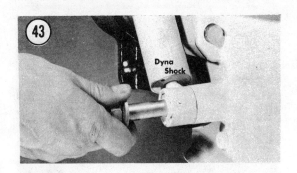

1. Remove gear housing from drive shaft housing, using the procedure above.

2. Place gear housing in an upright position in a vise, with the skeg held between 2 wood blocks.

3. Remove the O-ring from the upper end of the drive shaft.

4. Remove centrifugal slinger from drive shaft.

5. Remove water pump body assembly (see **Figure 41**) by removing nuts and lockwashers plus a cap screw and lockwasher.

6. Remove impeller, impeller drive pin, gaskets, and face plate.

7. Remove flushing screw (if present), seal, and gasket and lift out water pump base.

NOTE: *Later model gear housings do not have flushing screws. Water pump bases with flushing screw holes cannot be used with these models.*

8. Remove O-ring and oil seal from base plate assembly.

9. Check water pump impeller and inspect closely for wear. If evidence of wear or damage is present, replace the defective part.

### Water Pump Reassembly

This procedure applies to MerCruiser 110, 120, 140, 150, 160, 165, 470, 888, 200, 225S and 233.

1. Position water pump base assembly and gasket in gear housing.

2. Install water pump base to face plate gasket and install face plate (see Figure 41).

3. Place drive pin on drive shaft, holding it in position with a small amount of multipurpose lubricant.

CAUTION
*If drive shaft and/or drive pin show signs of wear, they should be replaced with new parts. Drive shaft removal and replacement requires special tools and techniques beyond the scope of this book. Take the gear housing to an authorized MerCruiser repair station.*

4. Set impeller (new part if inspection reveals wear or damage) in place over drive shaft.

5. Insert water pump cartridge into pump and place body-to-face plate gasket on water pump body (see Figure 41).

6. Slide water pump body over drive shaft and impeller (see Figure 41).

7. Turn drive shaft clockwise and press water pump body assembly into place, at the same time sealing the impeller.

NOTE: *Make certain impeller drive pin is in drive pin groove in impeller.*

8. Replace lockwashers and nuts. Insert cap screw and tighten. Torque nuts and cap screw to values shown in **Figure 42**.

9. Replace O-ring and slinger on drive shaft (using new O-ring).

10. Replace plastic water tube guide (if removed) in water pump body recess (Figure 42).

11. On gear housing with interconnected oil chambers, install O-ring in recess with adhesive (Mercury Part No. C-92-25234).

### Drive Shaft Housing Removal

1. Place unit in forward gear.

2. If so equipped, remove elastic stop nuts and washers from tilt adjustment or anchor studs and aft anchor pin.

3. Remove hydraulic cylinders and tilt adjustment stud.

4. If so equipped, remove bolt which secures dyna shocks to drive shaft housing (see **Figure 43**) and place reverse lock hook release in reverse position.

5. Remove elastic stop nuts or cap screw which secure drive shaft housing to bell housing. Remove drive shaft housing by pulling straight back (see **Figure 44**).

6

### Drive Shaft Housing Installation

Check engine and gimbal bearing alignment and gaskets, then install drive shaft housing by reversing removal procedure above.

### Water Pump Removal
### (MerCruiser 60, 80, and 90)

1. Remove 4 bolts holding top cover in place and remove top cover (see **Figure 45**). Remove gasket, face plate, impeller, drive pin, and water pump cartridge insert.

2. Remove bolts holding water pump body. Then remove O-rings from water inlet and outlet orifices in housing.

3. Remove O-ring and press or drift out 2 seals and bearing cup from water pump body.

### Water Pump Assembly
### (MerCruiser 60, 80, and 90)

1. Install new seals, one with lip up and the other with lip down, in water pump body.

> **CAUTION**
> *Do not damage seals when pressing them into water pump body. Use oil seal and bearing tool or, if not available, wood or soft metal drift bar.*

2. Install original shims and bearing cup in pump body.

3. Place new O-rings in water inlet and outlet orifices, and on water pump body assembly.

> NOTE: *Late model units use a small gasket in water pump housing to seal around insert locating tab.*

4. Install pump body assembly in drive shaft housing. Replace bolt and torque to 5-8 in.-lb.

5. Apply anti-corrosion grease (Mercury Part No. 3-92-45134 or equivalent) to water pump insert and place in pump body.

6. Place impeller drive pin on impeller shaft. Use a small amount of multipurpose lubricant to hold pin in place.

7. Install impeller over drive pin, then install gasket, face plate, and gasket over top of pump assembly.

8. Install top cover with 4 bolts and torque to 20-25 ft.-lb.

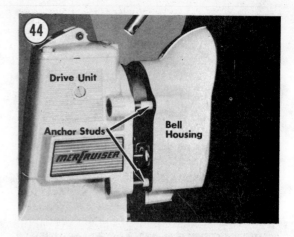

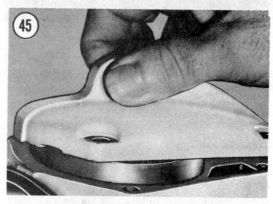

### MERCRUISER TYPE I
### (110, 120, 140, 150, 160, 165, 470, and 200)
### STERN DRIVE

Gear housing removal and installation procedures are found on page 81; water pump removal and installation on page 82.

### MerCruiser Engine Removal

### (110, 120, 140, 150, 160, 165, 470 and 200)

If the engine cannot be moved forward far enough to clear the drive shaft (4-6 in.) the stern drive unit must be removed prior to engine removal. See procedure below.

> *CAUTION*
> *Reinstallation of the engine requires use of a special alignment tool (MerCruiser Part Number C-91-57797A1 or A2). If this tool is not available, carefully note the placement of washers, spacers, shims, etc., when removing the engine so they may be reinstalled in the proper order. Also carefully measure the spacing of the*

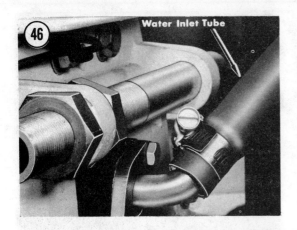

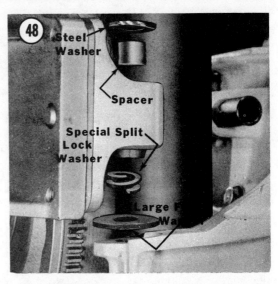

*front mounting bracket adjusting nuts and bolts. Then proceed with removal and installation bearing in mind that misalignment of the engine could cause damage to engine bearings and seals and/or the gimbal bearing. Installation in a different boat or in a boat from which forward engine mount has been removed or replaced (or installation of a new or different engine), should be attempted only if alignment tool is available.*

1. Disconnect battery cables and unplug instrument panel harness connector from engine harness receptacle.

CAUTION

*Before disconnecting fuel line, shut off fuel tank valve and have a container at hand to catch any gasoline spillage. Do not smoke in the boat while performing this operation, and keep a Coast Guard approved fire extinguisher handy.*

2. Disconnect fuel line and throttle and shift control cables.

3. Locate and disconnect shift interlock switch wires, trim indicator sender wires, and hydraulic pump motor wires from engine.

4. Remove the water inlet and exhaust tubes (see **Figures 46 and 47**).

5. Using a suitable sling or chains through the engine lifting eyes, support the engine with an overhead hoist and remove bolts from the front and rear engine mounts.

6. If stern drive unit has not been removed, move the engine 4 to 6 in. forward to clear drive shaft.

7. Lift engine straight up and out of boat.

**Engine Installation and Alignment**

**(110, 120, 140, 150, 160, 165, 470, and 200)**

NOTE: *Install engine before installing stern drive unit.*

1. Attach a suitable sling or chains to the engine lifting eyes and support engine with an overhead hoist.

2. Place large fiber washer and special split lockwasher on inner transom plate engine mounting brackets, as shown in **Figure 48**.

NOTE: *Engine heights on MerCruiser 120, Serial No. 2050045 and up, and MerCruiser 160, Serial No. 2051445 and up, have been lowered 3/32 inch by narrow spacers above engine*

6

*mounts in the flywheel cover, to help overcome engine misalignment made at time of engine installation. To lower engine height on all Model 110, 140, 150 and 120-160 below the serial numbers above, cut the special lockwasher (Part No. B-13-33734) in half as shown in* **Figure 49**. *This will give the same effect as installing new spacers. DO NOT cut lockwashers on the 120 and 160 engines with serial numbers higher than those listed above.*

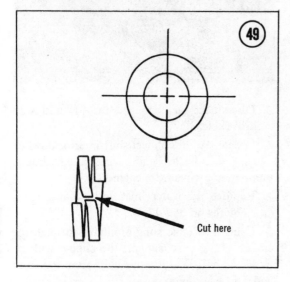

Cut here

3. Raise engine up and into boat, and position over transom plate mounting brackets. Install hose clamp over rubber exhaust tube or bellows, and position over manifold outlet (see **Figure 50 or 51**, as appropriate). Tighten clamps securely.

4. Install washers and spacers on mounting bolts in order shown in Figure 48, and insert bolts through engine mounts, washers, and transom plate mounting brackets. Thread elastic stop nuts on bolts, but do not tighten at this time.

5. If required, adjust front mounting bracket (by turning adjusting nuts) until bracket rests firmly on mount location in boat (see **Figure 52**). Relieve hoist tension.

6. Torque rear mounting bolts to 35-40 ft.-lb.

> NOTE: *See note regarding special alignment tool (Mercury Part No. C-91-57797A1 or A2) in engine removal procedure. If tool is available insert small diameter end through gimbal bearing and insert into engine coup-*

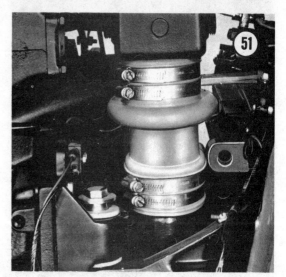

*ling spline (see* **Figure 53**). *Move gimbal bearing with alignment tool, if necessary. If tool shaft enters coupling freely, alignment is correct. If not, adjust engine front mounting bracket nuts until tool enters coupling freely. If tool is not available, note and duplicate measurements made during removal procedure.*

7. After completing alignment, secure adjustment nuts tightly and recheck alignment (if tool is available).

8. If required, secure front mounting bracket to boat.

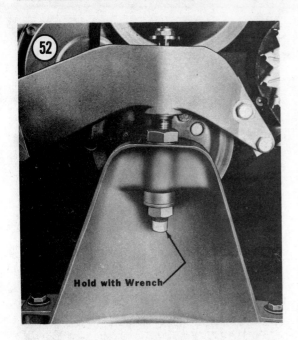

Hold with Wrench

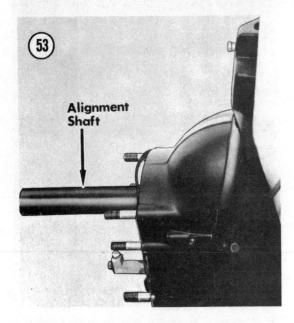

Alignment Shaft

9. Install hose clamp over water inlet tube. Place tube over inlet pipe and tighten clamp securely (see **Figure 54**).

**Stern Drive Removal**

1. Remove nuts holding tilt or shock cylinders and/or Dyna-Shocks, then remove cylinders.
2. Remove elastic stop nuts securing drive shaft housing to bell housing.

Water Inlet Tube

3. Attach lifting device to stern drive unit or arrange for help in supporting the unit during removal.
4. Remove unit by sliding it straight back.

**Stern Drive Installation**

Before installing stern drive unit, correct gaskets must be available to install between drive shaft housing and bell housing. Also, parts must mate properly to seal water intake passages (see procedures later in this section).

CAUTION
*Do not attempt to install a MerCruiser I drive shaft housing on a MerCruiser IA, IB or IC bell housing (or vice versa). Although the bolt patterns are identical, drive shafts will not align with gimbal housing bearings.*

1. Lubricate the shifting slide assembly (see **Figure 55**), and also lubricate drive shaft housing pilot and drive shaft splines. Apply light coat of lubricant to bell housing bore surfaces (see **Figure 56**). Use multipurpose lubricant.

CAUTION
*If locating slot of shift lever in bell housing and coupler of intermediate shift shaft in drive shaft housing are not aligned as described below, couplers will be damaged when installation is attempted.*

6

2. Align shift lever coupler slot straight by moving shift lever to right. Lubricate slot and reverse lock roller with multipurpose lubricant (see **Figure 57**).

3. Align intermediate shift shaft coupler for straight entry into locating slot of shift lever while in forward gear (see **Figure 58**).

> NOTE: *Rotate propeller shaft, if required, to align intermediate shift shaft coupling with upper shift shaft slot.*

4. Place small amount of multipurpose lubricant on coupler cam surface and lower roller.

5. Position drive shaft housing gasket.

> NOTE: *Place reverse lock hook release lever in "lock" position (on drive shaft housing), if so equipped.*

6. Use hoist or obtain assistance, and insert stern drive unit into bell housing bore (see Figure 56), as follows. Lubricate universal joint (U-joint) O-rings with multipurpose lubricant and guide U-joint shaft splines through gimbal bearing into drive coupling. At the same time, guide shift slide into opening in drive shaft housing. Do not move shift slide assembly or coupler.

7. Rotate propeller shaft counterclockwise, if necessary, to align drive shaft splines with engine coupling splines so drive unit can be pushed into place.

8. Replace elastic stop nuts and washers on studs connecting drive shaft housing to bell housing (**Figure 59**). Torque nuts 50 ± 5 ft.-lb.

9. Reinstall shock or tilt cylinders, or Dyna-Shocks (see procedures below). Secure with washers and elastic stop nuts. Tighten nuts securely, then back off ½ turn (see **Figure 60**).

10. Check that drive unit tilt adjustment bolt is installed in gimbal ring. Tighten nut on bolt securely, then back off ½ turn to allow bolt to rotate freely.

**Transom Plate Removal**

1. Remove stern drive unit as described earlier.
2. Remove the engine.
3. Remove the steering link rod. See **Figure 61A** for inline and **Figure 61B** for V8 transom plate installations.

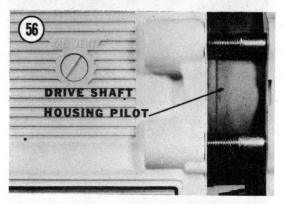

DRIVE SHAFT
HOUSING PILOT

Locating Slot of
Shift Lever Coupler

Reverse
Lock
Roller

4. Remove the cotter pin from the locking sleeve. Remove the sleeve (b, **Figure 61A** or a, **Figure 61B**).
5. Remove the clevis pin (b, **Figure 61B**) from the cable end adaptor on V8 installations.
6. Remove the steering cable coupler nut. Slide the steering cable from its support tube.
7. Remove the black hydraulic hose from the base of the trim pump. On inline installations, remove the gray hose at the reverse lock valve. Cap all hoses and plug all hose connections.

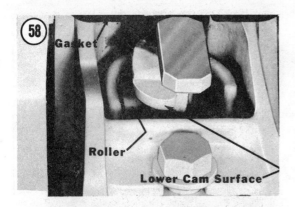

Figure 58 — Gasket, Roller, Lower Cam Surface

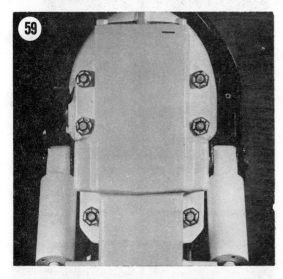

Figure 59

8. Remove the exhaust elbow assembly from the gimbal housing.

9. Disconnect the trim switch leads at the trim wiring harness.

10. Remove the power steering lines from the control valve, if so equipped.

11. If the pump is mounted to the transom plate on inline installations, disconnect the power trim panel wiring harness at the pump. Remove the drive unit and remote shift cables. See **Figure 61C**.

12. Remove the screws and nuts holding the inner and outer transom plates together. Remove the inner plate. Remove the outer plate.

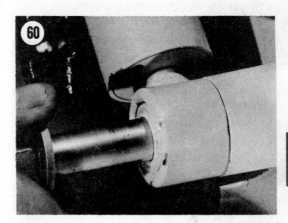

Figure 60

Figure 61A

a. Steering link rod
b. Locking sleeve
c. Steering cable coupler nut
d. Black hydraulic hose
e. Gray hydraulic hose
f. Trim wire harness
g. Exhaust elbow
h. Allen head screw

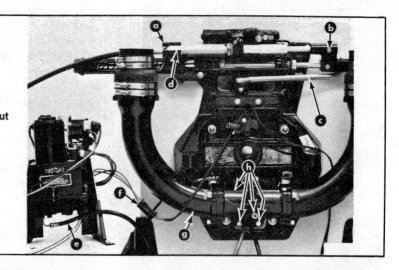

 **61 B**

a. Locking sleeve
b. Clevis pin
c. Steering link rod
d. Steering cable coupler nut
e. Black hydraulic hose
f. Trim wire harness
g. Exhaust assembly
h. Cap screws

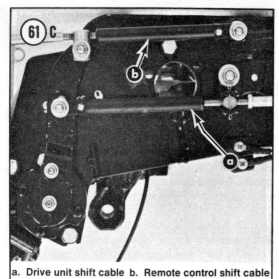

**61 C**

a. Drive unit shift cable  b. Remote control shift cable

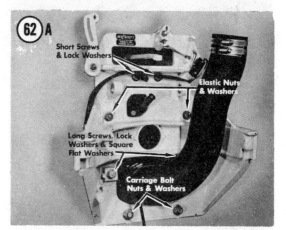

**62 A**

Short Screws
& Lock Washers

Elastic Nuts
& Washers

Long Screws, Lock
Washers & Square
Flat Washers

Carriage Bolt
Nuts & Washers

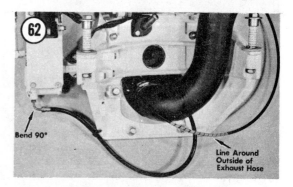

**62**

Bend 90°

Line Around
Outside of
Exhaust Hose

## Transom Plate Installation

1. Set gimbal housing assembly and inner transom plate in position. **Figure 62A** shows the inline installation; V8 installation is similar.

2. Insert shift cable, switch leads, hydraulic lines, etc., through proper openings in transom and inner transom plate. **Figure 62B** shows the inline installation; V8 installation is similar.

3. Hold gimbal housing and inner transom plate in position. Fasten with nuts and bolts as shown in **Figure 62A**. Torque fasteners evenly to 20-25 ft.-lb.

4. Reverse Steps 1-11 of *Transom Plate Removal* to complete installation.

## Ride-Guide Steering Cable Attachment—MerCruiser Type I

1. Insert end of cable through tube and thread large fastening nut securely on tube (see **Figure 63**).

2. For early type Ride-Guide cable, attach coupler halves to steering cable and link with

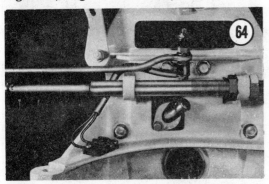

flat washer and locknut (see Figure 63 and **Figure 64**). Tighten nut securely.

3. For later type Ride-Guide cable, assemble spacer and cable on steering link rod as shown in **Figure 65**. Tighten nut securely, then back off ¼ turn (**Figure 66**), or torque to 12 foot-pounds (**Figure 67**). Attach steering link rod to lever with spacer, flat washer and locknut. Torque nut ot 12 foot-pounds maximum (see Figure 67).

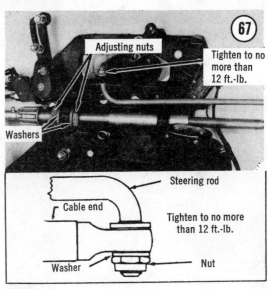

6

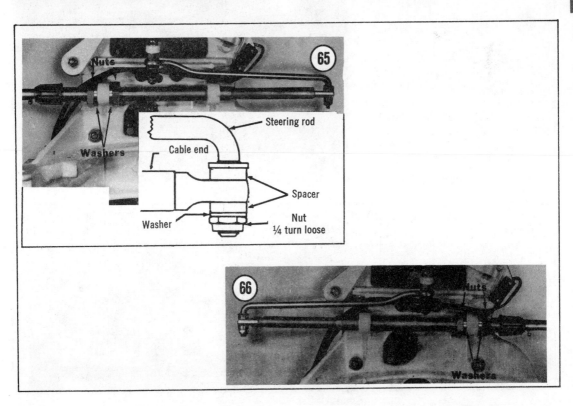

**EARLY 4-CYLINDER ENGINE**

 **LATER 4-CYLINDER ENGINE**

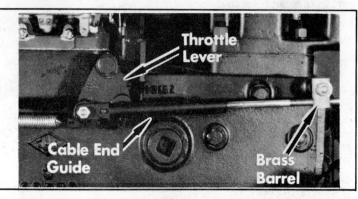

 **4-CYLINDER 140 ENGINE**

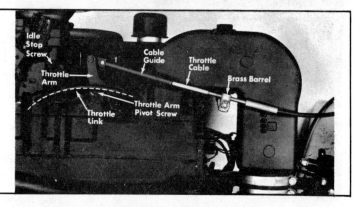

 **6-CYLINDER ENGINE WITH DUAL CARBURETORS**

**WITH CONVERSION KIT
(DUAL AND SINGLE CARBURETION)**

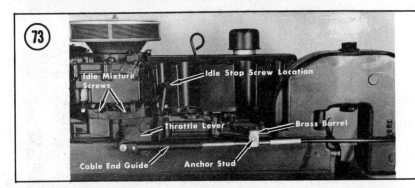

**6-CYLINDER ENGINE**

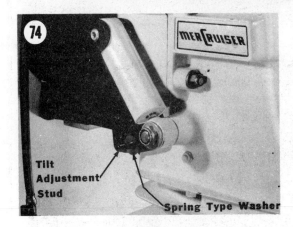

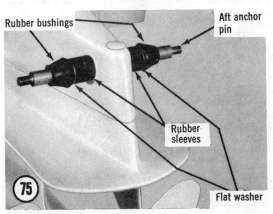

### Attaching Throttle Cables

1. Place remote control in neutral.

2. Fasten cable end guide to throttle lever arm (see **Figures 68 through 73**).

3. Grasp throttle cable behind brass barrel and push cable toward throttle lever. Adjust barrel to align with anchor stud and fasten barrel to the stud.

4. Check that throttle valves in carburetor are fully open when remote control lever is forward. Return control lever to neutral and check that idle stop screw is against stop.

### Installing Shock Absorber Cylinders

1. Insert tilt adjustment stud through desired set of holes in gimbal ring (see **Figure 74**).

> NOTE: *Place one spring washer, dished side out, on tilt pin stud on each side of gimbal ring.*

2. Install aft anchor pin in drive shaft housing and assemble rubber sleeves, flat washers, and rubber bushings on pin as shown in **Figure 75**. Apply a light coat of multipurpose lubricant to rubber bushings.

3. Place cylinders on tilt pin and aft anchor pin.

CAUTION
*Note the position of the aft end of cylinders, as shown in* **Figure 76**. *Do not turn outer housing of cylinders, as internal damage will result.*

4. Place bushings in aft end of cylinder, then secure with flat washers and nuts on both sides of tilt pin stud and aft anchor pin (Figure 76). Secure tightly.

### Installing Tilt or Trim Combination

1. Install tilt adjustment stud (see **Figure 77**) through location in gimbal ring that will cause anti-cavitation plate to be parallel with bottom of boat.

NOTE: *It may be necessary to change tilt position after test run, depending upon boat riding angle.*

2. Insert forward anchor pin in gimbal ring (see Figure 77).

3. Place flat washer, rubber bushing, and spiral spring on each side of forward anchor pin.

4. Install aft anchor pin in drive shaft housing. Place washer, rubber bushing, and spiral spring on each side of anchor pin (see **Figure 78**).

5. Install the cylinders on the forward and aft anchor pins.

CAUTION
*Make certain a grounding spring is installed between rubber bushings on each side of aft anchor pin.*

6. Insert rubber bushings in forward and aft ends of each cylinder.

7. Place flat washer and nut on each end of both anchor pins and tighten securely (see **Figure 79**).

### Attaching and Adjusting Shift Cable (Starboard Control)

Use this procedure when remote control is mounted on starboard side of boat.

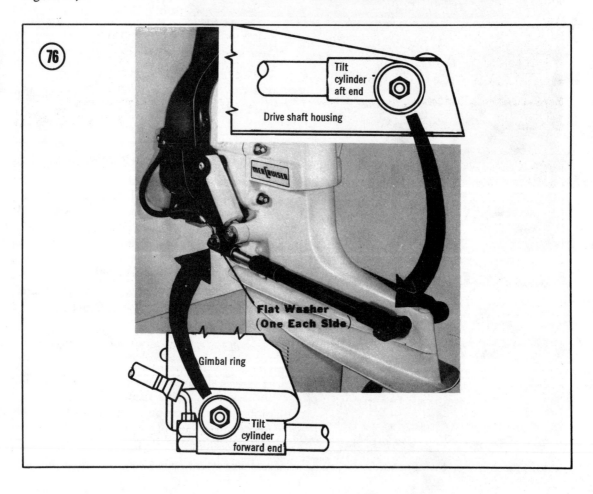

Figure 76

1. Attach control cable in bottom of slot in shift lever (see **Figure 80**) and move lever as far to right as it will go. This shifts stern drive unit into forward gear. While shifting, turn propeller shaft counterclockwise as far as possible to ensure full clutch engagement.

NOTE: *On E-Z shift through 160 models, place lockout screw through cutout switch lever as shown in Figure 80. Some early MerCruiser models have unit shift cable routed on left side of transom plate.*

2. Move remote control lever fully forward.

3. Anchor remote control shift cable end guide to transom plate anchor point. Pull outer conduit away from cable guide to eliminate cable slack. Adjust brass barrel on shift cable to align with mounting hold in shift lever (see **Figure 81**).

4. Fasten brass barrel and spacer to shift lever, using cap screw as shown in **Figure 82**. Tighten nut securely.

5. Disconnect shift cable end guide from transom plate anchor point and move remote control lever to full reverse position.

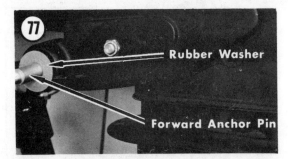

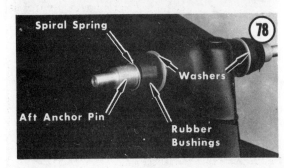

6

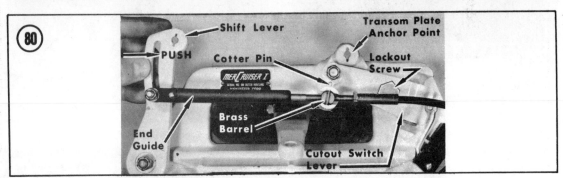

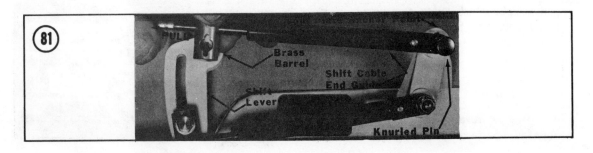

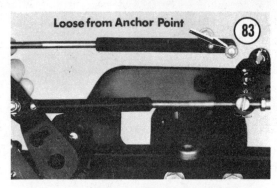

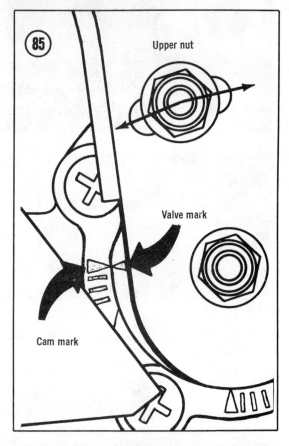

6. Move shift lever by hand as far to the left as it will go (see **Figure 83**). This shifts unit into reverse. While shifting, rotate propeller shaft clockwise as far as it will go to ensure full clutch engagement.

7. Loosen and move end guide of stern drive shift cable up in slot in shift lever until end guide can be reinstalled to transom anchor point (see **Figure 84**). Secure stern drive cable end guide to shift lever.

> NOTE: *The following 2 steps apply to models equipped with Power Trim or E-Z Shift.*

8. To adjust reverse lock valve (Power Trim units only) perform the following:

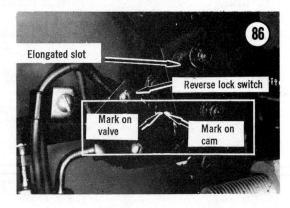

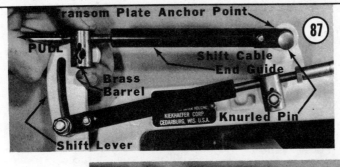

6

a. Shift into full reverse. While shifting, rotate propeller clockwise until shaft stops.

b. Loosen 2 nuts on shift lever and move nut as required to align raised triangular marks on cam and reverse valve. See **Figures 85 and 86.** Retighten nuts.

CAUTION

*Unit may be locked in neutral if reverse lock valve is overadjusted.*

9. Remove screw that was attached through shift cutout switch lever (see note after Step 1 above).

**Attaching and Adjusting
Shift Cable (Port Control)**

Use this procedure when remote control is located on port side of boat.

1. On E-Z Shift through 160 models, place lockout screw through cutout switch lever (see Figure 80).

2. Attach shift cable in bottom of slot in shift lever, move lever as far right as it will go (Fig-

ure 80). This shifts unit into forward gear. Turn propeller shaft counterclockwise until shaft stops while shifting to ensure full clutch engagement.

3. Move remote control handle to full forward position.

4. Anchor shift cable end guide to shift lever (see **Figure 87**). Pull outer conduit away from cable guide to eliminate slack in cable. Adjust brass barrel on shift cable to align with anchor point on transom plate.

5. Fasten brass barrel with spacer to anchor point on transom plate (see **Figure 88**).

6. Disconnect the shift cable end guide from the shift lever.

7. Move remote control lever to full reverse position.

8. Move shift lever as far to left as it will go (see **Figure 89**). This places unit in reverse. While shifting, turn propeller shaft clockwise until it stops to ensure full clutch engagement.

9. Loosen and move end guide of shift cable up in shift lever slot until cable end guide can be reinstalled on shift lever (see **Figure 90**).

10. Securely tighten nut on stud which fastens cable end guide to shift lever.

> NOTE: *The following steps apply to models equipped with Power Trim or E-Z Shift.*

11. Adjust reverse lock valve (Power Trim models only) by shifting into reverse. While shifting, turn propeller shaft clockwise until it stops to ensure full clutch engagement. Loosen 2 nuts on shift lever and move upper nut until raised triangular marks on cam and reverse valve cover align with each other (see Figures 85 and 86). Tighten nuts on shift lever.

12. Remove screw installed through shift cutout switch lever in Step 1 above.

### MERCRUISER TYPE I (888, 225S, AND 233) STERN DRIVE

Gear housing removal and installation is found on page 81; water pump removal and installation is on page 82.

### Engine Removal

> NOTE: *The procedure for removing the MerCruiser 888, 225S, and 233 engines is identical to that for the MerCruiser III. See Chapter Seven.*

### Engine Installation

> NOTE: *If engine is being replaced in same boat from which it was removed, and front engine mounts and supports have not been moved or readjusted, the following procedure can be used to install engine. If engine is being installed in a different boat, or front engine mounts and supports have been tampered with, or if new engine is being installed, engine must be aligned (use alignment procedure given for MerCruiser 215-H in Chapter Seven) using alignment tool (C-91-57797A1).*

To install the engine, proceed as follows:

1. Place a double-wound lockwasher and a fiber washer on each inner transom plate engine support.

2. Lift engine with overhead hoist, using suitable sling and lifting eyes on engine.

3. As engine is being lowered into position, connect exhaust bellows to exhaust elbows. Continue lowering until rear engine mounts rest on transom plate engine supports, but do not relieve hoist tension.

4. Place a steel washer and a spacer on each rear mounting bolt and insert bolts through engine mounts and supports. Thread an elastic stop nut on each bolt and torque to 35-40 foot-pounds.

5. If engine requires alignment, use procedure for MerCruiser 215-H. See Chapter Seven.

6. Install front mounting bolts and tighten securely.

7. Place hose clamp on water inlet hose and connect hose to water inlet tube (see **Figure 91**). Tighten clamp securely.

### Removing and Installing Stern Drive Unit

To remove the stern drive unit, reverse the following procedure.

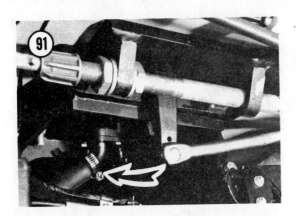

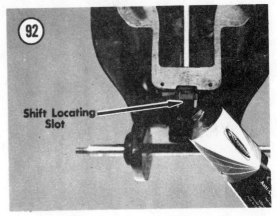

1. Lubricate shifting slide assembly with multi-purpose lubricant.

> NOTE: *Slide assembly is free to rotate on core wire; be sure slide is located in upright position during installation.*

2. Lubricate band on drive shaft housing pilot with multipurpose lubricant. Also apply light coat of lubricant to bell housing bore.

CAUTION

> *If components are not carefully aligned as described in Steps 3 and 4, couplers will be damaged when drive unit is installed.*

3. Align locating slot of shift lever coupler in bell housing straight to rear by moving shift lever to right (facing transom from inside boat). Lubricate slot with anti-corrosion grease (see **Figure 92**).

4. Align coupler of intermediate shift shaft in drive shaft housing (see **Figure 93**) for straight entry into locating slot of shift levers. Drive unit must be in forward gear. Lubricate coupler surface with anti-corrosion grease.

> NOTE: *It may be necessary to rotate propeller shaft to align shift shaft coupling with shift shaft slot.*

5. Coat universal joint O-rings with multipurpose lubricant.

6. Place drive shaft housing gasket on bell housing.

7. Insert stern drive unit into bell housing bore. Guide drive shaft through gimbal housing into drive coupling. At same time, guide shift slide into opening in drive shaft housing.

8. Be careful not to move shift slide assembly or coupler. Unit will not align out of position.

6

If drive shaft splines do not align with engine coupler splines, rotate propeller shaft counterclockwise until they are aligned.

9. Push unit into position and install elastic stop nuts on 6 mounting studs. Torque evenly to 50 foot-pounds.

**Throttle Cable Installation**

1. Place remote control in neutral, idle position.

2. Remove nut and washer from screw passing through carburetor throttle lever.

3. Place cable end guide over spacer on throttle lever. Replace washer and nut on screw and tighten securely (see Figure 93).

4. Grasp throttle cable behind brass barrel and push toward throttle lever. Adjust brass barrel to align with anchor stud. Fasten barrel to stud with flat washer and nut. Tighten nut securely.

**Attaching and Adjusting Shift Cable (Starboard Control)**

Use this procedure when remote control is located on starboard side of boat.

1. Push shift lever as far to left as it will go while turning propeller shaft counterclockwise until it stops. This shifts unit into forward gear and ensures full clutch engagement (see **Figure 94**).

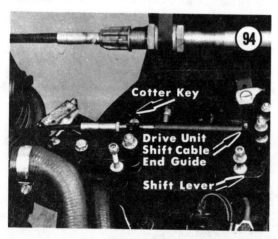

2. Move remote control handle to full forward position.

3. Anchor remote control shift cable end guide to shift lever anchor point. Pull outer conduit away from cable guide to remove slack from cable. Adjust brass barrel on remote control shift cable to align with anchor point (see **Figure 95**).

NOTE: *Do not allow position of brass barrel on cable to change during following steps.*

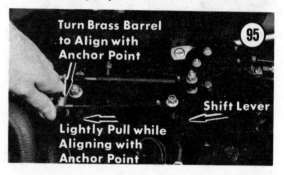

4. Move shift lever as far right as it will go while rotating propeller shaft clockwise until it stops. This places drive unit in reverse with full clutch engagement (see **Figure 96**).

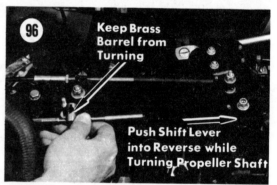

5. Move end guide of stern drive shift cable in shift lever slot so brass barrel of control shift cable can be installed on anchor point (see **Figure 97**).

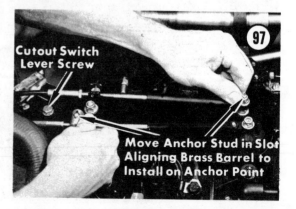

6. Securely tighten nuts holding anchor stud to shift lever and brass barrel to anchor point.

7. Shift unit into reverse. Loosen 2 nuts on shift lever and move upper nut until triangular marks on cam and reverse valve cover align with each other. Tighten nuts securely.

8. Remove screw extending through shift cutout switch lever (see Figure 97).

### Attaching and Adjusting
### Shift Cable (Port Control)

Use this procedure when remote control is located on port side of boat.

1. Move shift lever as far to left as it will go while turning propeller shaft counterclockwise until it stops. This places unit in forward gear and ensures full clutch engagement.

2. Move remote control handle to full forward position.

3. Hold remote control shift cable end guide to anchor point with washer and stop nut (see **Figure 98**). Pull outer conduit away from cable guide and adjust brass barrel on remote control shift cable to align with anchor point.

4. Hold brass barrel to anchor point with spacer, washers, and stop nut.

5. Remove stop nut holding remote control shift cable end guide to anchor point.

6. Move remote control handle to full reverse position.

7. Move shift lever as far right as it will go while turning propeller shaft clockwise until it stops. This places drive unit in reverse with full clutch engagement (see **Figure 99**).

8. Move end guide of stern drive shift cable in shift lever slot until control cable end guide can be reinstalled to anchor point (see **Figure 100**).

Push Shift Lever into Reverse while Turning Propeller Shaft

Cutout Switch Lever Screw
Move Anchor Stud in Slot to Install Cable End Guide to Anchor Point

9. Securely tighten nuts fastening anchor stud to the shift lever and cable end guide to the anchor point.

10. Shift unit into reverse, aligning raised triangular marks on cam and reverse valve. Loosen 2 nuts on shift lever and move top nut as required to align triangular marks on cam and reverse valve cover. Tighten nuts securely.

11. Remove screw passing through shift cutout switch lever (see Figure 100).

### Installing Trim and Shock Cylinders

Procedure for installing combination trim and shock cylinders is identical to that for MerCruiser III. See Chapter Seven.

### Ride-Guide Steering Installation

Procedure for installing and adjusting Ride-Guide Steering is identical to that for MerCruiser 215-H. See Chapter Seven.

Anchor Point
Lightly Pull to Align with Anchor Point
Brass Barrel Must Be Positioned as Shown

Table 1    TORQUE SPECIFICATIONS (MERCRUISER MODEL I)

| Location | Ft.-Lb. | In.-Lb. |
|---|---|---|
| Steering lever coupler nut | 20 | |
| Gimbal ring-to-upper swivel shaft bolt | 20 | |
| Steering lever-to-upper swivel shaft nut | 45-50 | |
| Hydraulic connector-to-gimbal housing stud nut | 10 | |
| Exhaust bellows clamp | | 35-38 |
| Universal joint bellows clamp | | 35-38 |
| Shift bellows clamp | | 35-38 |
| Bell housing stud-to-drive shaft housing nut | 50 | |
| Hydraulic pump bracket bolt | 14 | |
| Steering link rod castle nut-to-Ride-Guide cable | | 20 |
| Steering link rod castle nut-to-steering lever | 15-18 | |
| Gimbal housing stud-to-transom plate nut | 20-25 | |
| Transom plate carriage bolt nut | 20-25 | |
| Transom plate-to-gimbal housing bolt | 20-25 | |
| Gimbal housing stud nut | 20-25 | |
| Shift cable-to-core wire support nut | 15 | |
| Exhaust bellows bolt | 20-25 | |
| Engine mount nut | 60 | |
| Reverse lock valve nut | 14 | |
| Shift cutout lever arm spring retainer bolt | | 50-75 |
| Drive shaft housing-to-rear housing nuts | 35 | |
| Bell housing-to-drive shaft housing nuts | 50 | |
| Drive shaft housing top cover bolts | 20 | |
| Universal joint shaft pinion nut | 85 | |
| Universal joint cover retainer | 200 | |
| Trim tab bolt | | 180 |

Table 2    TORQUE SPECIFICATIONS (MERCRUISER MODEL O)

| Location | Ft.-Lb. |
|---|---|
| Transom plate carriage bolts | 20-25 |
| Transom plate-to-gimbal housing bolts | 20-25 |
| Hydraulic pump bracket bolt | 14 |
| Steering link rod nut | 30 |
| Ride-Guide bolt | 30 |
| Bell housing stud-to-drive shaft housing nut | 40 |
| Bell housing-to-gimbal ring hinge pin | 40 |
| Universal joint bellows clamp | 12 |
| Exhaust bellows clamp | 12 |
| Steering lever-to-upper swivel shaft nut | 35 |

# CHAPTER SEVEN

# MERCRUISER STERN DRIVES
## MODELS II, II-TR, II-TRS, III, AND 215

This chapter describes the removal, installation, and repair of the Model II, II-TR, II-TRS, III and 215 stern drives.

The procedures in this chapter can be performed by anyone with average mechanical skill and a well-equipped tool chest. This chapter does not include complete disassembly of the drive train as this requires special skills and tools that only an experienced MerCruiser mechanic and repair shop are likely to have.

Tightening torques are given in **Table 1** at the end of this chapter.

## MERCRUISER TYPE II STERN DRIVE
### (NON-TRANSOM MOUNTED)

**Engine Removal**

If engine cannot be moved straight forward sufficiently to clear drive shaft (4-6 inches), stern drive must be removed before removing the engine.

1. Disconnect battery cables and unplug instrument wiring harness from engine wiring harness connector.

### CAUTION
*Before removing fuel line, close fuel tank valve and have container handy to catch spilled gasoline. Do not allow smoking in or around the boat. Make certain a Coast Guard approved fire extinguisher is on hand.*

2. Disconnect fuel lines and throttle and shift control cables.

3. Disconnect reverse lock switch, trim indicator switch wires and hydraulic pump motor wires from engine.

4. Remove water inlet tube and exhaust tubes.

5. Support engine with a suitable sling or chains attached to engine lifting eyes and to an overhead hoist.

6. Remove the front and the rear engine mounting bolts.

7. If stern drive unit is attached, move engine straight forward to clear drive shaft.

8. Lift engine straight up and out of boat.

**Engine Installation**

Transom plates, if removed, must be installed before installing engine.

NOTE: *Alignment of engine requires a special tool (Part No. C-91-31620A3). If this tool is not available, the amateur mechanic should not attempt to install the engine in a boat different from the one from which engine was removed or in the same boat if mounting plates or engine mounts have been replaced, removed, or tampered with (or if new engine is being installed). Misalignment of engine can result in engine*

7

*damage and/or damage to gimbal housing bearing. Care should be taken when removing the engine to note and mark the parts' arrangements and positions.*

1. Attach suitable sling or chains to engine lifting eyes and lift with overhead hoist.

2. Lift engine into boat and lower into place on mounting plates. If mounting plates are in same position as when engine was removed, and adjusting screws and nuts on engine mounts have not been tampered with, install and tighten mounting bolts.

NOTE: *If alignment tool (see* **Figure 1***) is available perform Steps 3 through 13.*

3. Position small tool plate of alignment tool (see Figure 1) in bore of outer transom plate at engine end. Turn expander screw to hold plate in position.

4. Set larger tool plate in outer transom plate bore with shoulders of plate firmly against outer transom plate. Turn expander screw to hold in position.

5. Install pointed end of guide rod through tool plates, then install pointer on guide rod.

6. Place adjusting disc on machined shoulder of engine coupling.

NOTE: *Engine mounts are adjustable and are used in aligning engine (see* **Figures 2 and 3***). To raise or lower front or rear of engine, turn adjusting screw A (clockwise to raise, counterclockwise to lower). Loosen screw B to move engine to right or left.*

7. Position engine as required to place pointed end of adjusting tool guide rod within ⅛ inch or less of center of adjusting disc.

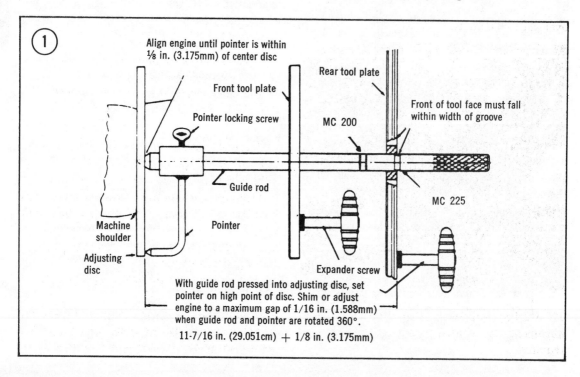

8. Move engine forward or backward as required to place back surface of rear tool plate within the width of the proper groove (see Figure 1) in guide rod.

9. With guide rod pressed into center of adjusting disc, rotate guide rod until pointer is positioned on highest point of adjusting disc. Tighten locking screw to secure pointer to guide rod.

10. Adjust engine mounts so that gap between pointer and adjusting disc is no more than 1/16 inch when pointer is rotated 360 degrees.

11. Fasten mounting plates securely to boat stringer. Tighten screws and nuts (B in Figures 2, 3, and **Figure 4**) and bend tabs of tab washers over edge of mounts.

12. Recheck alignment (Steps 7 through 10). If alignment has shifted, make adjustments as required.

13. Remove alignment tool.

> NOTE: *The following steps apply to all installations.*

14. Connect fuel line to engine.

15. Connect throttle and shift control cables using the procedures following.

16. Plug instrument wiring harness into engine wiring harness connector.

17. Connect battery cables and wires to reverse lock switch, trim indicator switch, and hydraulic pump motor.

### Stern Drive Removal (except 220-225)

To remove the MerCruiser Type II stern drive unit, reverse the stern drive installation procedure which follows. Use hoist attached to lifting eye in stern drive top cover for lifting the unit.

### Stern Drive Installation (except 220-225)

1. Lubricate outer transom plate bore and drive unit splined shaft with multipurpose lubricant.

2. Install tilt adjustment bolt in one set of gimbal ring holes, and thread nut on bolt and tighten. Back nut off ½ turn so bolt will rotate freely.

> NOTE: *Tilt adjustment bolt may require reinstallation later. When installation of stern drive unit is complete, check to see if anti-cavitation plate is parallel to bottom of boat. If not, remove bolt, align anti-cavitation plate, and reinstall bolt in proper set of holes. Further adjustment may be required when boat is operated to arrive at proper boat operating attitude.*

3. Insert shift cable and tilt switch cable through transom plates opening.

4. Support stern drive unit with hoist attached to lifting eye in top cover and align unit with hole in transom plates. Rotate stern drive unit clockwise 15 degrees (as viewed from rear) to clear stop screw; then push unit into opening (see **Figure 5**). Align shaft splines with splines in engine coupler, turning propeller shaft if required.

5. Install crank on crank extension. Press down on crank and slowly turn clockwise until a slight inward movement of the unit indicates thread

engagement. Now turn crank counterclockwise to thread gimbal housing into clamp nut.

> NOTE: *If cranking is difficult, turn crank in opposite direction. Then try Step 5 again. Do not force crank; cross-threading will strip threads.*

6. Continue cranking until stop on gimbal housing is located over the stop screw (see **Figure 6**).

7. Align drive unit as near as possible to perpendicular with boat bottom.

8. Operate crank to tighten clamp nut securely.

9. Hold free end of latch spring away from steering lever housing and assemble latch to housing with flat head nylock screw (see Figure 6). Tighten screw, then back off ¼ turn so latch can pivot freely. The free, formed end of the latch spring must be in contact with step in latch (see Figure 6).

10. The catch on the clamp nut must be in the one o'clock position (when viewed from inside boat). Reposition catch in another set of holes on clamp nut, if necessary, to achieve proper latch and catch engagement.

> NOTE: *If catch is not properly positioned, teeth on gimbal housing and outer transom plate will be meshed when catch engages latch, and unit cannot be raised to* UP *position.*

11. Loosen 6 clamp nut cover mounting screws and rotate cover until latch seats firmly in notch (see Figure 6).

> NOTE: *Latch must prohibit clockwise rotation of clamp nut cover.*

12. Tighten 6 cover mounting screws.

13. Adjust stop screw against stop on steering lever housing.

14. Press down on crank and turn clockwise to raise unit up for check.

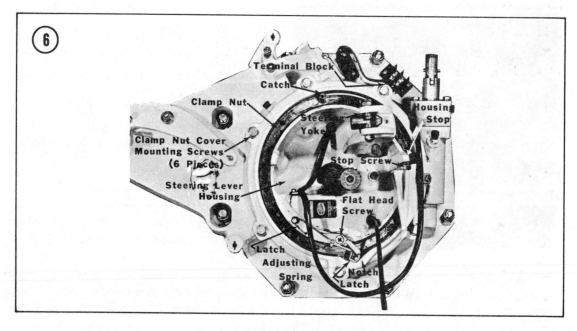

15. Crank unit down to running position, then crank about 25 more turns until firmly locked.

> NOTE: *Latches and catches must be properly matched to steering lever housing to assure proper raising and lowering of stern drive unit. See* **Figures 7, 8, 9, and 10.**

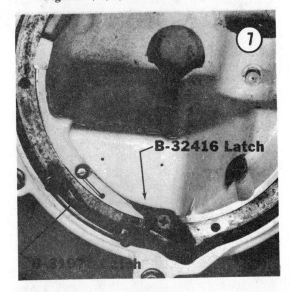

B-32416 Latch

Figure 7

B-32619 Latch

Figure 8

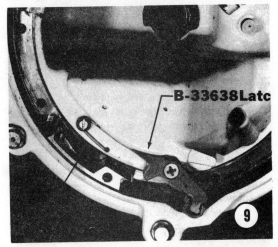

B-33638 Latch

Figure 9

B-35249 Latch

B-33639

Figure 10

Tightening Rod

Eccentric Locking Washer and Screw

Clamp Nut

Figure 11

## Stern Drive Removal (MerCruiser 220-225)

1. Remove eccentric locking screw and washer (see **Figure 11**).

2. Insert a tightening bar (MerCruiser Part No. C-91-49670, or any metal bar of suitable diameter) in clamp nut as shown in Figure 11

and turn counterclockwise to loosen nut. Remove nut from steering drum.

3. Attach hoist to lifting eye on stern drive top cover to support drive during removal.

4. Carefully pull stern drive unit to the rear until it clears transom plates.

### Stern Drive Installation (MerCruiser 220-225)

1. Lubricate outer transom plate bore O-rings and splined shaft of drive unit with multipurpose lubricant (see **Figure 12**).

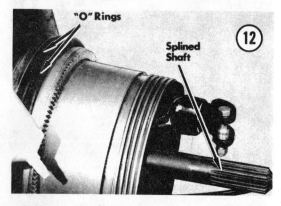

2. Use hoist attached to lifting eye in top cover of stern drive unit to lift and handle unit.

3. Insert drive unit shift cable and tilt switch cable through transom plate opening.

4. Place clamp ring over engine coupling with tapered edge toward flywheel.

5. Push unit into transom plate opening, aligning shaft spline with splines in engine coupling. Also align locating pin with recess in drive (see **Figure 13**).

6. Thread clamp nut onto steering drum while holding stern drive unit in place.

### CAUTION
*Thread clamp nut onto steering drum carefully to avoid cross-threading, which could damage parts. If tightening is difficult, back off clamp nut and rethread.*

7. Insert tightening bar (MerCruiser Part No. C-91-49670 or equivalent) into clamp nut as shown in Figure 11 and tighten nut. Align clamp nut flute with one of 6 holes and install locking screw and washer (see Figure 11).

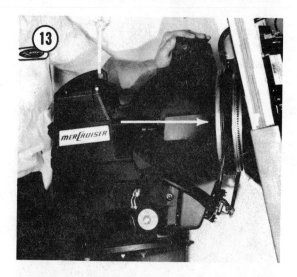

NOTE: *If original locking screw and washer will not hold clamp nut, obtain locking screw (Part No. C-10-35192) and eccentric washer (Part No. C-12-54208) from dealer and install.*

### Transom Plate Installation

1. Place outer and inner transom plates in position over holes drilled in transom as shown in **Figure 14**. Insert lock-in switch lead through opening in inner transom plate.

2. Insert 8 transom bolts with rubber seals under heads through holes in transom (from outside boat). Install washers and nuts on bolts (inside boat) and torque evenly to 30 ft.-lb.

3. Place lock-in switch cover in position and fasten with 2 screws. Position switch lead as shown in **Figure 15**.

> NOTE: *If stern drive is not locked in operating position and remote control lever is not in neutral, starter cannot operate.*

Switch Lead

**ENGINE ROTATION**

### Shift Cable Adjustment

To avoid damage to the stern drive unit, perform the steps in this procedure exactly and carefully. In addition, keep the following points in mind.

a. Early MerCruiser II model does not have reverse lock valves. Disregard instructions for reverse lock valve adjustment below for early II model.

b. The MerCruiser II stern drive normally produces left-hand rotation (counterclockwise when viewed from rear) and must use a left-hand propeller. Instructions for changing from left- to right-hand rotation are given below. If change is made, a right-hand propeller must be installed.

c. Do not install propeller until shift cable is installed and adjusted.

d. Do not attach throttle cable to carburetor before shift cable is installed and adjusted.

e. Engine must be running and power shift operating when cable adjustment procedure calls for remote control handle to be

placed in full forward and full reverse positions. After handle has been moved, engine may be stopped.

f. When installing shift cables, adjustment ment must be made so that remote control lever synchronizes with stern drive unit, and full clutch engagement is made in both forward and reverse positions of remote control lever.

1. Place unit in full reverse (left-hand rotation) or full forward (right-hand rotation) and remove cable and guide. Inner core wire of stern drive unit shift cable must extend exactly 1⅜ in. from end of cable guide insert, as shown in **Figure 16**.

2. Reinstall cable end guide and leave unit fully in gear. The distance from center line of brass barrel to center line of cable end guide mounting hole (see **Figure 17**) must be exactly 6¼ in. Adjust brass barrel as required.

> NOTE: *Steps 3-9 adjust reverse gear on models with left-hand propeller rotation (L-H) and forward gear on models with right-hand rotation (R-H).*

3. Tighten nut on switch lever pivot stud so that lever cannot be moved. See **Figure 18** (L-H) **or Figure 19** (R-H).

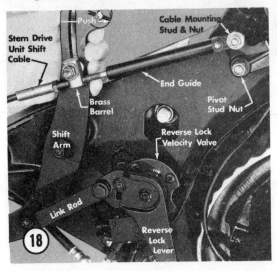

4. Fasten stern drive shift cable end guide to mounting stud on switch lever with washer and elastic stop nut. Nut must be loose enough to allow end guide to pivot freely on stud. See Figure 18 (L-H) or Figure 19 (R-H).

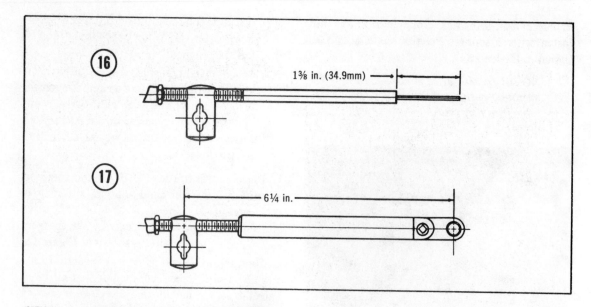

1⅜ in. (34.9mm)

6¼ in.

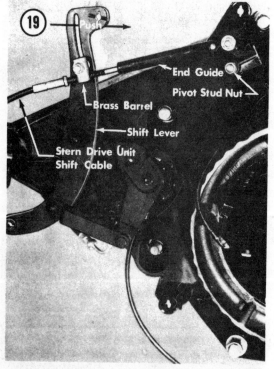

End Guide

Pivot Stud Nut

Brass Barrel

Shift Lever

Stern Drive Unit
Shift Cable

engaged it will stop. See **Figure 20** for diagram of proper and improper clutch engagement.

CAUTION
*This adjustment is very important; improper clutch engagement will damage the clutch.*

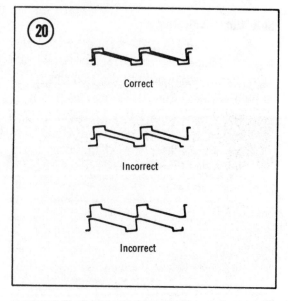

Correct

Incorrect

Incorrect

5. Mount brass barrel loosely in curved slot of shift lever, using cap screw, spacer, 2 washers, and nut. Washers must be on either side of shift lever (see Figure 18 or 19). Do not tighten nut.

6. Push top of shift lever as far to right (viewed from inside boat) as possible. At same time, turn propeller shaft counterclockwise to shift unit fully into gear. When clutch is properly

7. Move remote control handle to full reverse (left-hand rotation) or forward (right-hand rotation).

8a. On boats with starboard-mounted shift control, anchor remote control shift cable end guide to transom plate anchor point with cap screw, 2 washers, and nut. Push outer conduit toward cable guide as far as possible to eliminate slack in cable, and adjust brass barrel to align with mounting hole in shift lever. See **Figure 21** (L-H) **or Figure 22** (R-H).

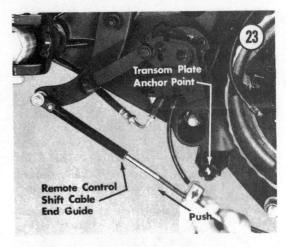

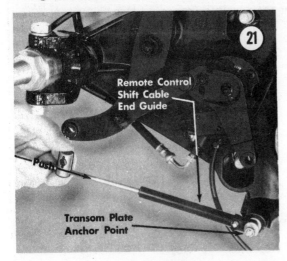

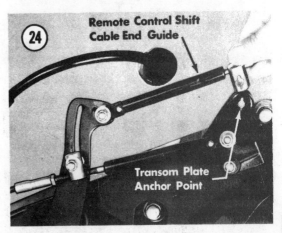

8b. On boats with port-mounted shift control, anchor remote control shift cable end guide to shift lever with screw, washer, and nut. Push outer conduit toward cable guide as far as possible to eliminate slack in cable, and adjust brass barrel to align with mounting hole in transom plate anchor point. See **Figure 23** (L-H) **or Figure 24** (R-H).

9a. On boats with starboard-mounted shift control, fasten brass barrel to shift lever with cap screw, spacer, washers, and nut. Tighten the nut securely. Refer to **Figure 25** (L-H) **or Figure 26** (R-H).

9b. On boats with port-mounted shift control, fasten brass barrel to anchor point using cap screw, washers, spacers, and nut. Tighten nut securely. See **Figure 27** (L-H) **or Figure 28** (R-H).

NOTE: *Steps 10-16 adjust forward gear on models with left-hand rotation (L-H) and reverse gear on models with right-hand rotation (R-H).*

10. Disconnect remote control shift cable end guide from transom plate anchor point (starboard control) or shift lever (port control).

11. Move remote control lever to full forward (left-hand rotation) or reverse (right-hand rotation).

12. Pull top of shift lever to left as far as possible while turning propeller shaft clockwise (viewed from behind boat) until it cannot be turned further. This shifts unit into forward gear, see **Figure 29** (L-H) **or Figure 30** (R-H), with clutch properly engaged (see Figure 19).

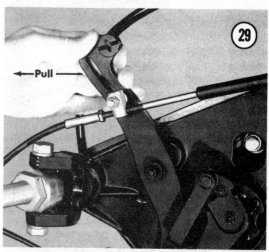

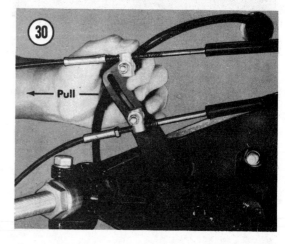

13. Raise brass barrel of stern drive shift cable up in a slot of shift lever until remote control

shift cable can be installed in transom plate anchor point. For starboard installations see **Figures 31** (L-H) **and 32** (R-H). For port installations see **Figures 33** (L-H) **and 34** (R-H).

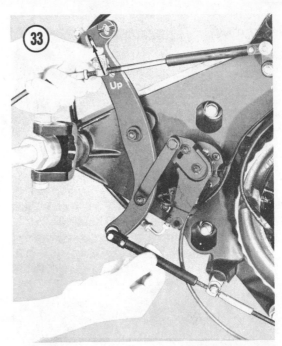

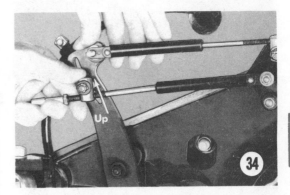

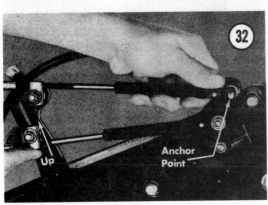

7

14. Continue to slide brass barrel up in slot to remove slack from remote control shift cable, then securely tighten cap screw and nut holding brass barrel to shift lever.

15. Loosen nut on pivot stud of switch lever one full turn. Lever must pivot freely when shifting with engine running. See **Figures 35** (L-H) **and 36** (R-H).

16. On later models with reverse lock valve, shift unit into full reverse. At the same time rotate propeller shaft counterclockwise until shaft stops. Loosen 2 nuts on reverse lock lever

and move upper nut as required to align raised triangular marks on cam and reverse lock valve cover with each other. Tighten 2 nuts on reverse lock lever (see **Figure 37**).

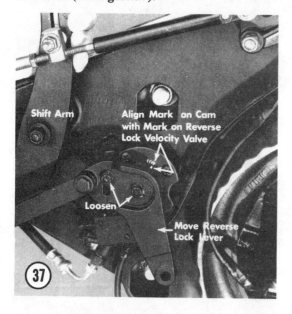

**Throttle Control Cable Attachment (MerCruiser 200-225)**

1. Place remote control handle in neutral and neutral warmup lever fully down.

> NOTE: *If knurled pin is in cable guide end, remove pin and spring.*

2. Remove nut and washer from bolt passing through carburetor throttle lever.

3. Place cable end guide over spacer. Place washer and nut on bolt and tighten nut securely (see **Figures 38 and 39**).

4. Grasp cable behind brass barrel and push toward throttle arm. Adjust barrel to align with anchor stud in bracket. Place flat washer, sleeve, and barrel, in that order, on stud. Then place

another flat washer and stop nut on stud and securely tighten nut (see Figures 38 and 39).

5. Confirm that primary throttle valves in carburetor are fully open when remote control handle is fully forward.

6. Adjust engine idle speed to 500-600 rpm in forward gear with idle stop screw on carburetor. See Chapter Three. Turn screw in to increase speed and out to decrease speed.

**Throttle Control Cable Adjustment (MerCruiser II)**

1. Place remote control handle in neutral position and neutral warmup lever in fully down position.

2. For early model carburetors, attach cable end guide and brass barrel as follows (see **Figure 40**).

  a. Remove roll pin which passes through knurled pin in cable end guide and remove pin and spring.

  b. Remove nut and washer from bolt passing through carburetor throttle lever.

  c. Place cable end guide over spacer and replace washer and nut. Tighten securely.

  d. Grasp throttle cable behind brass barrel and push toward throttle arm. Align brass barrel with anchor stud in bracket. Place flat washer, sleeve, and barrel, in that order, on stud, then install flat washer and stop nut on stud and securely tighten nut.

3. For late model carburetors, attach cable end guide and brass barrel as follows (see **Figure 41**).

  a. Remove roll pin which passes through knurled pin in cable end guide and remove pin and spring.

  b. Attach cable end guide to throttle arm with bolt, sleeve, and elastic stop nut.

  c. Position throttle arm so that 2 throttle link pivot points are in line with throttle arm pivot stud as shown in Figure 41. Hold arm in this position and grasp throttle cable behind brass barrel and push toward throttle arm. Adjust barrel to align with anchor stud in bracket. Place flat washer, sleeve, and barrel, in that order, on stud. Place

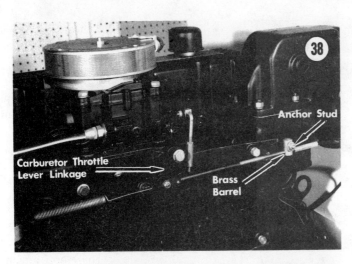

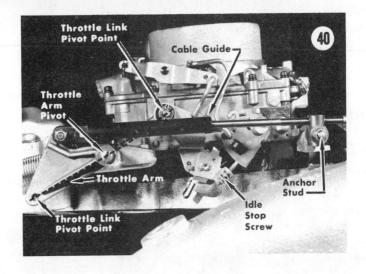

7

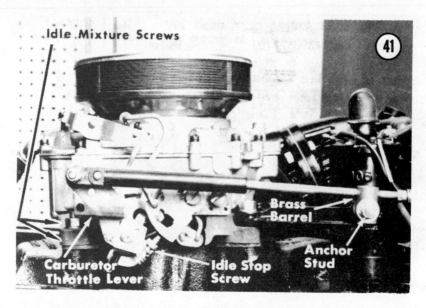

another washer and stop nut on stud and securely tighten nut.

4. Confirm that primary throttle valves in carburetor are fully open when remote control handle is fully forward. Return handle to neutral and confirm that throttle valves are fully closed.

5. Set engine idle speed to 500-600 rpm in forward gear with idle stop screw on carburetor. See Chapter Three.

**Ride-Guide Attachment**

1. Lubricate steering cable tube end with multipurpose lubricant.

2. Thread steering pivot yoke into bracket until it seats firmly. Back off one turn to prevent binding when unit is rotated 180 degrees (see **Figure 42**).

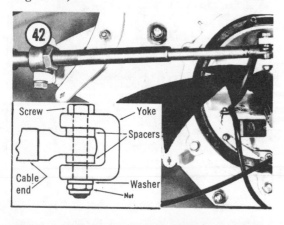

3. Insert cable end through tube and thread large fastening nut loosely on tubes.

4. Remove coupler valves from steering arm yoke. Do not lose sleeves in yoke.

5. Thread steering arm yoke into steering arm until it seats. Back out one or two turns to prevent yoke from binding when unit is rotated 180 degrees.

6. Turn steering wheel until cable end extends out far enough to attach coupler halves into groove at end of cable.

7. Place coupler halves in cable tube groove and place cable with coupler halves into steering arm yoke.

8. Place sleeves in yoke and insert cap screw from top. Secure coupler assembly with elastic stop nut (see Figure 42).

9. Turn steering wheel to extreme right position.

10. Verify that steering cable tube is fully threaded in against yoke locknut.

11. Turn steering tube out until steering wheel start to move to left.

12. Secure locknut on tube against swivel and tighten large fastening nut on cable.

**Gear Housing Removal**

1. Mark trim tab position. Remove propeller and trim tab.

2. Remove cap screws (**Figure 43**) and Allen head screw and nut (**Figure 44**) from anti-

Hex Head Cap Screws

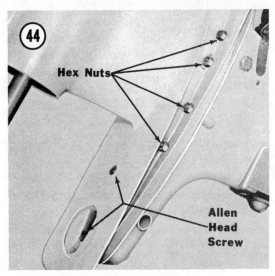

Hex Nuts

Allen Head Screw

cavitation plate area, and then separate gear housing from drive shaft housing.

## Gear Housing Installation

1. Place new gasket on mating surface between gear housing and drive shaft housing.

2. Position trim tab Allen head screw and, on later models, install oil tube in drive shaft housing.

> NOTE: *If unit serial number is below 1602186, drive shaft housing is not machined to accept oil tube. Oil tube seal must be removed from ball bearing retainer. Also, it is not necessary to install oil tube when late model drive*

*shaft housing is replaced on units below serial number 1602186.*

3. Join gear housing and drive shaft housing by inserting drive shaft through sliding clutch. Then install screws and nuts removed during disasasembly. Tighten securely.

4. Install trim tab in place, using markings made during removal, for alignment. Tighten Allen head screw securely and install plastic plug in drive shaft housing.

5. Fill drive unit with fresh lubricant (see Chapter Two for type and amount).

## Tilt Stop Switch Removal

1. Lock stern drive unit in normal running position.

2. Remove switch leads from terminal block on inner transom plate.

3. Remove 2 nylon clips holding switch to steering lever housing and to clamp nut cover.

4. Support weight of unit with overhead hoist, using lifting eye in top cover of drive shaft housing.

5. Remove lubricaps and grease fittings in ends of hinge pins, if so equipped.

6. Remove pins that lock hinge pins in gimbal ring, using thin punch.

7. Remove hinge pins, using slide hammer and adapter (if available).

8. Remove tilt adjustment bolt and slide entire unit back about 4 in. This will allow clearance for switch removal.

9. Remove 2 screws holding switch actuating lever to gimbal ring.

10. Remove 2 screws holding switch retaining plate to gimbal ring.

11. Remove nylon clip fastening switch leads to gimbal housing.

12. Remove 2 screws holding switch lead retainer to gimbal housing.

13. Cut switch leads and remove switch.

## Tilt Stop Switch Installation

1. Install new switch in gimbal housing.

2. Install spacer and retainer plate, with shoulder toward spacer.

7

3. Thread switch leads through gimbal housing and install switch lead retainer.

4. Replace nylon clip and check leads carefully to be sure that they cannot rub against the gimbal ring.

5. Replace switch actuating lever.

6. Check bellows carefully for kinking and uneven folding; remedy as required.

7. Slide entire unit into gimbal ring and align hinge pin holes.

8. Install greased anti-galling washer between drive shaft housing and gimbal ring.

9. Hold washers in place and install hinge pins.

10. Install hinge pin retaining pins.

11. Install grease fittings and lubricaps, if so equipped.

12. Install 2 nylon clips to secure switch leads to steering lever housing and clamp nut cover.

13. Install switch leads on terminal block.

14. Check tilt stop circuit with meter to make sure that circuit is open when unit is down and closed when unit is tilted.

15. Check trim limit circuit with meter to make sure that circuit is closed when unit is down and open when unit is tilted.

### Converting Left-Hand to Right-Hand Rotation

Propeller rotation is converted from left- to right-hand by repositioning cam and cable on inner transom plate. No internal changes are necessary.

To convert 1.33:1 drives, serial No. 1602186 and above, from left-hand to right-hand rotation, proceed as follows.

1. Rotate the unit to inverted position with hand crank.

2. Push gear housing end of drive unit toward transom. Hold unit in this position and press both reverse lock hook arms down and allow drive unit to pivot downward.

3. Remove nut from bolt fastening shock absorber to drive shaft housing and remove bolt. Pivot shock absorber up toward gimbal ring.

4. Carefully note positions of components of reverse assembly for reference when reassembling the unit.

5. Remove cotter pin passing through reverse lock tube and shaft.

6. Push pivot shaft out of drive shaft housing and remove reverse lock assembly.

7. Loosen set screw fastening cam to shaft, and remove cam from shaft.

8. Hold drive unit shift cable brass barrel and push cable end guide toward brass barrel while rotating propeller shaft. Continue to push end guide toward brass barrel until it stops.

9. Replace cam on shaft in position shown in **Figure 45**, and securely tighten set screw.

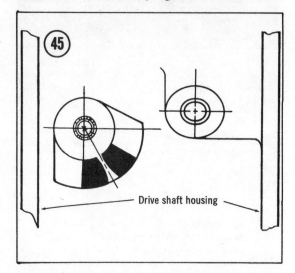

Drive shaft housing

10. Install reverse lock assembly, pivot shaft, and cotter pin. Make certain reverse lock arm tension spring is over top of drive shaft housing lug and nylon roller is on top of cam.

11. Install shock absorber, bolt, and nut.

12. Pivot drive unit up until reverse lock hooks lock on tilt adjustment bolt.

13. Rotate drive unit down to operating position with crank until unit is tight and locked in this position.

14. Install right-hand rotation propeller of proper pitch and diameter.

To change the rotation of 1.78:1 drive units from left to right rotation, proceed as follows.

1. Install right-hand rotation propeller of proper pitch and diameter.

2. Reposition and adjust shift cables following *Shift Cable Adjustment* procedure described earlier.

3. Remove link rod from upper reverse lock lever arm and reinstall on lower arm as shown in **Figure 46**.

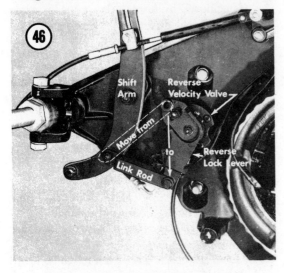

## MERCRUISER II (TRANSOM MOUNTED) STERN DRIVE

### Engine Removal

NOTE: *If engine cannot be moved forward far enough to clear drive shaft (because of obstructions, etc.), stern drive unit must be removed prior to engine removal.*

1. Disconnect battery cables and unplug instrument panel harness connector from engine harness connector.

2. Shut off fuel tank valve and disconnect fuel line and throttle and shift control cables.

3. Disconnect reverse lock switch wires, trim indicator switch wires, and hydraulic pump motor wire from engine.

4. Remove the water tube inlet tube and the exhaust tubes.

5. Support engine with suitable sling attached to engine lifting eyes and overhead hoist. Remove front and rear engine mounting bolts.

6. Lift engine up and out of boat.

### Engine Installation

1. Place one large steel washer, one double-wound lockwasher, and one neoprene washer on top of each inner transom plate engine support.

2. Using overhead hoist, lift engine into boat. Lubricate engine coupling spline with multi-purpose lubricant.

3. Position engine over transom plate and carefully lower to allow rear mounts to rest on supports and washers (installed in Step 1 above).

4. Place one neoprene washer and one steel washer on top of each rear engine mount and insert mounting bolts from top. Place a steel washer and nut on each bolt and torque nuts to 100 ft.-lb.

5. Verify that front engine mounts have not been moved or readjusted.

6. Replace front engine mounting bolts and tighten securely.

NOTE: *If front engine mounts have been readjusted (or if engine is being installed in new boat), an alignment rod must be used to properly align engine. This rod must be inserted as shown in* **Figure 47**. *Adjust front engine mounts up or down so rod fits tightly enough without fore and aft play, but loose enough to be removed by hand. Rod is 9.775 ± 0.010 in. in length.*

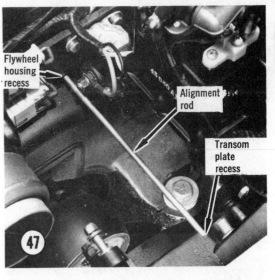

7. Replace cables, wires, and fuel line removed during engine removal procedure.

### Stern Drive Removal/Installation

To remove stern drive unit, reverse this procedure.

To install the stern drive unit, proceed as follows.

1. Lubricate bore of outer transom plate, O-rings, and splined shaft of drive unit with multipurpose lubricant.

2. Using hoist connected to lifting eye in top plate to support unit, insert shift cable and tilt switch cable through transom plate opening and clamp nut. Then push unit into opening, aligning shaft spline with engine coupling spline and locating pin with recess in drive.

3. Hold drive unit in place and thread clamp nut onto steering drum.

### CAUTION
*Avoid cross-threading. Do not force nut.*

4. Use a bar of suitable length and diameter, as shown in Figure 11, to tighten clamp nut, aligning clamp nut flutes with backing screws. Fit locking screws snugly and tighten locknuts.

**Shift Cable Adjustment**

To avoid damage to the stern drive unit, perform the steps in this procedure exactly and carefully. In addition, keep the following points in mind.

  a. Do not attach throttle cable to carburetor until after shift cable is installed and adjusted.

  b. This model drive unit is normally assembled for left-hand propeller shaft rotation (counterclockwise when viewed from rear) and must be used with a left-hand propeller.

  c. Propeller shaft rotation can be changed from left- to right-hand by using the prodedure given later in this chapter. If this change is made, a right-hand propeller of the proper pitch and diameter must be installed.

  d. It is very important that the clutch be fully engaged when adjusting the shift cable in both forward and reverse positions. This is achieved by turning the propeller while shifting as directed in the procedures below.

1. With cable end guide removed and unit in full reverse (left-hand rotation) or forward (right-hand rotation), inner core wire of stern drive unit shift cable must extend exactly 1⅜ in. from end of cable guide insert as shown in Figure 16.

2. With cable end guide installed and unit still fully in gear, distance from center line of brass barrel to center line of cable end guide mounting hole must be exactly 7¾ in. (see **Figure 48**).

  NOTE: *Steps 3-7 adjust forward gear on boats with left-hand propeller rotation (L-H) and reverse gear on boats with right-hand propeller rotation (R-H).*

3. Attach stern drive shift cable to mounting stud in shift lever slot and place brass barrel in recess of cutout switch lever. Secure it with cotter key (see **Figure 49**).

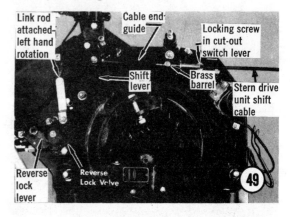

4. Move top of shift lever as far to left as it will go while turning propeller shaft clockwise (when

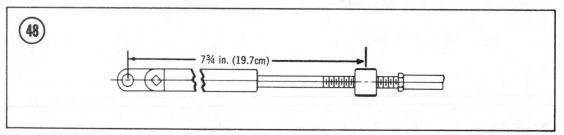

viewed from rear of boat) as far as it will go. This shifts unit into forward gear (see **Figure 50**).

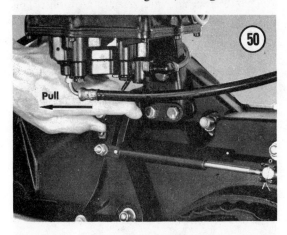

5. Move remote control handle to full forward (L-H) or full reverse (R-H).

6. Anchor remote control cable end guide with spacer, washer, and nut. Pull outer conduit away from cable guide as far as possible to eliminate slack in cable and adjust brass barrel to align with mounting stud (see **Figures 51 through 54**).

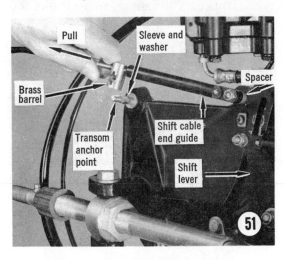

7. Fasten brass barrel to shift lever or transom anchor stud with sleeve, washers, and nuts.

> NOTE: *Steps 8-14 adjust reverse gear on boats with left-hand propeller rotation (L-H).*

8. Disconnect remote control shift cable end guide from shift lever or transom anchor stud.

9. Move top of shift lever as far right as it will go while turning propeller shaft counterclock-

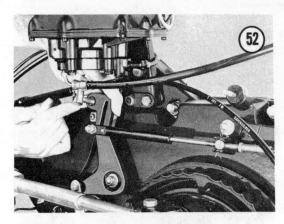

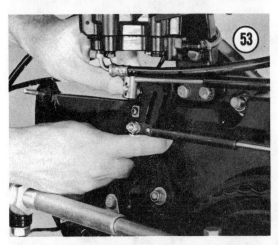

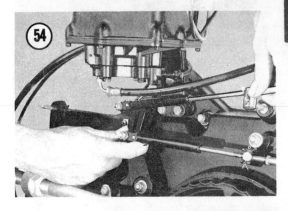

wise as far as possible (see **Figures 55 and 56**). This places unit in gear.

10. Remove remote control handle to full reverse (L-H) or forward (R-H).

11. Raise cable end guide of stern drive shift cable up in shift lever slot until remote control shift cable can be reinstalled (see **Figures 57 through 59**).

7

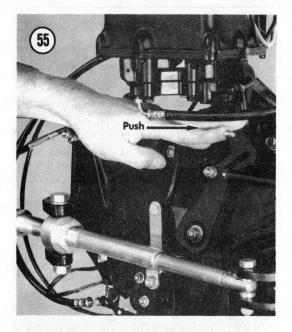

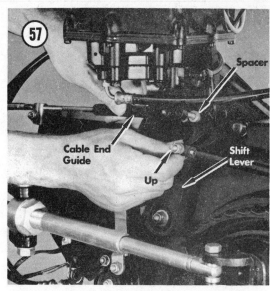

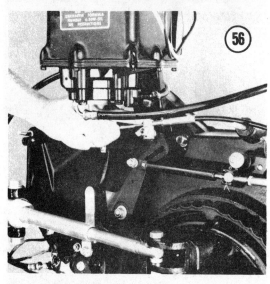

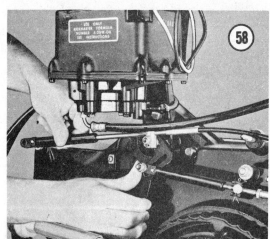

12. Continue to slide cable end guide up slot until slack is removed from remote control shift cable. Tighten anchor stud and nut which fasten cable end guide to shift lever.

13. Shift into full reverse and check alignment marks on reverse lock valve cover and cam. If adjustment is required, loosen 2 nuts on reverse lock lever (see **Figures 60 and 61**) and align marks. After alignment, tighten the 2 nuts securely.

14. Remove screw extending through shift cut-out switch lever (see **Figure 62**).

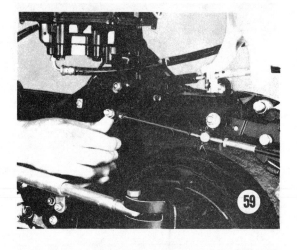

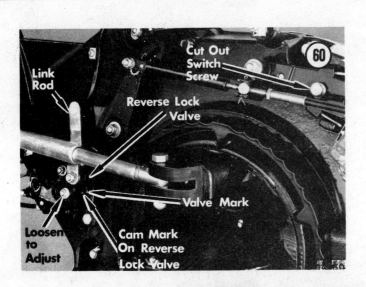

60

Cut Out Switch Screw

Link Rod

Reverse Lock Valve

Valve Mark

Loosen to Adjust

Cam Mark On Reverse Lock Valve

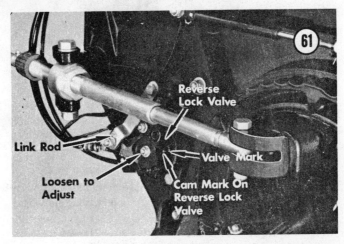

61

Reverse Lock Valve

Link Rod

Valve Mark

Loosen to Adjust

Cam Mark On Reverse Lock Valve

7

62

Cutout Switch Lever Screw

**Throttle Control Cable Attachment**

> NOTE: *The procedure is identical to the one for non-transom Mer-Cruiser II earlier in this chapter.*

## MERCRUISER II-TR AND II-TRS STERN DRIVE

**Engine Removal**

1. Remove stern drive unit and loosen 6 rear engine mount couplings.

2. Disconnect battery cables and unplug instrument panel harness from engine harness connector.

3. Shut off fuel tank valve and disconnect fuel line from engine.

> CAUTION
> *Have suitable container available to catch gasoline spillage and have a Coast Guard approved fire extinguisher handy.*

4. Disconnect throttle cable, shift control wires, trim indicator switch wires, and hydraulic pump motor wires from engine.

5. Disconnect power steering hoses from steering valve assembly and, if so equipped, remove power trim hoses from reverse lock.

> CAUTION
> *Cap all hydraulic hoses and plug connecting passages to prevent loss of hydraulic fluid and to prevent contamination of hydraulic system.*

6. Remove the water inlet tube and the transom exhaust elbows.

7. Support engine with overhead hoist and suitable sling attached to lifting eyes. Remove front engine mounting bolts.

8. Pull the engine forward to disengage the rear engine mount.

> CAUTION
> *Do not lift engine until rear mount is disengaged.*

9. Remove engine from boat.

**Engine Installation**

Unless the engine is being replaced in the same boat from which it was removed and the adjustment of the front engine mounts and supports has not been tampered with, alignment tool C-91-57797A3 and extension C-91-63618 must be used to properly install and align the engine. The following procedure includes instructions for using these tools.

1. Coat O-ring on rear mount (see **Figure 63**) and gimbal housing bore with multipurpose lubricant.

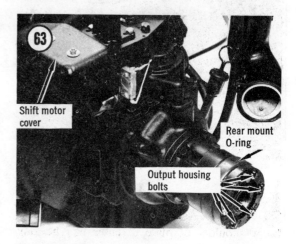

2. Attach suitable sling to engine lifting eyes and lift engine into boat with overhead hoist.

> NOTE: *Make certain that 6 nuts holding bearing retainer to output housing are loose before installing into gimbal housing.*

3. Position engine ahead of inner transom plate so transmission output housing and rear mount (see Figure 63) are aligned with large opening in inner transom plates.

4. Move engine to rear and guide transmission output housing into gimbal housing bore. Handle carefully so output housing and rear mount are not damaged.

5. Adjust hoist tension as required to allow transmission output housing to seat in gimbal housing bore.

> CAUTION
> *Do not relieve hoist tension entirely at this time, as damaged to transmission and output housing could result.*

6. Position plate of alignment tool C-91-57797A3 on shaft, as shown in **Figure 64**. Thread extension C-91-63618 onto alignment shaft. Insert end of alignment tool into bell housing opening and into transmission output housing. Insert shaft until it bottoms out in transmission output housing.

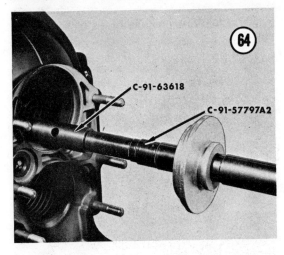

C-91-63618

C-91-57797A2

7. Slide alignment plate toward bell housing. Raise or lower front of engine with hoist to allow shoulder of plate to enter bell housing opening (see **Figure 65**).

8. Front engine mount supports should be adjusted so mounts rest on top of supports without disturbing position of alignment tool plate in bell housing when hoist tension is relieved.

9. Relieve hoist tension and fasten front mount bases to supports with bolts, washers, and locknuts.

10. Push alignment shaft and plate toward engine and check for gap between plate and rear surface of bell housing at 12, 3, 6, and 9 o'clock positions.

11. If gap exists at 12 o'clock, raise front of engine by turning adjusting bolts clockwise in both front engine mounts (see **Figure 66**). Turn each bolt an equal distance, alternating from one side to the other until gap disappears.

CAUTION
*Damage to exhaust elbows may result if engine mounting bolts are not adjusted evenly.*

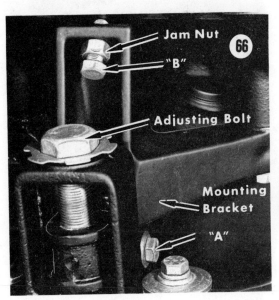

Jam Nut

"B"

Adjusting Bolt

Mounting Bracket

"A"

12. If gap exists at 6 o'clock position, lower front of engine by turning both adjusting bolts counterclockwise (see Figure 66) an equal amount.

13. If gap exists at 3 o'clock position, loosen screw and nut (A, Figure 66) on both front mounts and move front of engine to right until gap disappears.

CAUTION
*Mounts must not extend out more than ¾ in. from mount brackets (see Figure 66).*

14. If gap exists at 9 o'clock position, loosen screw and nut (A, Figure 66) on both front mounts and move front of engine to left until gap disappears. See CAUTION above.

15. Securely tighten all mount fasteners.

16. After correct alignment has been achieved, remove alignment tool and bend tabs of adjusting bolt tab washers down over edges of mounts and recheck all nuts and bolts to make certain they are tight.

17. Turn cap screws (B, Figure 66) finger-tight against engine and tighten jam nuts.

18. Torque 6 rear mount compression stud nuts evenly to 70 in.-lb. (see **Figure 67**). Remove lubrication cap and lubricate output bearing with multipurpose lubricant.

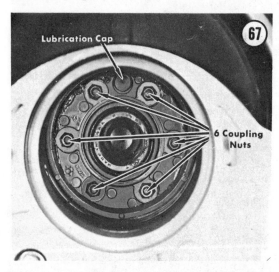

19. Connect all wires, cables, hoses, and fuel line that were disconnected during engine removal. Install transom exhaust elbows and water inlet.

**Stern Drive Installation/Removal**

> NOTE: *Reverse following procedure to remove stern drive unit.*

To install stern drive unit, proceed as follows.

> NOTE: *Engine must be installed and aligned before attempting to install stern drive unit.*

1. Verify that 6 rear mount retaining nuts (see Figure 67) have been tightened to 70 in.-lb. before installing stern drive.

2. Lubricate drive shaft housing pilot, O-ring, and end of universal joint shaft (internally and externally) with multipurpose lubricant (see **Figure 68**). Also apply light coat of lubricant to bell housing bore and position bell housing gasket (see **Figure 69**).

2. Install forward anchor pin in gimbal housing (see Figure 69).

3. Using hoist attached to top cover lifting eye, lift stern drive and insert unit into bell housing bore by guiding universal joint shaft through pilot bearing.

4. Push drive shaft housing into bell housing and fasten with 6 elastic stop nuts and flat washers. Torque to 35 ft.-lb.

> NOTE: *If universal joint shaft splines do not mesh with transmission splines, rotate propeller shaft slightly until drive unit can be pushed into place.*

5. Fill unit with fresh lubricant of proper type and amount (see Chapter Two).

**Throttle Cable Installation**

1. Place remote control handle in neutral, idle position.

2. Connect cable end guide to throttle lever with screw, bushing, washers, and nut (see **Figure 70**).

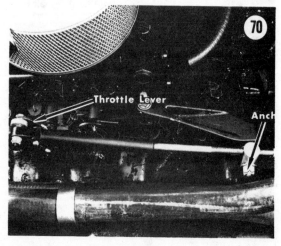

3. Grasp cable behind brass barrel and push lightly toward throttle lever. Adjust brass barrel to align with anchor stud and fasten barrel to stud with washers and nut (see Figure 70).

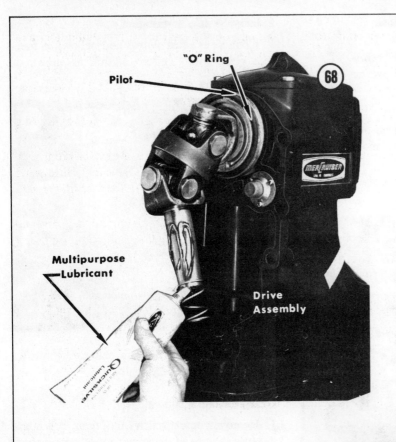

"O" Ring

Pilot

Multipurpose
Lubricant

Drive
Assembly

68

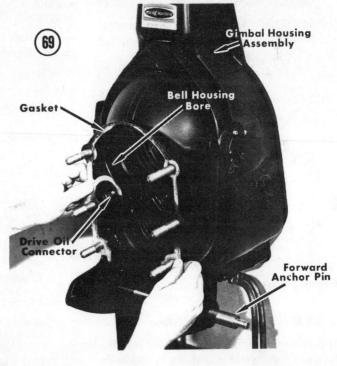

69

Gimbal Housing
Assembly

Bell Housing
Bore

Gasket

Drive Oil
Connector

Forward
Anchor Pin

7

**Shift Control Wiring Connections**

CAUTION
*Disconnect battery cables prior to connecting shift control wiring to shift motor.*

1. Remove shift motor cover.

2. Connect ring terminals located on shift control harness to terminals on shift motor, matching lead and terminal colors. Fasten harness clamp to shift motor bracket as shown in **Figure 71**. Reinstall cover.

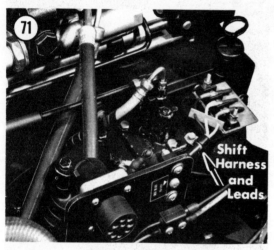

3. Connect white wire from remote control to 12V terminal (with white lead) on tachometer (see **Figure 72**). Use nut and insulating cap.

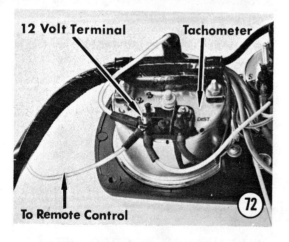

**Trim and Shock Cylinder Installation**

See procedure later in this chapter for installation of combination trim and shock cylinders on the MerCruiser III.

**Exhaust System Installation**

1. Connect exhaust elbows and bellows to transom plate and manifold elbows as shown in **Figure 73**.

2. Torque screws attaching exhaust elbows to transom plate to 20-25 ft.-lb.

**Gear Housing Removal**

1. Remove complete drive unit from bell housing (use reverse of drive unit installation procedure given above). Drain gear lubricant.

2. Remove propeller.

3. Mark position and remove trim tab.

4. Remove Allen head screw located under trim tab, then remove 7 nuts and separate gear housing from drive shaft housing.

**Gear Housing Installation**

CAUTION
*If gear housing, drive shaft housing, lower drive shaft, or lower drive shaft components have not been replaced, this procedure can be used. If any of the above have been replaced, the gear housing bearings and the drive shaft housing bearings must be preloaded. Preloading involves the use of tools and skills usually not available to the amateur mechanic, and should be done in a well-equipped shop by a qualified mechanic using factory instructions.*

1. Install trim tab Allen screw (if removed) in hole provided in gear housing.

2. Install O-ring around lower drive shaft bearing cup on drive shaft housing and O-ring in groove which is provided around oil recirculating passage in gear housing.

3. Connect gear housing to drive shaft housing with 7 nuts and tighten evenly.

4. Install Allen head screw located in trim tab cavity.

5. Install trim tab in position marked during removal, and trim tab access hole plug. Replace propeller and propeller components.

6. Fill unit with fresh gear lubricant, using the type, amount, and procedure specified in Chapter Two.

**Universal Joint Assembly**

1. Remove universal joint bearing snap rings, using a hammer and punch (see **Figure 74**).

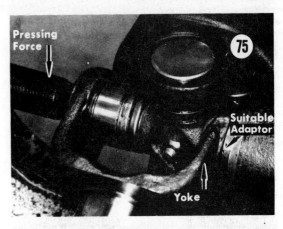

2. With a suitable adapter (see **Figure 75**) to support universal joint yoke (a suitably-sized socket can serve in a pinch), press on one bearing until opposite bearing is pressed into adapter. Remove loose bearing.

> NOTE: *An arbor press, large C-clamp, or a large vise can be used as a press.*

3. Remove opposite bearings in a like manner.

4. Repeat steps above to remove all bearings.

**Universal Joint Reassembly**

1. Place universal joint caps in yoke and start them on bearing cross members. Finish installation by pressing bearings through yokes and onto cross members (see **Figure 76**).

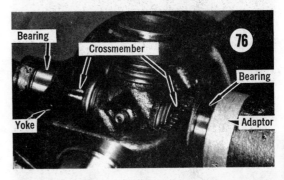

2. Install bearing cap retaining snap rings (see **Figure 77**).

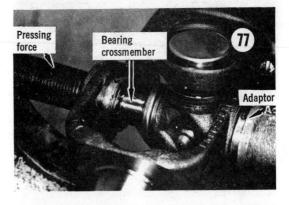

**MERCRUISER III STERN DRIVE**

**Engine Removal**

1. Remove stern drive unit using procedure later in this chapter.

7

2. Disconnect battery cables and unplug instrument panel harness connector from engine harness connector.

3. Shut off fuel tank valve and disconnect fuel line from engine.

#### WARNING
*Have a suitable container handy to catch gasoline and have a Coast Guard approved fire extinguisher readily available.*

4. Disconnect throttle arm and shift control cable. Disconnect reverse lock switch wire, hydraulic pump motor wire, and trim indicator wire from engine.

5. Remove water inlet tube and exhaust tube.

6. Support engine with overhead hoist and suitable sling attached to lifting eyes. Remove front and rear mounting bolts.

7. Lift engine up and out of boat.

### Engine Installation

1. Place one large steel washer, one double-wound lockwasher, and one neoprene washer, in that order, on each inner transom plate engine support.

2. Coat large O-ring seal (see **Figure 78**) with multipurpose lubricant.

**Bearing Support Housing"O" Ring**

3. Using overhead hoist, position engine ahead of inner transom plate so that bearing support housing and O-ring seal (see Figure 78) are in line with large opening in inner transom plate.

4. Move engine toward inner transom plate and guide the bearing support housing into transom plate opening. Do not damage O-ring. Continue

to move engine until holes in rear engine mounts line up with holes in washers and transom plate engine supports.

5. Relieve hoist tension as required to lower engine onto transom plate engine supports and washers.

6. Insert rear engine mount bolts through transom plate, washers, and rear engine mounts. Place a neoprene washer and nut on each mounting bolt. Torque nuts to 100 ft.-lb.

7. If front engine mounts and engine supports have not been moved or readjusted, install mounting bolts and tighten securely.

> NOTE: *If engine mounts and supports were moved or adusted after engine was removed, or if different engine is being installed, engine must be aligned. Alignment consists of inserting an alignment rod (9.775 ± 0.010 in. long for "325" engine) between recesses in inner transom plate and flywheel housing (see* **Figure 79**) *and adjusting front engine mounts up or down until alignment rod fits snugly, but can be easily removed.*

**Alignment Rod**

**Inner Transom Plate Recess**

**Flywheel Housing Recess**

8. Bend tabs of mount adjusting bolt tab washers down over edges of mounts.

### Stern Drive Unit Removal/Installation

> NOTE: *Reverse following procedure to remove stern drive unit.*

To install the stern drive unit:

1. Lubricate surface of drive shaft housing pilot and drive shaft splines with multipurpose lubri-

cant. Also apply light coat of lubricant to inside surface of bell housing bore.

2. Check that O-rings (see **Figure 80**) are properly seated (and remain so during installation) in their grooves for sealing. Otherwise installation will leak.

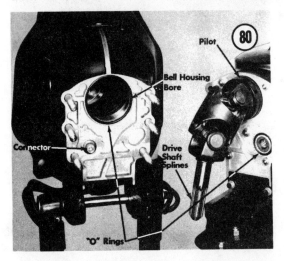

3. Attach hoist to lifting eye in top cap to support unit. Insert stern drive unit into drive shaft housing bell bore; guide drive shaft through guide spring in engine drive coupling. If drive shaft splines do not align with engine coupler splines, rotate propeller shaft slightly until splines mesh and drive unit can be pushed into position.

4. Install elastic stop nuts on 6 bell mounting bolts and torque to 100 ft.-lb.

## Throttle Cable Installation

Refer to **Figure 81** for this procedure.

1. Place remote control handle in neutral and warm-up lever in down position.

2. Remove roll pin from knurled pin in cable end guide and remove knurled pin and spring.

3. Remove nut and one washer from screw passing through carburetor throttle lever.

4. Place cable end guide over spacer, then replace washer and nut on screw and tighten nut securely.

5. Grasp throttle cable behind brass barrel and push toward throttle arm. Adjust brass barrel to align with anchor stud in bracket. Place flat washer, sleeve, and barrel on stud. Place flat washer and stop nut on stud and tighten nut securely.

## Shift Cable Installation

1. Place remote control cable in full forward position.

2. Place transmission in forward gear by moving shift cable lever to the right until detent ball (located behind transmission shift lever) is positioned in rear hole in transmission shift lever (see **Figure 82**).

3. Remove roll pin which passes through knurled pin in cable end guide and remove knurled pin and spring.

4. Place cable end guide on stud located on shift cable lever (see **Figure 83**).

7

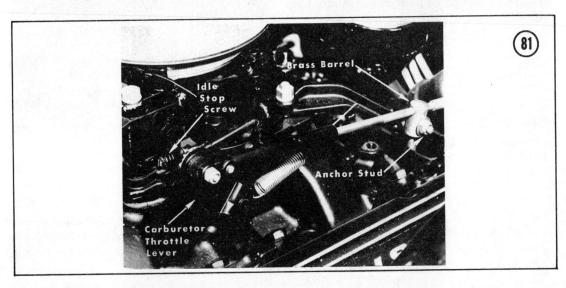

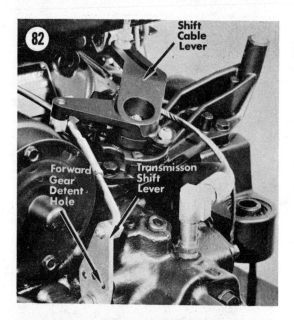

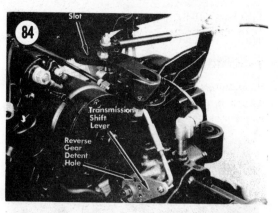

be centered in front hole (see Figure 84). If not, readjust until these conditions are achieved.

**Trim and Shock Cylinder Installation**

1. Install forward anchor pin through anchor pin holes in gimbal ring.

2. Place one flat washer and one rubber washer on forward anchor pin on each side of gimbal ring.

3. Insert aft anchor pin through hole in drive shaft housing and place a large washer and rubber bushing on each end of aft anchor pin (see **Figure 85**).

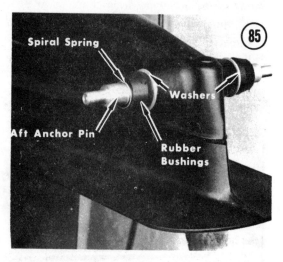

5. Adjust brass barrel on shift cable so barrel can be placed on anchor stud without disturbing shift cable lever position (see Figure 83).

6. Fasten end guide to shift cable lever stud with flat washer and nut. Tighten nut, then back off slightly so end guide can pivot freely.

7. Fasten brass barrel to anchor stud with flat washer and nut. Tighten nut securely.

8. Place remote control lever in full reverse position.

9. Loosen nut which fastens stud to shift cable lever. Move shift cable lever to left while sliding stud down slot in lever until detent ball is centered in front hole in transmission shift lever. Tighten nut securely (see **Figure 84**).

10. Check adjustment by moving remote control handle to full forward. Detent ball must be centered in rear hole in transmission shift lever (see Figure 82). Now move remote control handle to full reverse position. Detent ball must

4. Place cylinders in position on forward and aft anchor pins.

5. Place small spiral spring and a rubber bushing in forward and aft end mounting of each cylinder (make certain spring is between 2 rubber bushings). Small ends of bushings must face inboard.

6. Place a flat washer and a nut on each end of both anchor pins and tighten nuts securely.

### Power Trim Hose Connection

1. Remove cap from straight fitting on starboard hydraulic hose and connect hose to reverse lock valve as shown in **Figure 86**.

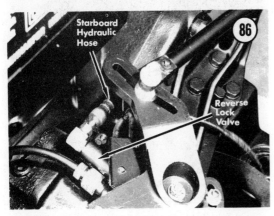

2. Remove cap from fitting on short plastic hydraulic hose and connect to reverse lock valve as shown in Figure 86.

### Reverse Lock Valve Adjustment

1. Shift unit into full reverse. Make certain transmission shift lever is in reverse detent.

2. Loosen 2 nuts on reverse lock lever. Move upper nut in direction required to align raised triangular marks on cam with those on reverse lock valve cover (see **Figure 87**). Tighten nuts on shift lever.

### Gear Housing Removal

1. Drain lubricant. See Chapter Two.

2. If stern drive unit has not been removed from boat, tilt unit up with hydraulic system to make gear housing removal easier.

3. Remove propeller. Mark position of trim tab and then remove it.

4. Remove Allen head screw and elastic stop nuts holding gear housing. Prepare to support gear housing so it will not fall when separated from drive shaft housing.

5. Separate gear housing from drive shaft housing.

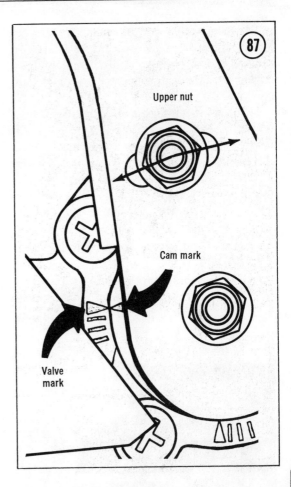

### Gear Housing Installation

1. Place new gasket on gear housing-to-drive shaft housing mating surface.

2. Position trim tab Allen head screw.

3. Joint gear housing and drive shaft housing by inserting drive shaft spline into gear splines. Install and tighten nuts and screws removed during disassembly.

4. Replace trim tab in position marked during disassembly and tighten Allen head screw.

5. Fill drive unit with fresh lubricant (see Chapter Two for type and amount).

6. Install propeller.

### MERCRUISER 215-H STERN DRIVE

#### Engine Removal/Installation

Removal and installation of MerCruiser 215-H engine are similar to removal and installation of MerCruiser III engine (procedures given earlier) if engine is being reinstalled in same boat and positions and settings of front engine mounts and supports have not been changed.

However, if positions and settings have been moved, or if engine is being installed in a different boat, or if new engine is being installed, the engine must be carefully aligned. To perform this alignment a special alignment tool (Mercury Part No. C-91-57797A1) must be used. The alignment procedure is as follows.

1. Install engine using MerCruiser III procedure earlier and torque rear engine mounting bolts to 100 ft.-lb.

2. Insert end of alignment tool shaft (C-91-57797A1) which has threaded hole through opening in bell housing into engine coupling (see **Figure 88**). Insert shaft until it bottoms out in coupling.

3. Position alignment tool plate on shaft as shown in **Figure 89**, and slide plate toward bell housing. Raise or lower front of engine with hoist to permit shoulder of plate to enter opening in bell housing.

4. With alignment tool positioned in bell housing and front of engine supported by hoist, adjust front engine mounts and supports so that alignment tool position will not be disturbed when hoist tension is removed.

5. Relieve hoist tension and fasten front mount bases to supports with ⅜ in. bolts, washers, and locknuts.

6. Push alignment shaft and plate toward engine and, while holding plate against bell housing, check for gaps between plate and rear surface of bell housing. If gap exists at 12 o'clock, raise front of engine with adjusting bolts on both front engine mounts until gap disappears. If gap exists at 6 o'clock, lower front of engine using same bolts until gap is corrected. If gap exists at 3 or 9 o'clock, front and rear mounting bolts must be loosened and the engine moved to right or left until gap is corrected. Then retighten nuts and bolts securely.

7. After alignment, bend tabs of adjusting bolt tab washers down over edges of mounts and recheck all mount fasteners for tightness.

8. Remove alignment shaft and plate.

9. Reconnect all wires, cables, and the fuel line that were disconnected during engine removal.

### Stern Drive Installation/Removal

Installation and removal of stern drive unit is identical to that for MerCruiser III, except that 6 elastic stop nuts in final step are torqued to 80 ft.-lb.

### Throttle Cable Installation

1. Place remote control handle in neutral gear, idle position.

2. Connect cable end guide to carburetor throttle lever with bolt, bushing, washer, and nut (see **Figure 90**).

3. Grasp cable behind brass barrel and push lightly toward throttle lever. Adjust brass barrel to align with anchor stud and fasten barrel to stud with washers and nut (see Figure 90).

### Shift Cable Adjustment

CAUTION
*Follow instructions closely. Failure to adjust shift cable properly will result in transmission failure.*

1. Place remote control handle in full forward position.

2. Place transmission in forward gear by moving shift cable lever to right until detent ball (located behind shift lever) is centered in rear hole in transmission shift lever (see **Figure 91**).

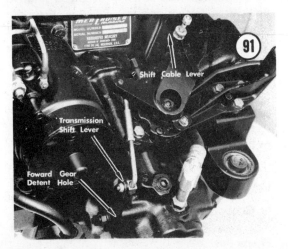

3. Place cable end guide on stud located in shift cable lever (see **Figure 92**).

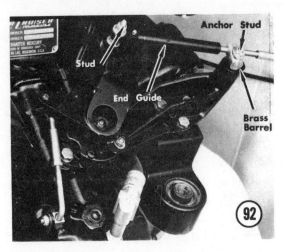

4. Adjust brass barrel on shift cable so barrel can be placed on anchor stud without moving shift cable lever (see Figure 92).

5. Fasten end guide to shift cable lever stud with flat washer and nut. Tighten nut and then back off slightly to allow end guide to pivot freely.

6. Fasten brass barrel to anchor stud with flat washer and nut, and tighten nut securely.

7. Move remote control handle to full reverse position.

8. Loosen nut holding stud to shift cable lever. Move shift cable lever to left while sliding stud down slot in lever until detent ball is centered in front hold in transmission shift lever (see **Figure 93**). Tighten nut securely.

9. Check adjustment by moving remote control handle to full forward position. Detent ball must be centered in rear hole in transmission shift

**7**

lever. Move control handle to full reverse position. Detent ball must be centered in front hole. If transmission lever does not position correctly, readjust by repeating this procedure.

## Trim and Shock Cylinder Installation

Installation of the combination trim and shock cylinders is identical to that for Mer-Cruiser III.

## Power Trim Hose Connections

> NOTE: *New hoses are filled with oil. All connections should be made as carefully and quickly as possible to prevent loss of oil.*

1. Connect gray hose to reverse lock valve (see **Figure 94**) as follows.

    a. Remove shipping plug and plastic seal from reverse lock valve (if present).

    b. Route gray hose under cable anchor bracket. Remove cap from end of hose and connect hose to reverse lock valve.

2. Connect black hose to reverse lock valve as follows.

    a. Remove ball from reverse lock valve (if present).

    b. Route black hose between shift cable and cable anchor bracket. Remove cap from hose fitting and connect hose to reverse lock valve as shown in Figure 94.

## Ride-Guide Steering Installation

1. Connect steering link rod with pivot bolt in rod, flat nylon washer and curved washer to steering arm as shown in **Figure 95**. Align curved washer and tighten nut.

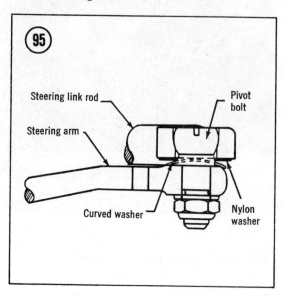

2. Lubricate inside of cable guide tube with multipurpose lubricant.

3. Insert cable end through tube and thread large fastening nut securely on tube.

4. Attach steering link rod to cable end and torque to 12 ft.-lb.

5. After engine and stern drive are installed, turn steering wheel to right and left. If drive unit turns farther in one direction than the other, loosen locknus and large fastening nut and move cable guide tube to left or right to allow full traverse. Tighten adjusting nuts securely.

6. Turn steering wheel until drive unit is centered. If steering wheel is not centered correctly, readjust cable guide tube to center wheel, then recheck Step 5.

## Exhaust System Installation

1. Connect exhaust elbows and bellows to transom plate and manifold elbows as shown in **Figure 96**.

2. Tighten clamp screws securely and torque elbow-to-transom plate screws to 20-25 ft.-lb.

## MERCRUISER 215-E
## STERN DRIVE

### Engine Removal

Procedure for removing MerCruiser 215-E engine is identical to that for MerCruiser III.

### Engine Installation

NOTE: *To install MerCruiser 215-E engine, use the installation procedure for MerCruiser III and the alignment procedure for MerCruiser 215-H.*

### Removing/Installing Stern Drive Unit

To remove stern drive unit, reverse the following procedure.

CAUTION
*Operating shift without drive shaft installed will cause clutch plate misalignment. Do not connect electrical shift control harness leads to actuator box unless battery is disconnected or fuse is removed from holder in red wire (over flywheel housing). If clutch plate has been moved out of position, an engine alignment tool (Part No. C-91-57797A1) with clutch alignment tool (Part No. C-91-57795) will be re-*

*quired to realign the clutch plate. The alignment procedure is given later in this chapter.*

1. Lubricate drive shaft housing pilot O-ring and oil and shift connectors with multipurpose lubricant (see **Figure 97**). Apply light coat of lubricant to inside surfaces of bell housing bore and position gasket (see **Figure 98**). Do not lubricate spline on shaft.

2. Place forward anchor pin in gimbal ring (see Figure 98).

3. Use hoist to raise and hold stern drive unit and position unit behind housing.

4. Insert drive shaft into bell housing bore. Pull shifter cable about 3 in. out of bell housing.

5. Insert square end of shifter cable into shifter shaft connector.

CAUTION
*Do not turn connector shaft in stern drive to insert shift cable.*

6. Push stern drive into bell housing and fasten housing to bell mounting studs with 6 elastic stop nuts and flat washers. Torque nuts evenly to 80 ft.-lb.

NOTE: *If drive shaft splines do not mesh with clutch disc splines, rotate universal joint shaft slightly until*

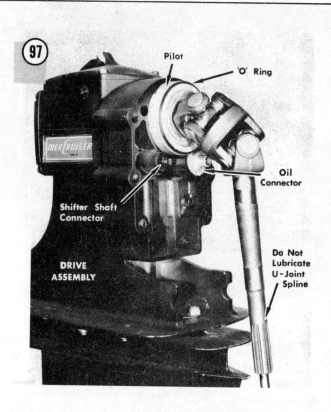

(97) Pilot    'O' Ring

Oil
Connector

Shifter Shaft
Connector

DRIVE
ASSEMBLY

Do Not
Lubricate
U - Joint
Spline

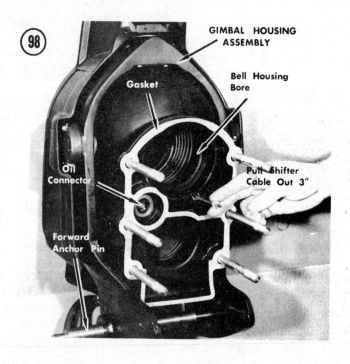

GIMBAL HOUSING
ASSEMBLY

(98)

Gasket    Bell Housing
Bore

Oil
Connector

Pull Shifter
Cable Out 3"

Forward
Anchor Pin

*splines mesh. If unit still cannot be pushed into position, perform clutch plate realignment procedures below.*

7. Install unit shifter shaft, using procedure given below.

8. Check shift harness installation to actuator box, and reinstall fuse in red wire fuse holder over flywheel housing.

### Clutch Plate Realignment

To realign clutch plate, proceed as follows.

1. Insert the engine alignment shaft (C-91-57797A1) with the clutch alignment tool (C-91-57795) through clutch plate splines with electric shift control connected and placed in neutral position. When tool is fully through clutch plate, shift the control into forward. This will hold clutch plate in alignment.

> NOTE: *To manually release clutch plate, remove fuse from holder and turn safety clutch toward forward gear (direction of decal arrow) until it reaches a firm stop. Then turn clutch in opposite direction until clutch plate is released. After positioning plate with alignment tool, return safety clutch to forward gear, as above.*

2. Remove fuse from holder in red lead to prevent a possible shift cycle with drive unit removed.

3. Remove the alignment tools and install the drive unit.

### Clutch Adjustment

> NOTE: *If stern drive unit does not shift smoothly when engine is operating, clutch requires adjustment. Also, model 215-E requires clutch adjustment after first 20 hours of operation.*

1. Place electric MerControl in forward gear and remove fuse from fuse holder on red wire over flywheel housing.

2. Loosen locknut on clutch lever and turn adjusting screw ½ turn, then tighten locknut and replace fuse (see **Figure 99**).

3. Start engine and shift into reverse gear and then into forward. If the unit does not shift

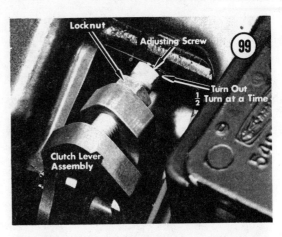

smoothly, readjust until smooth operation is obtained.

### Emergency Manual Shift Operation

If shifting the electric MerControl becomes difficult or impossible, stern drive can be shifted manually into forward gear as follows.

1. Remove fuse from fuse holder on red wire.

2. Turn the safety clutch in the direction of the decal arrow until it stops firmly. Drive is now in forward gear.

3. Remove jumper wedge from holder on rear of port rocker cover and jam wedge between 2 yellow terminals on port side of shift actuator box as shown in **Figure 100**. This permits unit to be started in gear.

> CAUTION
> *When starting engine, place throttle in idle and remember that stern drive is in gear. Cautiously start and stop engine to control motion of boat, as drive cannot be shifted into neutral or reverse.*

### Installing Unit Shifter Shaft

1. Route long flexible shaft and cable housing under engine mounts without sharp bends through brackets (see **Figure 101**) to actuator box safety clutch.

2. Route short cable housing over engine mount (**Figure 102**) through bracket to safety clutch.

3. Insert flexible shaft fully into safety clutch cover (see **Figure 103**) and tighten lock screw to 55 in.-lb.

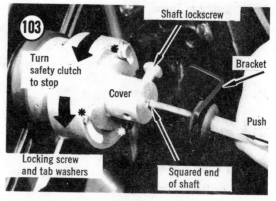

Jumper Wedge

Shift Actuator Box

Yellow Leads

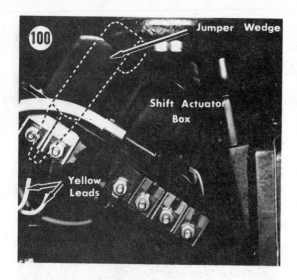

Bracket

Safety Clutch

Shift Cable Assembly

Engine Mount

Bracket

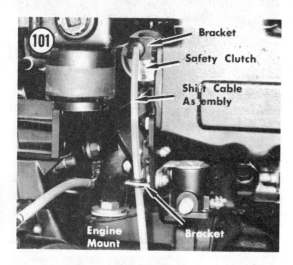

Bracket

Safety Clutch

Shift Cable Assembly

Engine Mount

Shaft lockscrew

Turn safety clutch to stop

Cover

Bracket

Push

Locking screw and tab washers

Squared end of shaft

### CAUTION

*Do not turn flexible shaft to align with safety clutch cover. If squared shaft end is not aligned, rotate safety clutch to forward gear stop (in direction of decal arrow). Loosen 3 screws in safety clutch cover (see Figure 103) and rotate in slots until shaft can be installed. Tighten set screws to 24 in.-lb. and bend tabs to lock screws.*

4. Attach electrical leads from shift control.

5. Cycle shift control 2 times to automatically set shift synchronization.

### Exhaust System Installation

1. Connect exhaust elbows and bellows to transom plate and manifold elbows as shown in **Figure 104**.

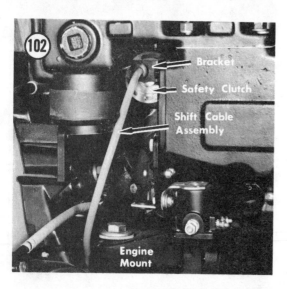

Hose clamps

⅜-16 x 4" long screws and lockwashers

⅜-16 x 1¼" long screw and lockwasher

Ground wire from flywheel housing

2. Connect ground wire to right side exhaust elbow attaching screw (see Figure 104).

3. Torque exhaust elbow-to-transom plate screws to 20-25 ft.-lb.

## Throttle Cable Installation

NOTE: *Installation of the throttle cable requires procedure identical to that for MerCruiser 215-H.*

## Power Trim Hose Connections

NOTE: *New hoses are filled with oil. Make connections as quickly and carefully as possible to prevent oil from draining out.*

1. Connect gray hose (from transom plate) to reverse lock valve as shown in **Figure 105**, removing shipping plugs and seals as required.

2. Connect black hose (from trim pump) to reverse lock valve as shown in Figure 105, first removing shipping caps and ball.

## Installation of Trim and Shock Cylinders

The procedure for installing combination trim and shock cylinders is identical to that for MerCruiser III.

## Installation of Ride-Guide Steering

Procedure for installing Ride-Guide steering is identical to that for MerCruiser 215-H.

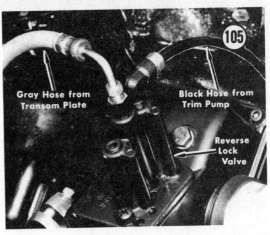

Gray Hose from Transom Plate

Black Hose from Trim Pump

Reverse Lock Valve

### Table 1     TORQUE SPECIFICATIONS
### (MERCRUISER MODELS II, II-TR, II-TRS, III, AND 215)

| Location | Ft.-Lb. | In.-Lb. |
|---|---|---|
| Gimbal ring-to-upper swivel shaft bolt | 20 | |
| Steering lever-to-upper swivel shaft nut | 45-50 | |
| Hydraulic connector-to-gimbal housing stud nut | 10 | |
| Oil hose clamp | | 12-15 |
| Exhaust bellows clamp | | 35 |
| Universal joint bellows clamp | | 35 |
| Valve guide cover-to-bell housing bolt | 15 | |
| Bell housing-to-gimbal ring hinge pin | 60 | |
| Bell housing stud-to-drive shaft housing nut | 80 | |
| Reservoir cover-to-transom plate bolt | 20 | |
| Exhaust cover-to-transom plate bolt | 12 | |
| Hydraulic pump bracket bolt | 20 | |
| Steering link rod castle nut-to-Ride-Guid cable | | 20 |
| Steering link rod castle nut-to-steering lever | 15-18 | |
| Gimbal housing stud-to-transom plate nut | 25-30 | |
| Exhaust elbow bolt | 20-25 | |
| Reverse lock valve bolt | 14 | |
| Drive shaft housing-to-gear housing stud nut | 35 | |
| Bell housing-to-drive shaft housing stud nut | 75-85 | |
| Drive shaft housing rear cover bolt | 20 | |
| Drive shaft housing top cover bolt | 20 | |
| Universal joint shaft pinion nut | 200 | |
| Valve guide-to-drive shaft housing bolt | | 30 |
| Trim tab bolt | | 180 |

7

# CHAPTER EIGHT

# VOLVO STERN DRIVES

This chapter contains procedures for installing, removing, and aligning the Volvo Aquamatic series. The procedures cover the following models: 100, 200, 250, 270, 270T, 280, and 280T. Internally, these models are essentially identical, the main difference being gear reduction ratios. The 270-270T and 280-280T series differ only externally; the latter series have a different lower gear housing designed to offer lower water resistance at high speeds. The "T" designation in 270T and 280T means that the units are equipped with internal power trim. This permits adjustment of the stern drive trim while underway to compensate for loading of boat, etc.

This chapter contains only those procedures that an average amateur mechanic with a well-equipped tool box could be expected to perform. Repairs which require special skills and tools are best left to the professional mechanic who has access to the required special tools and measuring devices. If these repairs are improperly performed, extensive damage to the drive mechanism will result.

Power from the engine is transmitted to the upper gear housing by a double universal joint which passes through the transom mounting collar. The universal joints are connected to the forward and reverse gears by an input drive which is in constant mesh with the gears. The

forward and reverse gears are carried on a countershaft so they can be rotated independently of the shaft. A cone clutch is located between the gears for disengagement and reversal of the vertical drive shaft. The lower end of the vertical shaft is geared to mesh with the geared end of the propeller shaft. Engine-to-drive reduction ratio is accomplished by these gears. The following reductions are available.

| | | |
|---|---|---|
| 280/280T | - B | 1.61:1 |
| 280/280T | - C | 1.89:1 |
| 280/280T | - D | 2.15:1 |
| 270/270T | - B | 1.61:1 |
| 270/270T | - C | 1.89:1 |
| 270/270T | - D | 2.15:1 |
| 250 | - A | 1.35:1 |
| 250 | - B | 1.61:1 |
| 250 | - C | 1.89:1 |
| 250 | - D | 2.15:1 |
| 200 | - B | 1.59:1 |
| 200 | - C | 1.85:1 |
| 100 | - B | 1.66:1 |

Since reduction takes place after the forward/reverse gear location in the power train, the reduction ratio is the same for forward and reverse gears.

Left-hand propeller rotation is standard on all models. Rotation can be changed to right-hand on all models, except 100B, by a simple procedure (given later in this chapter). If rotation is changed to right-hand, however, a right-hand propeller must be installed.

An electromechanical lift device is standard equipment on the 200, 250, 270, and 280 models and is an opentional extra on Model 100. The power trim mechanism on 270T and 280T also provides for tilting the drive unit to 30 degrees for shallow water operation, and to 60 degrees for mooring or transporting the boat.

The lubrication system is common to the upper and lower gear housings. An oil pump in the lower gear housing provides oil circulation.

**Stern Drive Removal**

It is important that the workbench and tools are kept clean when working on the outboard drive unit to prevent dirt from damaging internal parts. Clean outside of unit before removing from boat.

1. Remove propeller by bending tabs on the lockwasher (**Figure 1**) for propeller cone (1) and unscrewing cone. Take off the lockwasher, propeller, and spacer sleeve.

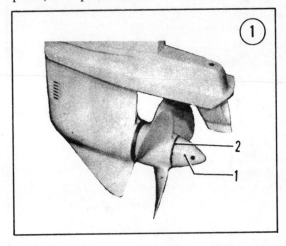

2. Remove 2 screws (1, **Figure 2**) for the zinc ring and remove the ring.

3. Drain oil from outboard drive by removing dipstick (71, **Figure 3**) and oil drain plug on lower end of unit.

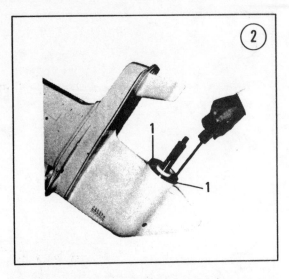

4. Remove casing (76, Figure 3) over control mechanism and disconnect control cable from yoke (2, **Figure 4**). Unscrew securing block (39, Figure 4) and remove control cable locking plate (35, Figure 4) mounted at front end of intermediate housing.

5. Loosen steering casing (12, **Figure 5**) and rubber bellows from upper gear housing, exhaust bellows from intermediate housing, and water hose from cooling water connection (28, Figure 4) on yoke.

6. Unscrew both lock screws (27, Figure 5) retaining pivot pins (26, Figure 5) in mounting collar. Place block under drive end, knock out pivot pins and lift off drive unit. Place it in a suitable jig.

NOTE: *Do not lose 2 bushings (38, Figure 4) on yoke.*

7. Loosen control rod (18, Figure 4) from yoke, unscrew bolts (15, Figure 4) and undo nuts (17, Figure 4) which hold upper gear housing to intermediate gear housing. Carefully tap either housing with rubber mallet until they separate.

8. Keep count of number of shims between different housings and on all the gear assemblies. If no gears, housings, or bearings are replaced, the same number of shims must be refitted when assembling.

9. Unscrew 7 bolts securing lower gear housing to intermediate housing and carefully tap either housing with rubber mallet until they separate. Lift off the spline sleeve (41, **Figure 6**).

8

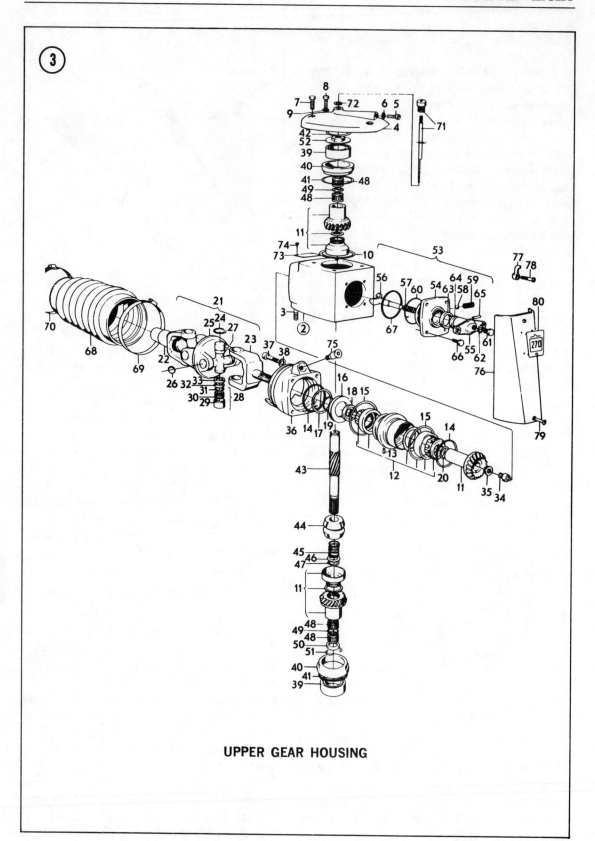

**UPPER GEAR HOUSING**

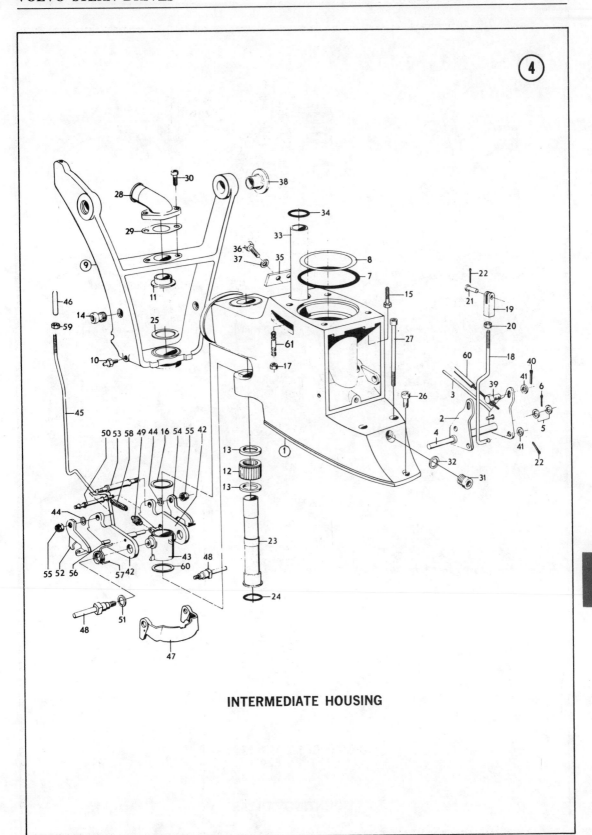

**INTERMEDIATE HOUSING**

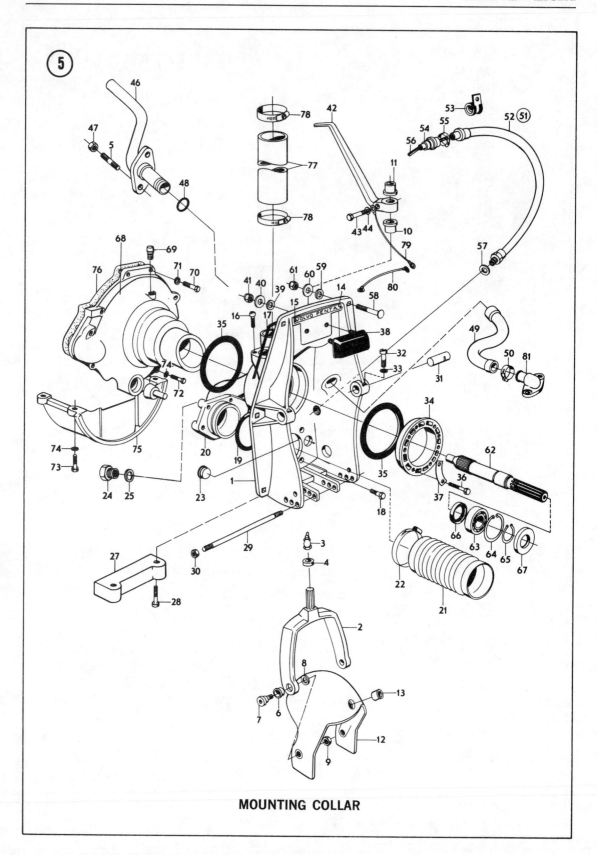

**MOUNTING COLLAR**

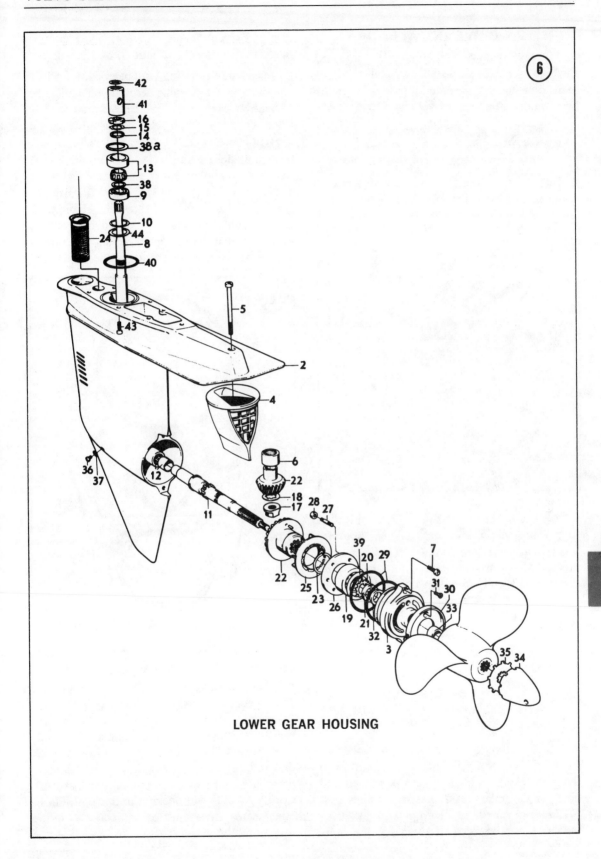

**LOWER GEAR HOUSING**

## STERN DRIVE INSTALLATION

1. Fit new bellows (21, Figure 5, and 68, Figure 3) for exhaust installation and universal joint. Connect cooling water hose (49, Figure 5) between drive and transom shield.

> NOTE: *The cooling-water hose is marked "Engine" on end to be fitted to connection in the transom shield.*

2. Lift drive to transom shield and block it under fin at right height. See **Figure 7**.

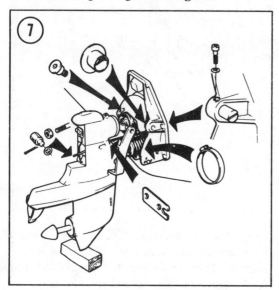

3. Place hose clamp (69, Figure 3) for universal joint rubber bellows on neck of gear housing. Smear universal joint and shaft splines with grease. Move drive toward drive shaft while turning universal joint at same time so that splines on drive shaft can engage with splines on universal joint.

### CAUTION
*Make sure when fitting not to burr the splines as this would make assembling difficult.*

> NOTE: *Lubricate the shaft pins with grease or Molykote or similar.*

4. Move outboard drive mounting yoke (9, Figure 4) into mounting collar and line it up so that pivot pins (26, Figure 5) can be pushed into holes in the yoke. Fit 2 plastic bushings (38, Figure 4) in yoke holes. Turn pins so that locking bolts can be fitted. Tighten locking bolts

firmly. Torque tapered lock bolt (75, Figure 3) in steering casing (11, Figure 5) to 36 ft.-lb.

5. Install universal joint rubber bellows. Place clamp so that tightening screw is on underside of bellows. Make sure that bellows are correctly fitted and that both clips are tightened to prevent leakage.

6. Install hose clamps (19, 44, Figure 5) on exhaust and cooling water hoses. Connect hoses and tighten hose clamps. Clamps for exhaust hose should be turned as shown in **Figure 8**. It is important that clamps are fitted properly, otherwise they may damage adjacent hoses as well as hinder the movements of the drive.

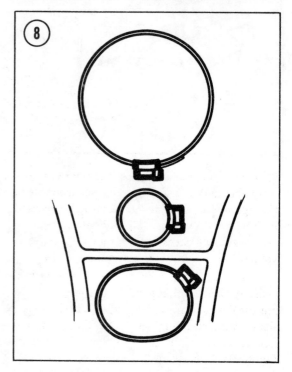

7. Install locking plate (35, Figure 4) for shift cable so it locks in cable groove.

8. Check that control lever and drive shaft lever are in neutral. Slacken locknut for yoke (11, **Figure 9**). Turn yoke on thread of control rod (10) so that when it is connected to shift lever position of reverse check rod (6) is such that rod comes in contact with (without force being used) bracket of retaining pawl at "A". Lock yoke (11) with locknut in this position. In other words, there must be no axial play in the reverse inhibitor rod (6).

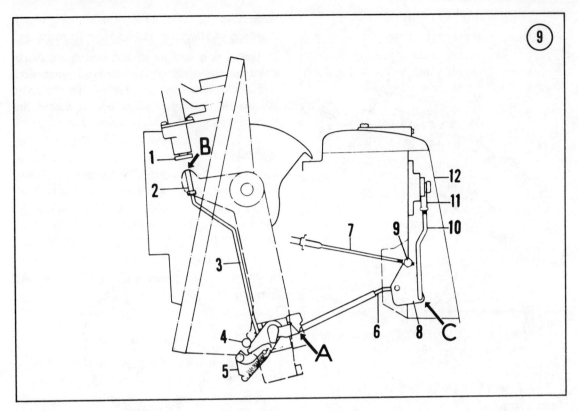

9. Thread locknut and securing block on control cable and adjust shift cable securing block (9, Figure 9) so that block can easily be inserted in hole in shift yoke. Move control lever to FORWARD and check that corner "C" on shift yoke (8) does not catch in housing.

10. Pull retaining pawl against stop lugs on bearing sleeve (43, Figure 4) and release locknut for thrust sleeve (2, Figure 9). Adjust thrust sleeve with retaining pawl still down so that sleeve comes to the level of the yoke (see B, Figure 9). Lock thrust sleeve with counternut. Then press drive forward toward the locating pin and check that upper end of thrust rod (3) does not contact lift thrust plate. When lift (1) is tilted up, retaining pawl releases.

11. Make certain retaining pawl hooks securely on locating pin by pulling drive backward and then to both outer steering positions. Check that electro-mechanical lift (1, Figure 9) releases retaining pawl from locating pin when drive tips up. With drive released fully downward and locating pin in the inside hole, there must be clearance between left thrust plate and retaining pawl release rod.

12. Check free travel of retaining pawl. Press drive forward and secure retaining pawl in this position. Then move the drive backward and check that retaining pawl does not hook on locating pin.

13. Fit protective cover (12, Figure 9) over shift mechanism, and fill drive unit with oil. Lubricate the steering yoke grease fitting (see Chapter Two for capacities).

14. Check retaining pawl when test running by pulling drive backward so that spring hooks of retaining pawl grip locating pin.

 a. Check that retaining pawl rests against underside of locating pin. If it does not, then probably counternut of thrust sleeve is incorrectly adjusted or thrust rod is deformed.

 b. Check that there is full overlapping between the tabs of the locking brackets and the connecting surfaces of the spring hooks (5, **Figure 10**) when "reverse" is engaged.

 c. The clearance between the tabs of the locking bracket and the contact surfaces of the spring hook in "neutral" should be

8

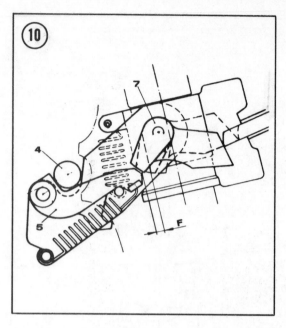

approximately 0.08 in. (2mm). See measment at F, Figure 10.

## REPAIRING UNIVERSAL JOINTS

### Disassembly

1. Remove snap rings (24, Figure 3) which hold needle bearings in the yokes.

2. Use a hammer and drift to drive out the needle bearings (see **Figure 11**). Remove spider.

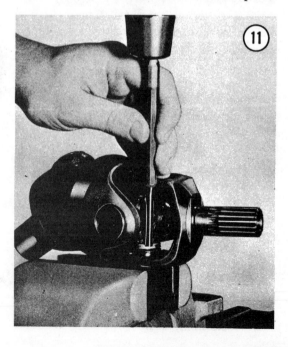

### Inspection

Check the spider and needle bearings for looseness and scoring in the bearing races. If there are any faults replace the spider complete with the needle bearings. Also make sure that the needle bearing cages are not loose in the yokes. If there is looseness, install new yokes.

### Assembly

1. Fit new seal washers on spider trunnions. Insert spider in flange yoke.

2. Push spider far enough in one direction that needle bearing can slide into the trunnion. Then press in the needle bearing far enough that snap ring can be fitted.

3. Fit the other needle bearing and snap ring in the same way.

## ANTI-CORROSION

Before installing the drive unit in the boat, check it for any corrosion damage as follows.

1. Check the contact surfaces of the zinc protectors. If these are eroded more than 50%, they should be replaced.

2. Touch-up paint work which is exposed to mechanical abrasion if damaged.

> CAUTION
> *In order to protect the drive unit against marine growth, the entire outboard drive, including the retaining pawl, cooling water inlet, and mounting collar must be painted with anti-marine growth paint. It must not contain bronze or copper. The zinc protectors must not be painted.*

> WARNING
> *Anti-fouling paint should not be sprayed on since it contains chemicals which are dangerous to inhale.*

## REPAIRING ELECTRO-MECHANICAL LIFT UNIT

1. Remove protective cover and take off switch (26, **Figure 12**) and bracket with relays (23, 24).

2. Loosen nuts and remove electric motor (22).

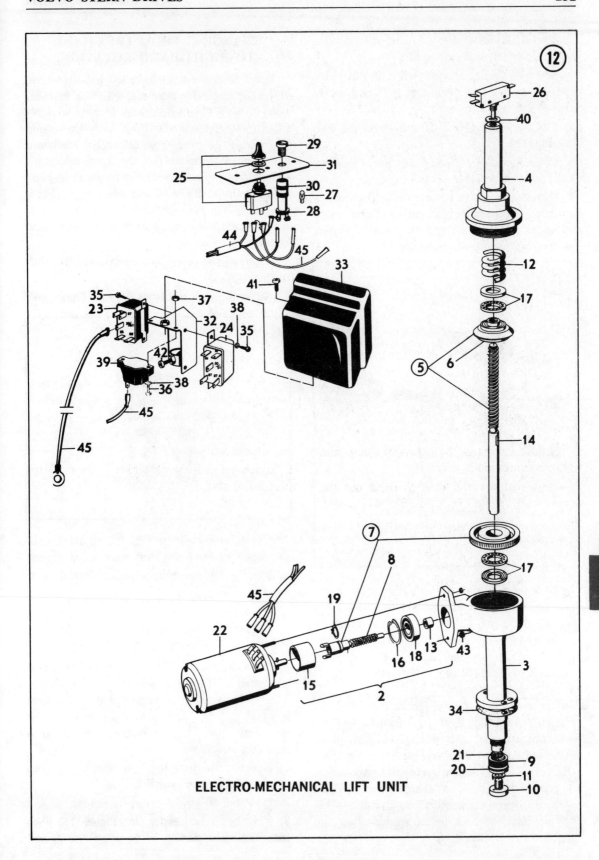

ELECTRO-MECHANICAL LIFT UNIT

3. Straighten lockwasher (11) and unscrew limiting screw (10) and sealing nut (9).

4. Screw off upper section (4) and lift out worm rod (5), spring (12), bearings (17) and worm gear (7).

5. Pull out guide ring (15) and worm (8) with bearing (18).

6. Clean the parts and check for wear. Replace any parts if necessary.

7. Reassemble lift in reverse order. Before assembling, grease parts with universal grease and fill upper part of housing with grease. Connect ground cable as shown in **Figure 13**.

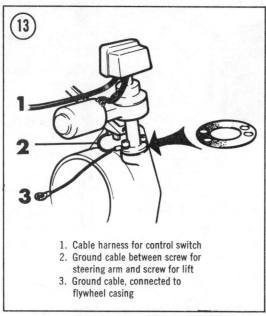

1. Cable harness for control switch
2. Ground cable between screw for steering arm and screw for lift
3. Ground cable, connected to flywheel casing

After reconditioning, check that drive tip-up and retaining pawl mechanism function satisfactorily. During tilting, lift should clear the retaining pawl completely from setting pin before drive tilts up. See stern drive installation instructions, Step 10, above, for pushrod adjustment. When outboard drive is lowered, lift motor should be run until it automatically cuts out and the warning light goes out. If drive does not straighten out, this means that the spring (12, Figure 12) has poor tension. Place a washer (Part No. 955901) under spring. If drive cannot be pressed down by hand (approximately 165 lb. at the fin), loosen upper section (2) slightly. It is not necessary to lock upper section since the spring thrust latches it.

## CHANGING FROM LEFT-HAND TO RIGHT-HAND ROTATION

Drive units normally have left-hand rotation. In certain cases (for example, with twin installation) it may be advantageous to have a right-hand rotating starboard drive. Very light rapid boats with the steering wheel on the starboard side can compensate for the boat operator's weight and the torque with a single right-hand rotating drive. By a simple adjustment, Models 270-270T and 280-280T can be altered from standard left-hand rotation to right-hand rotation as follows.

1. Remove the protective cover over the shift mechanism.

2. Move the shift rod from A to B (**Figure 14**).

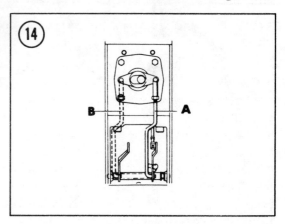

3. Check to make sure that the adjustment of the retaining pawl and shift mechanism agrees.

4. Remove left-hand propeller and install right-hand propeller.

## ADJUSTING TRIM INDICATOR (MODEL 270T)

The adjustable sender for the trim indicator is located on the collar next to the lift cylinder. The sender is set at the factory, but final adjustment should be made when the boat is first launched. Make final adjustment of the trim indicator as follows.

1. Run out the drive until the trim piston goes to its extreme outer position.

2. Loosen 3 adjusting screws on sender.

3. Turn cover on sender (see **Figure 15**) until trim indicator needle is between TRIM and

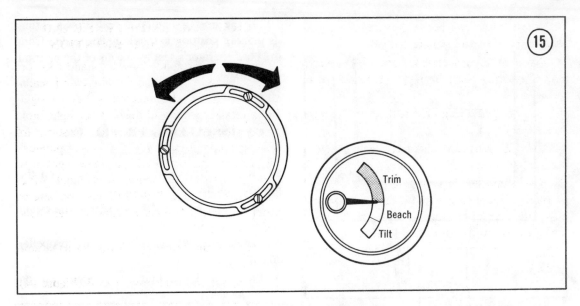

BEACH. Fix sender cover in this position by tightening screws.

### TEST RUN

1. Check engine oil level and, if necessary, add oil.

2. Check the oil level in the outboard drive. Add oil if required.

3. *Drive 270T and 280T*: Remove bolt from filler plug of hydraulic system (see **Figure 16**) if present. This bolt should not be present when the drive is being used. It is only intended as a plug during delivery from the factory. Check the oil level in the hydraulic system.

> NOTE: *The hydraulic system may require bleeding after the drive has been installed on the boat. Bleeding occurs automatically when the drive is lifted and lowered a couple of times.*

4. Make sure the hull drain plugs are installed. Close all drain cocks on the cooling system of the engine, and inspect boat and stern drive installation to make sure that the boat is ready for launching. Launch the boat.

5. After launching, check for and correct any leaks. Start engine as described in Chapter Two.

6. Make sure that there is no leakage of water, oil, or fuel from engine.

7. Test run the boat and check that controls operate satisfactorily by shifting repeatedly between FORWARD and REVERSE. Check instruments for the engine. Check that steering is smooth from one extreme to the other.

8. If the boat shows a certain tendency to go off course, loosen the mounting bolt and slightly turn the exhaust outlet tab, which is mounted under the drive cavitation plate. Turn rear edge in the direction the boat is twisting. Adjust "toe out" angle between drive in twin installations until cavitation-free running has been obtained. The angle between drives is increased with deeper V-bottom (see **Figure 17**).

9. If boat does not run flat at planing speed, minor adjustments can be made with the adjusting pin in the mounting collar. There are 3 or 4 alternative holes, depending on the model. If at planing speed the boat sets its stern in the water, move the adjusting pin forward. If the boat's bow dips (so-called overplaning), move the adjusting pin aft.

**8**

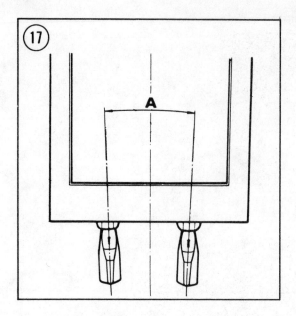

10. If the boat is equipped with Power Trim, its planing position is infinitely adjustable from the boat operator's seat by means of the internal power trim.

## INSTALLING PROPELLER

To install propeller, proceed as follows.

1. Fit the spacer sleeve (33, Figure 6) on the propeller shaft.

2. Coat propeller shaft with water-resistant grease and slide on propeller.

3. Install lockwasher (35) and propeller cone (34).

4. Lock cone by peening all the lock teeth on the lockwasher.

# CHAPTER NINE

# STERN-POWR STERN DRIVES

The Stern-Powr stern drive transmits inboard engine power through the boat transom. Features include an allowable kick-up of 55 degrees to avert damage from underwater obstacles and permit easy beaching and trailering. Automatic interlock retains the unit in reverse. Through the transom-mounted steering arm, the outdrive can turn up to 30 degrees to port or starboard for craft maneuverability.

This chapter covers Models 80, 81, and 91. The models are similar in external appearance and use many interchangeable parts. These procedures pertain to all unless otherwise noted.

> NOTE: *STERN-POWR stern drive units also are marketed under various "private labels," such as Dieseldrive, Aqua Flite, Chrysler Drive 90°, Perkins Engines, Sea-Glide, and many others. The units were marketed previously under the Dana brand.*

Component groups of the drive unit can be removed and serviced separately without removing the main unit from the boat. For example, each section of the exterior group, such as shift mechanism or steering control, may be serviced without removing the outdrive or disturbing the engine mounting. Similarly, the lower case group may be removed and serviced without removing the upper case.

If both the upper and lower case groups are removed together, hoist the assembly with an S hook through the eye on the upper case. Leave the assembly suspended with the S hook and secure skeg in vise with soft jaws (see **Figure 1**).

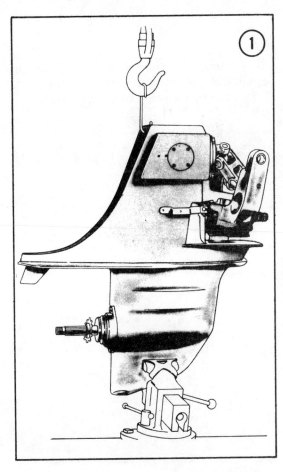

9

## SERVICE HINTS

The general precautions and procedures listed below should be followed.

1. Replace all oil seals, O-rings, roll pins, cotter pins, gaskets, and other expendable parts that may be distorted upon removal. Also, replace all star type lockwashers.

2. Lubricate new oil seals and O-rings liberally with petroleum jelly, castor oil, or equivalent lubricant, to avoid seal damage and ensure proper installation.

3. Install all gears, bearings, and oil seals using suitable tools. Use an arbor press, if possible, to install bearings and seals accurately.

4. Inspect interior and exterior of all castings for cracks or other defects. Replace as required.

5. Check all painted surfaces for scratches or chips. Retouch all bare spots with the touch-up paint kit which is a special epoxy compound that resists corrosion.

## PROPELLER

### Removal

For Model 91, remove cotter key on end of output shaft. Remove 2 propeller jam nuts. Using a standard inboard wheel propeller puller suited for use on a 1½ in. diameter shaft, remove propeller (see **Figure 2**).

For Models 80 and 81, bend out lock tangs of propeller lockwasher (**Figure 3**). Insert ⅜ in. diameter steel rod through hole in propeller locknut. Remove locknut (right-hand thread). Remove lockwasher, propeller, and hub support from output shaft.

If nuts will not loosen easily, place wood block between propeller blade and underside of cavitation plate to keep propeller from turning.

### Installation

For Model 91, install key into output shaft keyway. Slide propeller onto shaft, making sure key remains in middle of keyway. Install thin jam nut and tighten securely. Install thick jam nut next. Install cotter pin in output shaft and bend both tangs over.

For Models 80 and 81, install propeller cushion hub support (M-18, Figure 3) on output shaft. Slide propeller into position on shaft spline. Install lockwasher (M-17) and propeller locknut (M-16). Jam propeller with wooden block and use ⅜ in. steel bar to tighten locknut. Secure by bending all tangs of lockwasher into detents of locknut.

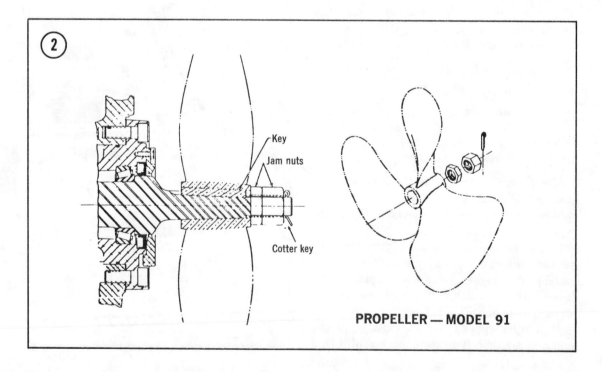

Key
Jam nuts
Cotter key

**PROPELLER — MODEL 91**

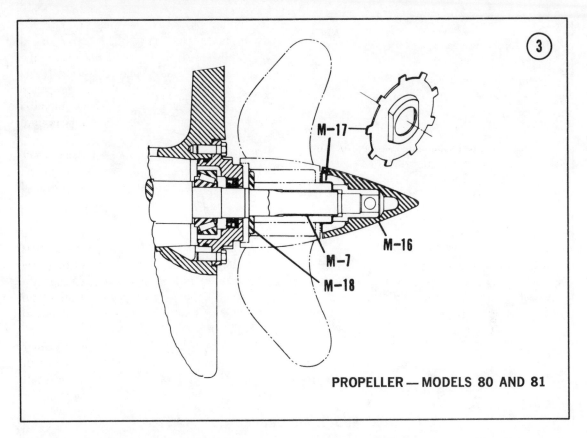

③

**PROPELLER — MODELS 80 AND 81**

## SHOCK ABSORBERS

NOTE: *The shock absorbers can be replaced without removing the marine drive from the transom. The shock absorbers "cushion" the unit against sudden propeller thrust as it return from an emergency kick-up position. Refer to* **Figure 4** *for this procedure.*

### Removal

1. Remove cotter pin (H-6) from upper shock pin (H-2) located in support yoke (F-1). Remove shock pin.

2. Tap lower cotter pin (H-4) free of anchor pin (H-3). Slide off shock absorbers and washers (H-5). Remove lower anchor pin from pivot housing.

### Installation

To install shock absorbers, reverse the above procedure. Always attach the rod end of the shock absorber to the pivot housing first. Upper shock pins (H-2) should always be installed with the legs inward.

## KICK-UP INTERLOCK

### Removal

Refer to **Figures 5 and 6** for Models 81 and 91. Refer to **Figure 7** for Model 80.

1. Loosen interlock clamp bolt (C-2) and remove the interlock lever (C-1) from the lever shaft (G-2).

2. Using a small drift, tap pin (G-3) out of lever shaft and interlock (G-1). Tap interlock lever shaft out of upper case and remove interlock.

3. If necessary to remove interlock bushing (G-21, Figure 6, or G-8, Figure 7), use ½ inch O.D. bar stock or tubing for a drift.

NOTE: *For removal and installation of locking arm and spring, see* Pivot Support Yoke.

9

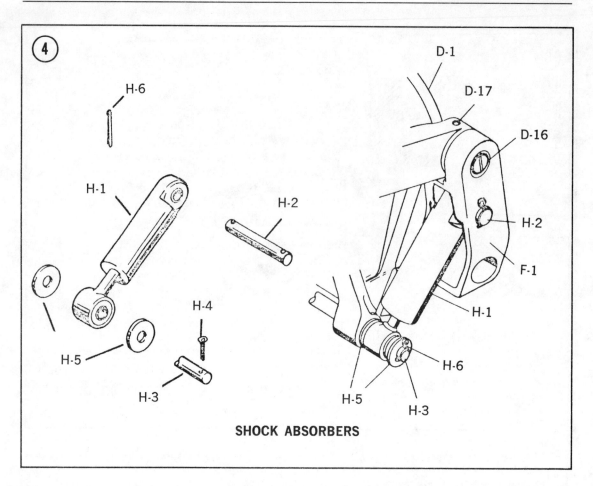

**SHOCK ABSORBERS**

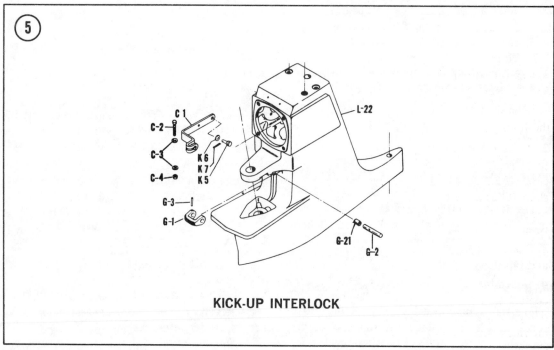

**KICK-UP INTERLOCK**

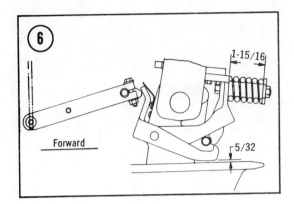

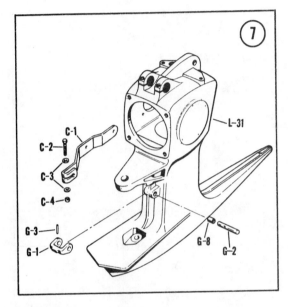

## Installation

Refer to Figures 5 and 6 for Models 81 and 91. Refer to Figure 7 for Model 80.

1. If bushing (G-21 or G-8) was removed from the housing, install new bushing.

2. Place the lugs of the interlock (B-1) around the boss located in the "throat" of the upper case (L-22 or L-31). Align pin hole in lever shaft (G-2) with hole in lug of interlock. Tap the shaft through the bores, long plain end first, from the shift control side of the case.

3. Place new pin (G-3) in the interlock lug hole and tap flush.

4. Assemble interlock lever (C-1) to the shift control side of interlock lever shaft. Do not tighten cap screw (C-2) and nut (C-4) until the interlock is properly adjusted and the interlock shift booster is attached.

### Adjustment

Shift the unit into forward, making sure the gear is completely engaged. The interlock (G-1) should release the locking arm from the adjusting pin. It allows kick-up when underwater obstacles are encountered. Shift the unit into reverse, making sure the gear is completely engaged. The interlock (G-1) should just clear the locking arm, allowing full engagement of the locking arm around the adjusting pin. This will prevent the outdrive from kicking up when in reverse gear.

> NOTE: *Interlock lever (C-1) must be horizontal to cavitation plate in neutral for proper operation of shift linkage.*

## STEERING ARM

### Removal and Disassembly

Replacement of steering control components is possible without removing the marine drive assembly. Refer to **Figure 8** (Models 81, 91) or **Figure 9** (Model 80).

1. To replace the steering rod (A-2), pull back on the quick disconnects (A-3) and free rod from ball studs. Loosen jam nut (A-4) and unscrew the 2 quick disconnects from the steering rod; replace parts as required.

2. To replace steering arm (A-6), disconnect from the steering rod (A-2) and remove the steering cable. Remove the 4 bracket bolts (A-12), flat washers (A-13), lockwashers (A-14) and nuts (A-15) securing bracket assembly to transom. Remove retainer plate (A-11), steering arm boot (A-10) and bracket (A-9) from transom. Discard gasket (A-16).

3. From the underside of bracket, punch out steering arm pivot (A-7) holding steering arm (A-6) in the bracket.

4. Unscrew quick disconnect ball from steering arm.

### Reassembly and Installation

Refer to Figure 8 (Model 81, 91) or Figure 9 (Model 80).

1. To facilitate installation, use 2 bolts (A-12) to "stack up" the steering subassembly before

**9**

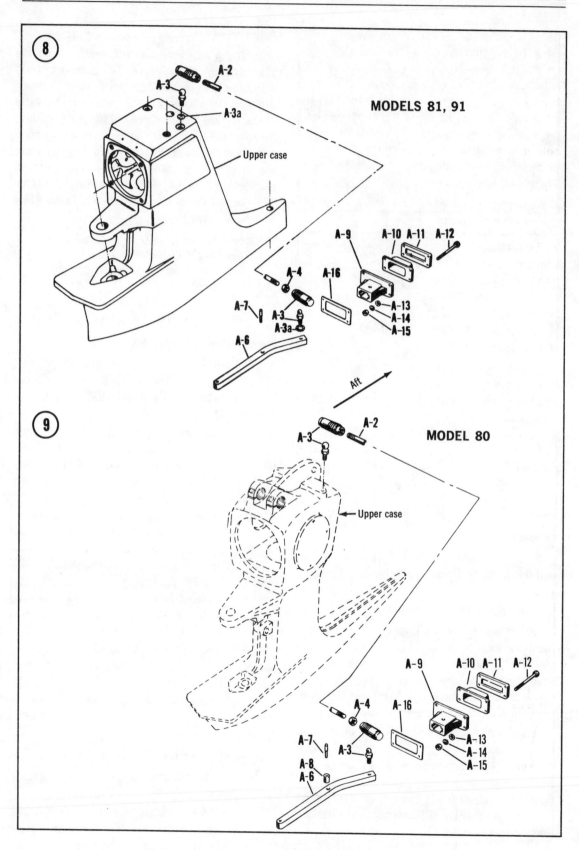

attempting to mount it in transom. Assemble the plate (A-11), boot (A-10), bracket and arm (A-9 and A-6) and the gasket (A-16, A-17) on 2 bolts, and place the group in the transom. The bend in steering arm should be outboard and away from drive unit. Assemble 2 nuts (A-15), flat washers (A-13) and lockwashers (A-14) to hold it in position before installing the second pair of bolts and nuts in the remaining holes. Tighten all nuts securely.

NOTE: *Install bolts with bolt heads outside the transom.*

2. To reassemble the steering bracket assembly, slip arm (A-6) with bushing (A-8, Model 80 only) in place through bracket (A-9). Insert pin (A-7) and press flush with the bracket housing.

3. Install the ball to the steering arm if removed in disassembly. Torque 20-30 foot-pounds.

4. Install a quick disconnect (A-3) to each end of the steering rod (A-2). Use jam nut (A-4) on end connecting to steering arm. Connect steering cable to the steering arm inside the boat.

## Adjustment

If removed, install the ball (A-3) on top of the case and on the side toward the steering arm. Torque to 20-30 foot-pounds. Place marine drive and steering wheel in a straight ahead position. Attach the steering rod quick disconnect to the ball stud on the marine drive. Turn the quick disconnects (A-3) equally in or out on rod (A-2) to achieve the proper steering angles. See **Figure 10** for proper steering angles. Make sure jam nut (A-4) on steering rod is tight.

NOTE: *Use jam nut (A-4) at one disconnect (A-3) only. Do not use on both of the disconnects.*

## TILLER BAR CONTROL
## (MODEL 80)

### Removal/Disassembly

Steering control components can be replaced without removing stern drive unit from boat.

1. Loosen one of the lug lock screws (T-13, **Figure 11**).

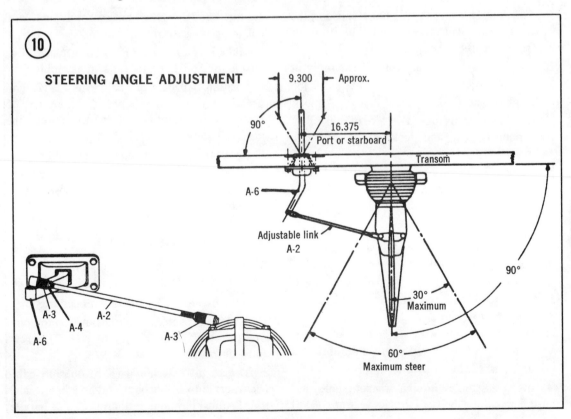

**10** STEERING ANGLE ADJUSTMENT

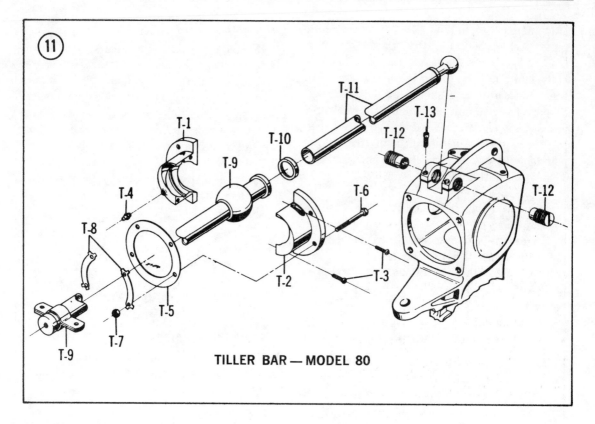

**TILLER BAR — MODEL 80**

2. Turn out ball seat (T-12) until outside tube is free of seats. Tilt tube up and slide it out of transom assembly.

3. Disconnect the steering control assembly at bracket inside boat.

4. Replace seal (T-10).

5. Bend lock strap tangs (T-8) free of nuts (T-7) and remove nuts and lock straps. Remove bolts (T-6).

6. Remove ball steering subassembly (T-1, T-2, T-3, T-4 and T-9) from transom.

7. To remove the assembly (T-9), remove 2 screws (T-3).

### Reassembly/Installation

1. Install assembly (T-9) in transom ball socket; install and tighten 2 screws. Lubricate ball surface before installing.

2. Grease assembly with water-resistant lubricant and pack seal (T-10) with same lubricant.

3. Place gasket (T-5) over assembly.

4. Insert assembly through transom hole and install mounting bolts (T-6), lock straps (T-8)

and nuts (T-7). Tighten nuts securely and bend lock strap tangs to retain nuts.

5. Make sure that seal (T-10) is in place, slide outside tube (T-11) into transom assembly.

6. Position ball between ball seats (T-12) and thread seats in until assembly is barely free to rotate. Adjust seats to center ball between the lugs. Tighten lock screws (T-13).

7. Connect the steering control assembly.

8. Should looseness develop between ball and ball seats, adjust seats to eliminate looseness yet allow free rotation.

### SHIFT CABLE

### Installation and Adjustment
### (Models 81 and 91)

Refer to **Figure 12** for this procedure.

1. Secure shift cable from transmission to upper case boss with shim (K-4), clamp (K-3), screws and lockwashers (K-8 and K-9).

2. Thread pivot terminal (K-5) on shift cable and insert outward through end hole in interlock lever. Adjust terminal until arm (C-1) is parallel

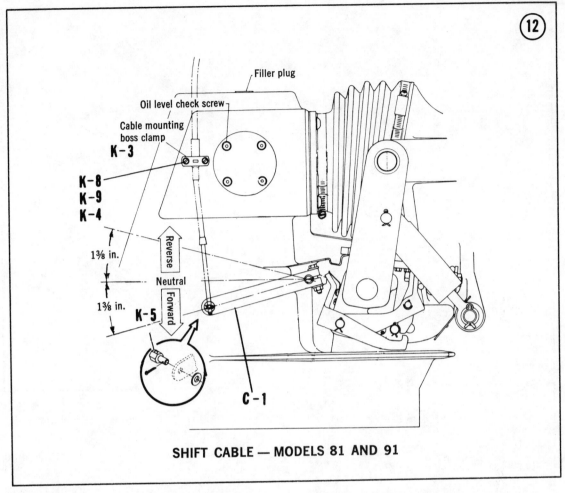

**SHIFT CABLE — MODELS 81 AND 91**

with cavitation plate when transmission is in neutral. Secure the terminal with washer and cotter pin.

3. Check interlock and adjustment as discussed in *Kick-up Interlock*.

### SHIFT BOOSTER (MODEL 80)

#### Removal/Disassembly

Refer to **Figure 13** for this procedure.

1. Unscrew and remove booster cylinder cap (B-3). Pull out rod (B-6), lockwasher (B-9), booster springs (B-5) and piston (B-4) from cylinder (B-2).

2. Loosen jam nut (B-8) and remove interlock rod clevis (B-7) from rod. Booster piston (B-4) is staked to rod; do not remove unless absolutely necessary.

#### Reassembly and Installation

1. Install bottom spring (B-5) into cylinder (B-2) and insert piston (B-4) and rod (B-6) assembly into cylinder. Install top spring (B-5) and close cylinder with lockwasher (B-9) and cap (B-3); tighten securely. Assemble locknut (B-8) and clevis (B-7) to rod.

2. Place booster assembly (B-1) in position on interlock lever (C-1). Secure lower end with clevis pin (B-10) and cotter pin (B-11).

3. Install jam nut (B-8) loosely, and screw clevis (B-7) in or out on interlock rod (B-6) until it fits properly over the interlock shift lever (J-11).

NOTE: *Interlock shift lever (J-11) should be approximately parallel to anti-cavitation plate when in neutral position.*

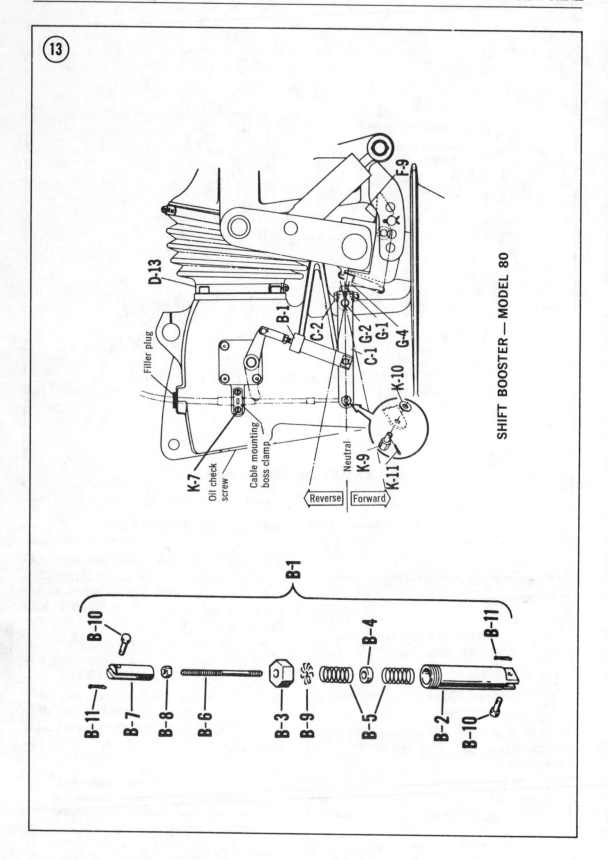

SHIFT BOOSTER — MODEL 80

4. Install clevis pin (B-10) and cotter pin (B-11) on clevis and shift lever. Temporarily turn jam nut against clevis end.

## SHIFT

### Removal and Disassembly (Model 80)

If unit is to remain on boat or in a vertical position, lower lubricant level by about one quart. Otherwise drain completely. Refer to **Figures 14 and 15.**

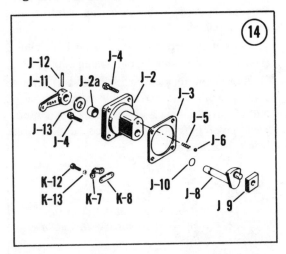

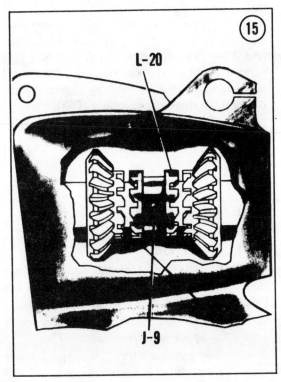

1. Remove the cotter pins (B-11) and clevis pins (B-10) which hold interlock shift booster assembly to interlock shift lever (J-11).

2. Remove the 4 cap screws (J-4) holding the interlock shift lever cap (J-2) to the upper case. Remove the interlock shift lever assembly from the case. Do not drop the shoe inside the case if it has worked free of the shaft.

3. Carefully rotate the shift lever arm (J-8) to release the spring (J-5) and poppet ball (J-6). Tap out the roll pin (J-12) from the shift lever (J-11) and remove the shift lever and shoe (J-9), shift lever arm (J-8) and washer (J-13) from the cap. Remove the O-ring (J-10) from the shift lever arm.

### Inspection

Check fit of shift lever shoe (J-9) in clutch collar (L-20). See Figure 15. Rotate shoe 90 degrees for the first "wearing", and thereafter replace the shift lever and shoe if worn excessively. Check shift lever and shift lever arm for bends, corrosion or other damage. Inspect shift lever cap. Inspect poppet spring retainer (within the shift lever cap) for wear or damage. Replace parts as necessary.

### Reassembly and Installation

Refer to Figures 14 and 15.

1. Lubricate and seat shift lever arm O-ring (J-10) in groove of shift lever arm (J-8). Install shift lever arm and shoe (J-9) through cap bore. Lever arm must be staked to secure shoe but still allow shoe rotation. Place shift lever (J-11) and washer (J-13) on shift lever arm and secure with roll pin (J-12).

NOTE: *Finger of shift lever arm (J-8) must be assembled in the* UP *position as shown. Shift lever (J-11) is marked* FRONT *on one side and* REAR *on the other. For left-hand output shaft rotation, assemble lever to arm so that word* FRONT *is showing outward. For opposite rotation, the word* REAR *must be visible.*

2. Rotate shift lever arm (J-8) to expose poppet hole in cap (J-2). Insert poppet spring (J-5) and ball (J-6) in the hole, depress spring and ball, and rotate shift lever arm back in place. Make sure poppet ball seats in all 3 ball detents when lever is shifted. Shift force should measure 8 to 15 pounds pull on spring scale.

3. Install shift lever cap assembly with new gasket (J-3) to upper case, making sure that shoe is in proper engagement with clutch gear (L-20). Secure cap to case with 4 Allen screws (J-4). Refill with lubricant.

**Shift Cable Installation and Adjustment**

1. Before installing shift cable, check the position of the interlock lever (C-1). This lever should be parallel to cavitation plate when drive is in neutral. Adjust booster clevis (B-7) to give overall lengths as shown in Figure 13. Do not reinstall cotter pin in clevis pin at this time.

2. Secure shift cable to upper case boss with shim (K-8), clamp (K-7), screws and lockwashers (K-12 and K-13). Do not tighten screws at this time. Thread pivot terminal (K-9) on shift cable and insert outward through end hole in interlock lever. Secure with washer (I-10) and cotter (I-11).

3. Shift control box into forward and make sure the outdrive gear is fully engaged. Rotate output shaft, if necessary, to check gear engagement. While in gear, the upper clevis pin on the booster should be free without bind. Readjust clevis if necessary.

4. Shift into reverse. Check for full gear engagement and free clevis pin. Cotter the clevis pin when adjustment is satisfactory.

## STERN DRIVE

### Removal

The following procedure covers removal of upper and lower case sections intact without disturbing engine or removing pivot housing assembly from transom.

The lower case may be separated from the upper case without removing complete unit from transom. See directions under *Separating Upper and Lower Units*.

Before attempting to remove outdrive assembly from pivot housing, support unit with an S hook and portable hoist. Place hook through lifting eye located on top of upper housing. Then proceed as follows (see **Figures 16 and 17**).

NOTE: *Figure 16 applies to Models 81 and 91, and Figure 17 applies to Model 80.*

1. Drain lubricant as described in Chapter Two. Disconnect shift cable, steering control and upper shock pins as described in earlier sections.

2. Loosen the front pivot housing boot clamp (D-12) and turn back pivot housing boot (D-11).

3. Raise unit to kick-up position and remove support yoke pins (D-17) by tapping upward out of pivot housing (D-1). Tap out support yoke pivot pins (D-16) to free support yoke from pivot housing.

### CAUTION
*Do not damage fiber bushings in support yoke when removing the pivot pins (D-16).*

4. To separate or remove upper and lower case assembly from the pivot housing, free interlock arm (G-4) from adjusting pin (D-14) and pull drive out and away from housing. Yoke shaft (E-2) attached to input shaft by universal joint will pull out drive sleeve splines (D-3).

5. To work on assembly, suspend unit with S hook and clamp skeg in vise. See Figure 1.

### Separating Upper and Lower Units

Refer to Figure 16 (Models 81, 91) or Figure 17 (Model 80).

1. Mark position of trim tab for proper reassembly. Remove screw (M-24) and trim tab (M-23) from lower case (M-1).

2. Remove 14 case screws with washers which secure the upper and lower cases.

3. Carefully separate upper case from the lower case. Pry them apart if necessary.

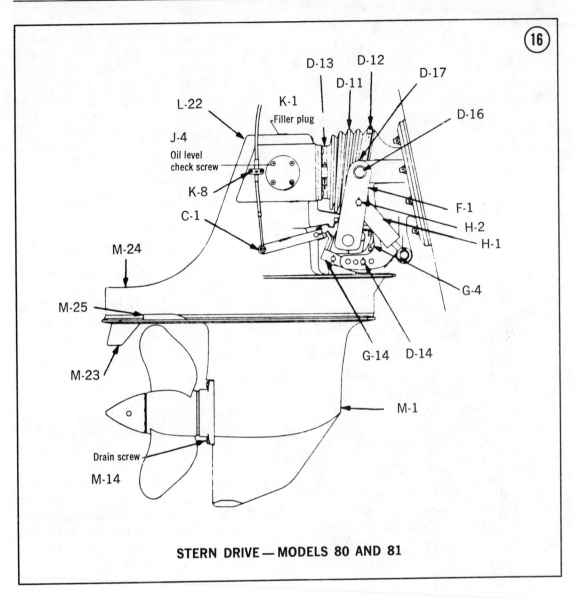

STERN DRIVE — MODELS 80 AND 81

CAUTION

*Do not damage the aluminum cases
with excessive force.*

NOTE: *Rotate output shaft slightly
to align the splines of upper stem gear
and coupling.*

4. Place upper case assembly aside. Remove drive coupling from stem gear. Discard gasket.

### Assembling Upper and Lower Units

1. Grip lower case skeg in vise as previously suggested and assemble drive coupling over spline of lower stem gear.

2. Install new gasket. Hoist upper case assembly with an S hook, align components carefully, lower to join assemblies.

3. Join cases with cap screws and washers. Tighten progressively down each side and final torque to 10-15 foot-pounds.

4. Install trim tab (M-23) with Allen screw (M-24). Torque to 10-15 foot-pounds. Set trim tab to mark made during assembly. If in doubt, set tab straight ahead and adjust after test on the boat.

9

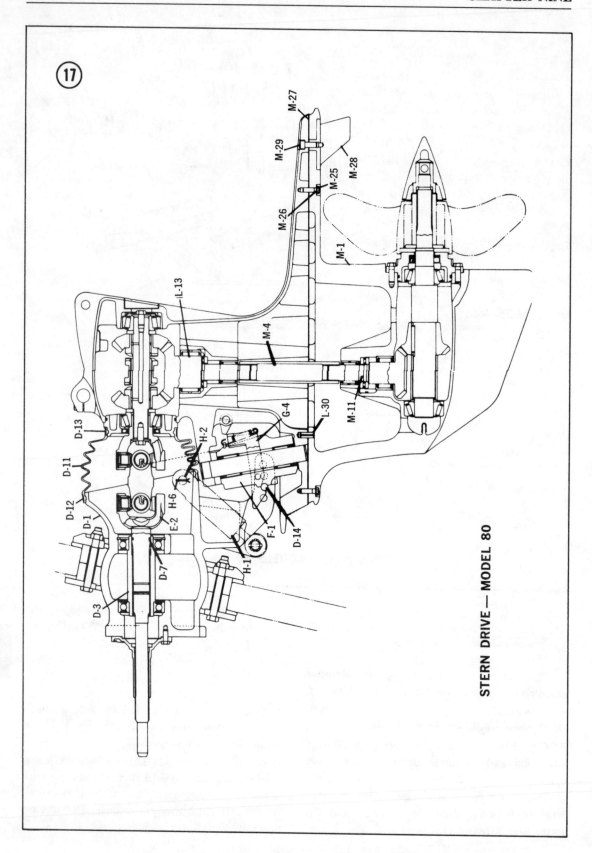

**STERN DRIVE — MODEL 80**

## Installation to Pivot Housing

Refer to Figure 16 (Models 81, 91) or Figure 17 (Model 80) unless otherwise specified.

1. Before installing outdrive unit, coat the universal joint yoke shaft splines with water resistant grease. Grease new O-ring (D-7) and install on yoke shaft (E-2).

2. Use chain hoist and S hook in lifting eye on top of marine drive. Position unit carefully while inserting splined yoke shaft (E-2) in the drive sleeve (D-3) of pivot housing. If splines do not readily engage, rotate universal joint slightly.

3. Align support yoke of outdrive with mounting bosses on pivot housing and start the two support yoke pins (D-16) into bosses.

4. Align cross-holes in yoke pins and housing bosses before tapping yoke pins in place. Secure with lock pins (D-17).

5. Tilt outdrive toward kick-up position and locate "cylinder" end of both shock absorbers (H-1, Figure 4) in the support yoke (F-1, Figure 4). Manipulate unit and install upper shock pins (H-2, Figure 4). Secure with cotter pins (H-6, Figure 4). Remove chain hoist and S hook.

6. Assemble large end of pivot housing boot (D-11), to mounting surface of pivot housing. Install boot clamp around boot and tighten. Locate boot clamp screw about 45 degrees (or halfway between horizontal and vertical) to avoid pinching boot in kick-up or turn positions and tighten securely.

7. Check relationship of cavitation plate to boat bottom. Plate should run parallel with bottom of boat. To adjust, remove the pivot housing adjusting pin (D-14) and relocate in one of the three remaining holes.

## Anodes

Two sacrificial anodes are mounted on the outdrive to prevent galvanic corrosion. One is located on lower corner of pivot support yoke on opposite side from shock absorber. The second is located on the output shaft bearing cap. Replace anodes when 50 percent used up.

## UNIVERSAL JOINT

### Disassembly

Refer to **Figure 18** for this procedure.

1. Loosen rear bearing cap boot clamp (D-13) and remove pivot housing boot (D-11) from upper case. See Figure 16.

2. Remove 2 snap rings (E-9) which hold journal bearing caps (E-7) in the universal joint end yoke (E-4). Use press or C-clamp to drive on one bearing cap to force opposite bearing part way out of yoke. If bearing cannot be worked free by hand, tap lightly on yoke lug and bearing should work out. Turn joint 180 degrees and remove remaining bearing in a similar manner. Tip journal cross to remove from end yoke lugs. Other journal cross and bearings can be removed in a similar manner. Discard O-ring (D-7) from yoke shaft (E-2).

### Inspection

Inspect the splines of the universal joint yokes for wear. Remove burrs. Replace worn or distorted parts. Check each individual joint by rotating journal cross assemblies; replace if roughness (brinnelled) or excessive play is present. Replace journal cross and bearings as a set. Lubricate bearings.

### Installation

Use journal cross kit as replacement. Refer to Figure 18.

1. Tip journal cross (E-6) into end yoke lugs (E-4) and start a bearing assembly into each lug. Do not lose bearings from caps during installation. Center the cross trunnion to match the bearing assemblies and, at the same time, press bearings flush in the lugs with a C-clamp or similar tool.

2. Tap each bearing into final position to expose snap ring groove inside bore of end yoke lug. Install snap rings (E-9) in each lug to secure bearings. Rotate joint to check operation. If other universal joint was disassembled, follow similar reassembly procedure.

3. Grease and install new O-ring (D-7) on yoke shaft (E-2).

4. Install pivot housing boot (D-11) and clamp (D-13) over universal joint assembly and around clamping surface of input shaft bearing cap (L-3). Locate clamp screw as shown in Figure 16 to avoid unnecessary abrasion of boot in kick-up position. Tighten clamp bolt securely.

9

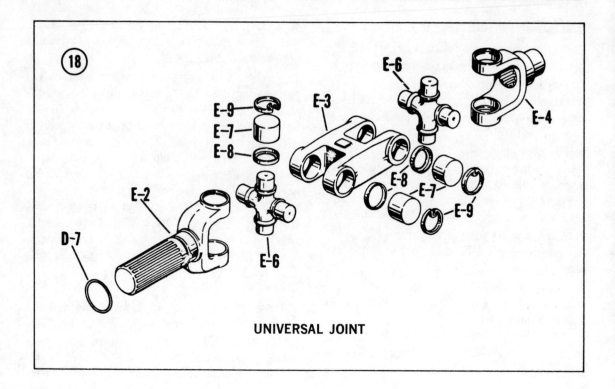

UNIVERSAL JOINT

# CHAPTER TEN

# BERKELEY AND JACUZZI
# JET DRIVES

This chapter includes Berkeley Models 12JB and 12JC and the Jacuzzi Model 12YJ. Instructions are given for removing the unit from the boat, disassembly, inspection, reassembly and reinstalling the jet drive unit in the boat.

Jet drives pump water from a water intake and discharge it through a nozzle at the stern of the boat. The reaction to the jet discharge provides propulsive thrust. For steering, the Berkeley jet employs a steerable nozzle while Jacuzzi uses a rudder-like deflector to deflect the jet stream. An optional rudder may be installed on Berkeley models to improve directional stability at lower speeds. Both manufacturers use a "gate" or "bucket", which drops down over the jet stream to reverse the direction of the stream and the boat. Neutral is achieved by partially lowering the reverse gate or bucket to balance fore and aft thrust.

Some disassembly and reassembly procedures require the use of special tools and skills that are unlikely to be found anywhere except in an authorized Jacuzzi or Berkeley repair shop. Take these jobs to your dealer.

## BERKELEY 12JB AND 12JC

### Removal

1. Disconnect universal at end of shift cable (Model 12JB only) by removing capscrew (44,

Figure 1) from reverse bucket (9, Figure 1). For Model 12JC, disconnect reverse cable from reverse bucket (9, **Figure 2**).

2. Disconnect outer jacket of reverse cable from top of tiller and clamp (12JB). Remove cable from tiller (12JC).

3. Disconnect steering cable from tiller.

4. Remove nut on steering tube. Pull tube and steering cable inside boat.

5. Remove screws holding transom housing.

6. Remove clamp and cooling hose connection to side of suction piece for engine cooling.

7. Remove 2 nuts securing hand hole extension to suction piece. Remove hand hole extension with lid in place (if so equipped).

8. Remove bolts holding suction piece to intake adapter.

9. Break gasket loose between suction piece and intake adapter and transom adapter, using broad chisel at each corner. Chisel also may be used to break loose gasket between transom adapter and boat.

10. When loose, withdraw unit through transom cutout.

### Disassembly

1. With soft mallet, tap transom adapter until it can be removed from bowl. It should go aft, over, and around steering nozzle.

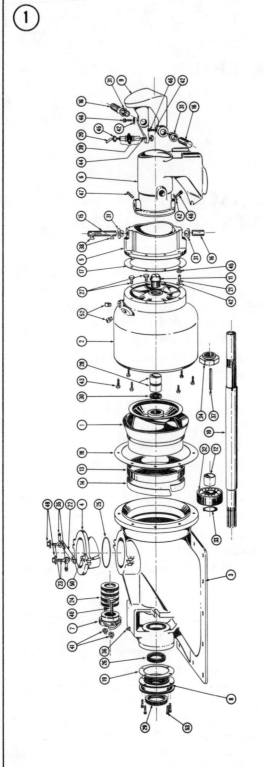

# BERKELEY 12JB

1. Aluminum or stainless steel impeller
2. Bowl
3. Suction piece
4. Hand hole cover
5. Nozzle housing
6. Steerable nozzle
7. Packing split gland
8. Bearing cap
9. Reverse bucket
10. Pump shaft
11. Bowl bearing end cap
12. Shaft seal sleeve
13. Impeller wear ring
14. Wear ring insulator
15. Tiller shaft
16. Lower nozzle and reverse bucket shaft
17. Bowl to nozzle gasket
18. Bowl to suction gasket

19. Bearing cap gasket
20. Reverse control shaft cable
21. Bowl to nozzle housing stud
22. Hand hole cover lock wrench
23. Hand hole cover rod end
24. Packing rings set (5)
25. Hand hole cover O-ring
26. Suction piece clipper seal
27. Bowl to nozzle housing capscrew
28. Bowl bearing (glacier)
29. Bearing cap clipper seal
30. Bowl clipper seal
31. Nyliner bearing
32. Thrust ball bearing
33. Bearing retaining ring
34. Impeller nut
35. Hand hole cover groove pin
36. Bearing grease fitting

37. Impeller key
38. Tiller shaft Woodruff key
39. Reverse control shaft universal joint
40. Packing gland bolt
41. Packing gland nut
42. Lower nozzle and reverse bucket shaft lockwasher
43. Bowl to suction capscrew
44. Reverse arm capscrew
45. Hexagon nut
46. Lower nozzle and reverse bucket shaft capscrew
47. Tiller shaft set screw
49. Hand hole cover flange nut
50. Lock wrench fastener
51. Fastener screw
52. Oil reservoir pipe plug
53. Bearing cap capscrew

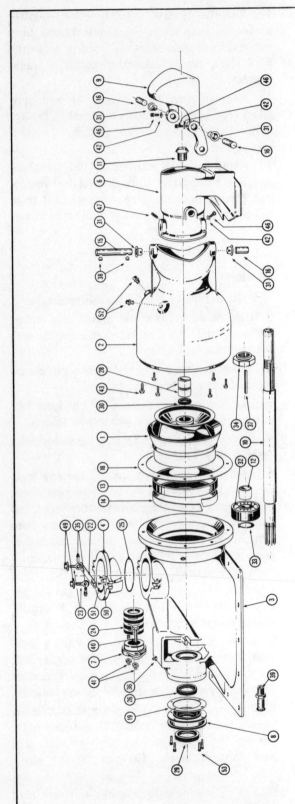

(2)

**BERKELEY 12JC**

1. Aluminum or stainless steel
   impeller
2. Bowl
3. Suction piece
4. Hand hole cover
6. Steerable nozzle
7. Packing split gland
8. Bearing cap
9. Reverse bucket
10. Pump shaft
11. Bowl bearing end cap
12. Shaft seal sleeve
13. Impeller wear ring
14. Insulator wear ring
15. Tiller shaft
16. Lower nozzle and reverse
    bucket shaft

18. Bowl to suction gasket
19. Bearing cap gasket
22. Hand hole cover lock wrench
23. Hand hole cover rod end
24. Packing rings set (5)
25. Hand hole cover O-ring
26. Suction piece clipper seal
28. Bowl bearing (glacier)
29. Bearing cap clipper seal
30. Bowl clipper seal
31. Nyliner bearing
32. Thrust ball bearing
33. Bearing retaining ring
34. Impeller nut
35. Hand hole cover groove pin
36. Bearing grease fitting

37. Impeller key
38. Tiller shaft Woodruff key
39. Engine cooling water barbed
    connector
40. Packing gland bolt
41. Packing gland nut
42. Lower nozzle and reverse bucket
    shaft lockwasher
43. Bowl to suction capscrew
46. Lower nozzle and reverse bucket
    shaft capscrew
47. Tiller shaft set screw
49. Hand hole cover flange nut
50. Lock wrench fastener
51. Fastener screw
52. Oil reservoir pipe plug
53. Bearing cap capscrew

**10**

2. For Model 12JB only, remove bolts and remove steering assembly from bowl.

3. Remove bolts holding bowl and tap bowl with soft mallet to break gasket loose. Carefully withdraw bowl parallel to shaft until it clears shaft. Be careful not to spill oil from back bearing.

4. Clean chrome end of shaft and tape surface to prevent damage.

5. Remove impeller nut (34, Figure 1).

6. Using a large gear puller, remove impeller. Tighten puller jacking screw, then tap it with hammer to break impeller loose. Repeat until impeller breaks loose and puller jacking nut turns easier. Remove impeller key.

7. Remove ball bearing cap (8, Figure 1) by removing screws (53, Figure 1). Use hammer and soft wood block to drive impeller shaft and thrust bearing out of suction piece.

CAUTION
*Do not remove bearing unless it is damaged and must be replaced. Using a bearing puller will probably damage the bearing.*

8. Remove snap ring (32, Figure 1). Remove thrust bearing (33, Figure 1) with gear or bearing puller.

9. Remove wear ring (12, Figure 1) with rolling head of a pry bar. Insert bar under wear ring and roll back, similar to using a claw hammer.

CAUTION
*Wear ring should not be removed unless it is to be replaced. Wear ring has a plastic liner which can be removed either before or after removing ring.*

10. Remove bowl bearing (28, Figure 1). To do this, remove end plug (11) using large screwdriver. Tap bearing out, using bearing removal drift tool. Do not remove bearing unless replacement is required.

11. Remove tiller shaft (15, Figure 1). First, remove set screw and tap shaft down with soft wood block and hammer until Woodruff key can be seen in nozzle housing. Then, remove Woodruff key with pliers or screwdriver and drive shaft upward with block and hammer while rotating tiller until shaft can be removed.

12. Remove reverse bucket. First, remove socket head cap screw (46, Figure 1) and drive out reverse bucket shaft (16) with a soft drift bar. Then, remove steerable nozzle in same manner.

13. Remove nuts (41, Figure 1) and split gland (7, Figure 1) with lock wrench (22). Remove packing rings (24, Figure 1) with screwdriver.

14. Remove thrust bearings (26, Figure 1) by inserting screwdriver through packing window and driving seal out. Remove seal (29) from bearing cap by pushing it out with screwdriver.

**Assembly**

Refer to Figures 1 and 2 for this procedure.

1. Remove all traces of old gasket from sealing surfaces, and clean surfaces thoroughly with solvent such as acetone.

2. Verify that wear ring and suction piece mating surfaces are clean and smooth.

3. Insert wear ring insulator (14) halfway into suction piece bore with L-shaped lip leading.

4. Insert wear ring (13) into insulator with beveled edge leading.

5. Push wear ring down evenly, keeping wear ring parallel to face of flange on suction piece. Tap wear ring into place with wooden block and hammer. Make certain wear ring enters bore straight by tapping evenly around circumference. If insulator folds or wrinkles, remove all parts and reinstall.

6. When wear ring is all the way in, tap sharply with wood block and hammer at 4 equally spaced points to firmly seat.

7. Insert packing rings (24) in stuffing box. Push them down with fingers as far as they will go. Rings must fit tightly against each other with joints staggered 180 degrees to prevent leakage.

8. Place split gland (7) in position and fasten loosely in place with bolts (40) and nuts (41). Smooth insides of packing rings so shaft will pass through easily. Do not tighten gland until later.

9. Verify that bearing housing and seal surfaces are clean.

10. Insert seal (26) in bottom of bearing bore with lip and spring toward stuffing box. Tap into place with wooden block and hammer until tightly seated.

11. Place seal (29) with lip toward bearing cap. Tap into place with block and hammer.

12. Slide sleeve (12) over spline and push against shoulder on shaft with beveled edge leading.

13. Slide thrust bearing (32) over spline and start it onto shaft, making certain it is true with shaft. Push onto shaft by hand as far as it will go.

14. Select a drift tube that will fit over shaft and rest on bearing inner race. Tap drift with hammer until bearing is tight against sleeve (12). Make certain that the bearing is true and square with the shaft.

15. Install snap ring in shaft groove to retain bearing.

16. Tape shaft end smoothly with one layer (only) of plastic tape; tape should cover shoulder where impeller fits. Carefully insert shaft through stuffing box and push into place until bearing contacts suction piece.

17. Push bearing into seat by hand, if possible. If not, tap in with wood block and hammer. Keep bearing clean.

18. Pack bearing and bearing cap (8) with Shell Alvania No. 2 grease (or equivalent). Install gasket (19) and bolt bearing cap into place.

19. Place key (37) in shaft keyway and tap in with wooden block and hammer. Make certain key is properly seated.

20. Coat bore of impeller with black Loctite, as well as end of shaft where impeller seats.

21. Slide impeller over shaft. Align key with keyway. Slide hollow drift bar over shaft and tap impeller into place tightly against shaft shoulder. Brace other end of shaft against a solid surface while tapping.

22. Thread nut (34) onto shaft and tighten securely.

23. Place bowl (2) on bench with large end up. Insert bowl bearing (28) into bore.

24. Tap bearing carefully into place with a soft metal drift against bearing inner race until bearing is flush with shoulder.

25. Turn bowl over and install other bearing in a like manner. Thread in bowl end cap (11); use black Loctite on threads.

26. Turn bowl over again and press seal (30) into counterbowl above bearing until flush. Make certain lip and spring of seal are forward.

27. Stick gasket (18) to face of suction piece with grease. Oil end of shaft with outboard motor lower gear oil.

28. Place bowl over impeller with oil holes and plugs (52) up. Guide end shaft into seal very carefully so that seal spring is not disturbed.

29. Bolt bowl into place with cap screws (43). Tighten bolts and rotate shaft to see that it turns freely. If not, loosen bolts and look for binding parts. Adjust as required and retighten bolts. Recheck shaft (it must turn freely).

30. Remove 2 plugs (52) and fill with outboard motor lower end gear oil.

31. When full, rotate shaft, and add oil if required. Replace plugs tightly.

32. Tighten nuts (41) on packing gland evenly until shaft does not turn easily by hand.

33. Leave in this condition until unit has run in boat, then retighten.

34. Insert nyliner bearings (31) into side holes in steering nozzle.

35. Slip reverse bucket (9) over bearings. Insert shaft (16) through reverse bucket and into bearings with threaded hole out. Line up with hole in boss of reverse bucket.

36. Screw in socket head screw (36) with lockwasher (32) in place. Use red Loctite on threads and tighten securely.

37. Insert nyliner bearings (31) into holes in nozzle housing (5) from inside. Bearing shoulders must be toward inside.

38. Slide steerable nozzle (6) into place against shoulders of bearings.

39. Insert lower nozzle shaft (16) into bearing and into steerable nozzle with thread end first. Align it so that screw (46) and lockwasher can be inserted through the steerable nozzle boss and into lower nozzle shaft. Use red Loctite on threads and tighten securely.

40. Insert tiller shaft (15) and push in until tiller contacts steering housing. Insert Wood-

**10**

ruff key (38) through nozzle housing and into keyway in tiller shaft. Tap in with wood block and make certain it is straight and parallel to the shaft.

41. Pull shaft upward and make certain Woodruff key goes into the keyway in the steerable nozzle boss.

42. Pull shaft up until counterbore in shaft centers with thread in steerable nozzle boss. Install and tighten set screw (47), using red Loctite on threads.

43. Install bowl-to-nozzle gasket (17) on bowl, using grease on bowl gasket surface. Make certain gasket holes are properly aligned.

44. Join nozzle housing to bowl and pull up tight with nuts (41), lockwashers (42), and cap screws (27). Install cap screws in 2 holes behind lever of reverse bracket.

## Installation

1. Make sure that intake adapter (1, **Figure 3**) mating surfaces are clean.

2. Apply grease and install gasket (3, Figure 3) on intake adapter.

3. Apply grease to shaft spline and slide jet unit into transom opening. Slide shaft spline into spline of double universal joint attached to the engine.

4. Slide unit in until holes in suction piece (3, Figure 1) match holes in intake adapter (1, Figure 3).

5. Bolt in place with cap screws and washers (5 and 6, Figure 3).

6. Install O-ring over bowl and into slot. Make certain O-ring fits tightly.

7. Lubricate O-ring and mating surface in bore of transom housing with silicone spray or grease.

8. Pull transom housing over steering assembly and bowl and over O-ring. Push housing on evenly.

9. When transom housing is about ¼ in. away from transom, install gasket with largest radius corners at bottom between transom adapter and transom and line up with bolts in transom housing. Make certain gasket remains in place as all bolts are installed.

10. Pull transom housing snug against transom by tightening bolts. Make certain O-ring has not pushed out of position. Otherwise a leak will certainly develop.

11. Insert steering cable through transom housing hole with rubber in place and hold steering tube in transom housing with nut. Do not tighten nut until steering cable is attached to tiller with cap screw and nuts. Center rubber hose in transom housing and tighten nut.

12. Connect shift cable to tiller with clamp and bolts. For Model 12JC, make sure clamp is in bolts. For Model 12JB, make sure clamp is in slot of outer jacket of the shift cable. For Model 12JC, attach cable to tiller.

13a. For Model 12JB, place end of universal joint (39) against lever of reverse bucket (9). Apply red Loctite to screw (44), install screw and pull up tight. Adjust reverse as required.

13b. For Model 12JC, apply red Loctite to threads at end of reverse cable. Thread one adjusting nut on cable (hex end up) and slide end of cable through reverse control arm pin. Attach other adjusting nut, hex end down. Do not crush shoulders of nyliner bearing with adjusting nuts.

14. Install hand hole extension, if so equipped, making sure that O-ring is in place. Tighten nuts evenly.

15. Connect cooling water hose to jet drive and clamp securely.

## JACUZZI 12YJ

### Removal

1. Disconnect steering and shift from tiller and reverse gate, respectively.

2. Remove rudder from deflector by removing 4 rudder bolts, lockwashers, and nuts.

3. Remove transom adapter-deflector assembly from transom of boat.

4. Disconnect engine water line and remove the pipe.

> NOTE: *To repair bowl bearing, impeller, or wear plate, it is not necessary to remove unit from boat.*

5. Remove inspection cap hold down bolts and inspection cap (see **Figure 4**).

6. Remove 8 bolts from top side of flange, and 2 bolts under aft section of flange (see **Figure 5**).

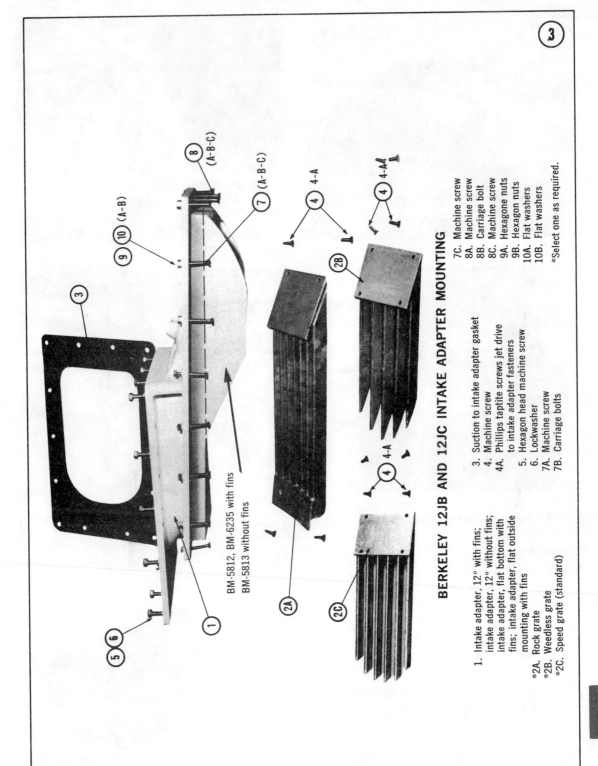

**BERKELEY 12JB AND 12JC INTAKE ADAPTER MOUNTING**

1. Intake adapter, 12° with fins;
   intake adapter, 12° without fins;
   intake adapter, flat bottom with
   fins; intake adapter, flat outside
   mounting with fins
*2A. Rock grate
*2B. Weedless grate
*2C. Speed grate (standard)

3. Suction to intake adapter gasket
4. Machine screw
4A. Phillips taptite screws jet drive
    to intake adapter fasteners
5. Hexagon head machine screw
6. Lockwasher
7A. Machine screw
7B. Carriage bolts

7C. Machine screw
8A. Machine screw
8B. Carriage bolt
8C. Machine screw
9A. Hexagone nuts
9B. Hexagon nuts
10A. Flat washers
10B. Flat washers

*Select one as required.

BM-5812, BM-6235 with fins
BM-5813 without fins

10

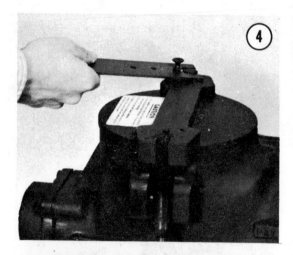

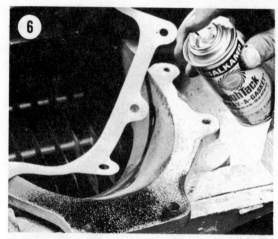

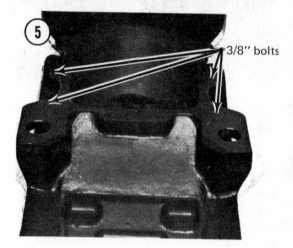

3/8" bolts

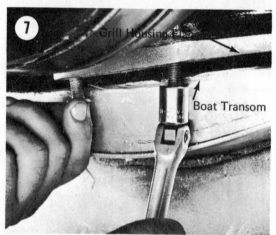

Grill Housing

Boat Transom

7. Remove jet unit through transom cutout.

## Installation

1. Clean flanges of suction piece and grille housing. Apply gasket sealer to grille housing and install new gasket (see **Figure 6**).

2. Insert jet unit through transom cutout and at same time engage engine coupling and splined shaft. Seat unit on grille housing, taking care not to disturb gasket.

3. Install 8 bolts on top side of flange and 2 aft bolts (see **Figure 7**). Torque to 20 ft.-lb.

4. Install new O-ring in groove in inspection cap (see **Figure 8**). Install cap and tighten hold-down bolts hand-tight. Lock by snapping lock wrench into place.

5. Install the water outlet pipe and the engine water hose.

O-ring

6. Place new O-ring in bowl groove and apply light coat of grease.

7. Apply Dow Corning 781 sealant or equivalent to transom adapter as shown in **Figure 9**, being careful to avoid breaks in sealant bead.

8. Place transom adapter over bowl. Press adapter over O-ring maintaining equal pressure on all sides. Check for correct O-ring placement and seal by inserting feeler guage between bowl and adapter as shown in **Figure 10**.

Insert Feeler Gauge Here

9. Install transom adapter bolts and torque to 11 ft.-lb.

## Steering and Reversing Controls Installation

1. Assemble steering tube to steering cable and tighten jam nut until rubber grommet com-

presses. Do not compress grommet too tightly or steering tube will become rigid. Make certain large flat washers are installed on either side of transom adapter (see **Figure 11**).

2. Pull shift cable through transom adapter and tighten until cable will not slip. Distance from cable locknut to cable end bracket groove should be 19¼ inches.

3. Hook steering cable to tiller arm and shift cable to reverse gate. See later procedures for adjustment of controls.

## Disassembly

The following procedure requries the use of precision measuring equipment and special tools, such as bearing pullers. If this equipment is not available, remove the jet from the boat and take it to an authorized Jacuzzi repair shop. If equipment shown or suitable substitutes are available, proceed as follows.

1. After unit has been removed from boat, remove eight ⅜ in. bolts holding bowl to suction piece (see **Figure 12**).

2. Carefully pry bowl from suction piece and remove bowl from end of impeller shaft.

3. Place special shaft holder over spline end of shaft and remove impeller nut (see **Figure 13**).

NOTE: *If special shaft holder is not available, remove bearing cap as described in Step 6. Hold spline with 2 pieces of wood bolted together at one end as shown in* **Figure 14**.

10

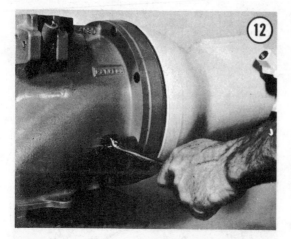

Shaft Holder

Wear Plate

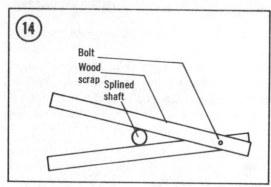

Bolt
Wood
scrap  Splined
shaft

4. Pull off impeller, using bearing puller as shown in **Figure 15**.

CAUTION
*Do not drop, hit, or bump exposed end of shaft after impeller is removed, as damage to seals and bearings could result.*

5. Remove wear plate (see **Figure 16**).

6. Remove 4 bolts holding bearing cap to suction piece (over spline end of shaft) and remove bearing cap (see **Figure 17**).

NOTE: *Make note of number of shims found between bearing cap and bearing housing.*

7. Place cap in vise and punch out lip seal from back side.

8. Pull impeller shaft and bearing assembly out of suction piece.

9. Hold impeller shaft between soft vise jaws and remove thrust bearing retaining pin (see **Figure 18**).

10. Remove thrust bearing from shaft as shown in **Figure 19**. Arbor press can also be used if available.

3⁄... Bearing Cap Bolts

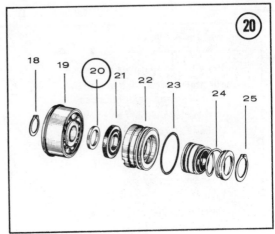

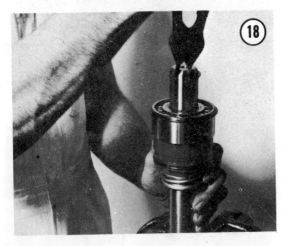

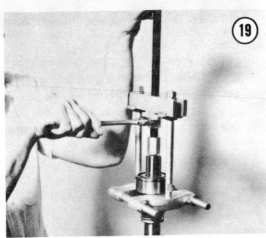

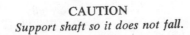

CAUTION
*Support shaft so it does not fall.*

NOTE: *Do not misplace thrust bearing located between seal housing and bearing (20, Figure 20).*

11. Remove seal housing.

12. Pull mechanical seal off shaft by hand. Retaining ring may remain on shaft. Place in vise and pry out lip seal. Turn over and tap out stationary seal seat, taking care not to crack or chip ceramic seal. Do not discard O-ring.

13. Remove 4 screws and remove bowl wear ring with inside bushing puller or screwdriver.

14. Check bowl bearing dimensions with inside calipers before removing and compare to **Table 1**.

15. Pry out lip seal and remove bowl bearings with blind hole puller (see **Figure 21**).

16. Disconnect shift and steering cables, and remove bolt from deflector bottom pivot pin. Use this bolt in end of pin to pull pivot pin. Remove trim cap bolts, lift off trim cap, and remove deflector (see **Figure 22**).

Table 1      DIMENSIONAL TOLERANCE

| Part Description | Tolerance (in.) |
| --- | --- |
| Impeller-to-wear plate clearance | 0.001 to 0.010 |
| Normal variation due to runout or blade length differences | 0.005 |
| Impeller adjustment shims | |
|     14-0829-03 (0.030 in. thick) | 0.010 impeller adjustment |
|     14-1903-00 (0.015 in. thick) | 0.005 impeller adjustment |
| Maximum shim adjustment | 7 (sets) |
| Bowl bearings-to-shaft | 0.011 maximum |
| Reverse gate pivot pin bushings | 0.015 maximum |
| Deflector pivot pin bushings | 0.015 maximum |
| Trim screw end plug | 0.013 maximum |
| Impeller hub wear ring | 0.020 to 0.010 maximum |

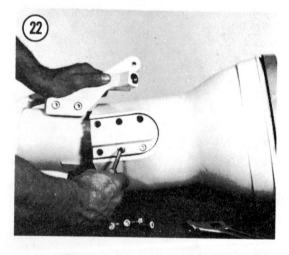

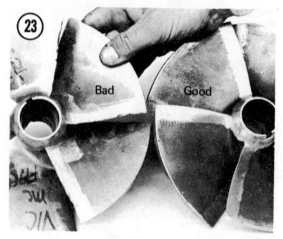

17. Remove bolt from reverse gate pivot pin and use bolt to pull pivot pins on both sides. Remove reverse gate.

18. Loosen set screw, remove cotter pin from trim screw nut, unscrew nut, and unscrew trim screw from assembly.

### Cleaning, Inspection, and Repair

1. Inspect leading edge of impeller for nicks and deformation (see **Figure 23**). Performance can be partially restored by filing edge back to original shape.

> **CAUTION**
> *Do not change basic contour of blade. Replace impeller if severely damaged.*

2. Inspect wear ring. Scoring on face of ring is normal and should not be reason for replacement unless correct impeller-wear plate clearances cannot be obtained (see adjustment procedure below).

3. Check impeller shaft spline for excessive damage or wear (see **Figure 24**).

4. Inspect impeller shaft tail section for wear or roughness. Minimum dimension is 1.1218 in.

> **CAUTION**
> *If tail section is rough, carefully check bowl bearings for damage before reassembly.*

5. Check thrust bearing washer inner shoulder. If not square, replace washer.

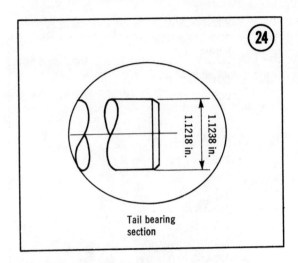

Tail bearing section

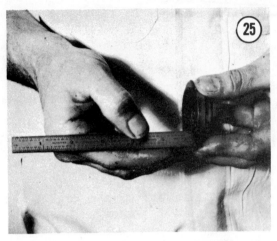

6. If bent impeller shaft is suspected, have shaft checked in lathe for runout of 0.003 in. maximum.

> NOTE: *Service bearings only in a clean area to avoid damage to bearings. Do not spin or roll bearings before they are cleaned, as dirt in raceway could cause damage.*

7. Immerse bearing in solvent (such as Solvasal) and agitate frequently until all grease and dirt is removed. Carefully turn one race while flushing to help dislodge internal dirt and grease. If available, use compressed air to dry bearing, taking care not to allow bearing to spin.

8. As soon as bearing is dry, lubricate at once with light oil to prevent rust.

9. Check bearing thoroughly and replace if any of the following conditions exist.

   a. Rusted balls or raceway

   b. Fractured ring

   c. Worn, galled, or abrased surfaces

   d. Badly discolored (bluish) balls or race (slight discoloration is not cause for discarding)

10. Clean thrust bearing seal assembly with solvent and inspect for cracks and wear. Replace damaged or suspect parts.

11. Measure shoulder on seal face (see **Figure 25**). New seal measures 3/32 in. Minimum allowable, 1/64 in. Replace if less than 1/32 in.

12. If seal face is distorted (not smooth and flat), replace seal assembly.

12. Replace friction ring if not resilient and flexible.

13. Clean seal housing lip seal with solvent and inspect lip area. Replace if worn flat or deteriorated.

14. Replace seal housing O-ring.

15. On suction piece, inspect water bleed hole on port side of bearing to verify that it is not plugged.

16. Clean flange area and inspect for damage such as nicks and cracks.

17. Verify that wear plate dowel pins are in the correct position.

18. Check inspection cap braces for cracks. If damaged, replace. Replace inspection cap O-ring.

19. Inspect bowl O-ring for cuts or hardness and replace if defective. Inspect bowl vanes and nozzle arc for chips and cracks. Minor nicks should be removed from vane leading edges with file.

20. Clean and inspect wear ring. Measure diameters of impeller hub and wear ring. Clearance between the 2 must be 0.010 to 0.030 in.

21. Clean bowl bearings and lip seal with solvent and dry.

22. Inspect bearings for wear and check inside diameter of bearings with outside diameter of shaft. Maximum difference is 0.011 in. If new shaft is installed, new bearing is required. If bearings are removed from bowl, replace them.

23. Examine lip seal. If worn or deteriorated, replace.

**10**

24. Clean and inspect transom adapter. Smooth minor scratches in bore with No. 20 emery cloth. Replace cable sealing gland and/or steering tube rubber grommet if hard or deteriorated.

25. Inspect tiller arm for corrosion or cracks. Inspect pivot pins for wear (maximum clearance between pin and bushing in holes is 0.015 in.). Replace nyliner bearings if worn or galled. Replace pivot pins if badly worn or galled. Inspect rudder flange area for damage.

26. Check rudder, reverse gate, and trim assembly. Replace badly worn or cracked parts and all gaskets.

**Assembly**

1. Install mechanical seal retaining ring (25, Figure 20).

2. Install seal housing O-ring (23) on seal housing (22).

3. Install lip seal (21), with lip facing inward in seal housing (22). Press in until seal seats against bottom of housing.

4. Verify that O-ring is installed in ceramic seal groove and press seal (24) into seal housing (22) by hand. Seal face will extend 1/16 in. when properly seated. Handle ceramic seal carefully and avoid getting ground surface dirty.

5. Apply light coat of clean oil to lip of lip seal.

6. Place lip seal ramp over impeller shaft and assemble mechanical seat to shaft as shown in **Figure 26**.

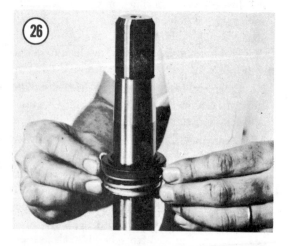

7. Compress mechanical seal assembly (Figure 26) and hold with 2 metal clamps which can

be made of 1/16 in. soft steel stock. Coat seal area of shaft with clean oil.

8. Place seal housing on shaft with ceramic seal facing mechanical seal (see **Figure 27**). Make certain lip seal rides over thrust washer shoulder and does not turn under. Remove seal protector.

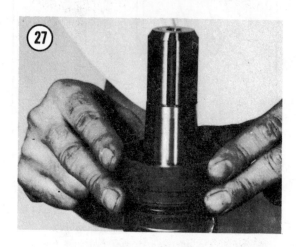

9. Place thrust washer (20, Figure 20) on shaft.

10. Place thrust bearing over shaft with outer race snap ring away from seal assembly (see **Figure 28**).

11. Push bearing down as shown in **Figure 29** until thrust bearing bottoms on thrust washer shoulder.

12. Install thrust bearing retaining ring (see **Figure 30**).

13. Remove metal clamps installed in Step 7 above and inspect to verify that seal faces are pressed together.

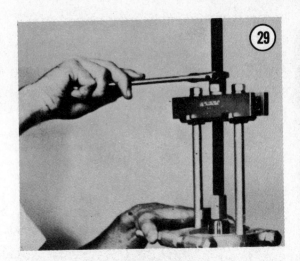

Bleed Hole

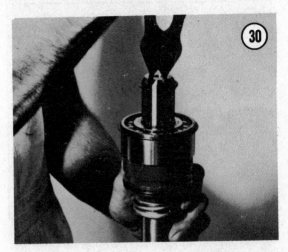

14. Apply clean oil to the bearing cavity in suction piece.

15. Install shaft, making certain bleed hole in seal housing is toward bottom of suction piece (see **Figure 31**).

16. Install bearing cap lip seal with lip facing inward. Press seal in squarely (see **Figure 32**).

17. Install bearing cap with lubrication pressure relief hole facing starboard, and bolt loosely in place.

18. Place impeller wear plate in impeller cavity; engage dowel pins at top and bottom.

19. Place square key in shaft keyway.

20. Install impeller over tail of shaft and engage keyway; avoid bumping shaft end.

21. Hold spline end of shaft and install impeller locknut with split side out. Tighten nut to no more than 20 ft.-lb. (do not overtighten).

22. Apply clean oil to bowl bearing cavity and to inside diameter of bearings.

NOTE: *Make certain splits in bearings are aligned when installing bearings.*

23. Use long end of bearing mandrel (Part No. 50-0064-or) to press fit bearing in until mandrel seats on lip seal shoulder.

24. Use short end of same mandrel to press second bearing in until tool seats on lip seal shoulder.

25. Press bowl lip seal squarely in with lips facing outward (see **Figure 33**).

26. Use 2 screws to align wear ring holes with tapped holes in bowl. Tap wear ring into place and torque screws to 2 ft.-lb.

27. Coat bowl end of impeller shaft with oil and place new O-ring on wear plate (see **Figure 34**).

**10**

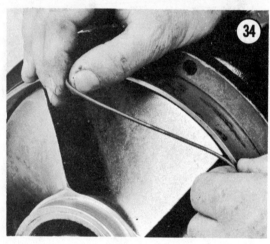

bolts with lock or tab washers. If lockwashers are used, torque to 6 ft.-lb. If tab washers are used, align flat of bolt head with tab and bend tabs to secure.

32. Oil threads of trim screw and insert in trim cap. Turn trim pivot assembly about halfway down screw and install nut.

33. Turn nut until it tightens up on trim cap, then back it off to first slot that aligns with cotter pin hole. Install cotter pin.

34. Check operation of trim screw. End-play should be 0.013 in. maximum. Measure between nut and trim cap with feeler gauge, at point shown in **Figure 35**.

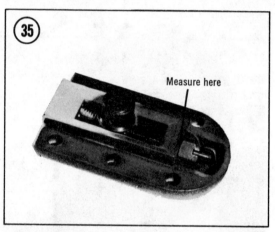

Measure here

35. Apply light oil to top and bottom pivot pin holes in deflector.

36. Insert nyliner bearings in holes and position deflector in bowl.

37. Insert flat washer between bushing and bottom pivot pin hole (see **Figure 36**).

38. Insert bottom pivot pin, and align hole in pin with hole in bowl. Install bolt and washer through holes.

39. Install gasket on trim cup flange with sealing compound.

40. Install trim cap on bowl while inserting trim pivot assembly into bushing in top of deflector.

41. Check free movement of deflector and bolt trim cap down. Torque bolts to 11 ft.-lb.

**Impeller/Wear Plate Adjustment**

See Table 1 above for clearances.

1. Remove inspection cap.

Install bowl on suction piece and torque bolts to 20 ft.-lb. Install auxiliary water outlet and torque to 15 ft.-lb.

CAUTION
*Do not allow end of shaft to reverse bowl bearing lip seal.*

28. Loosen bearing cap and install shims (removed earlier) between suction piece and thrust bearing outer race retaining ring.

29. Adjust impeller wear plate clearance using *Impeller Wear Plate Adjustment* procedure in this chapter.

30. Install bearing cap; torque screws 20 ft.-lb.

31. Lubricate bearings and install them in reverse gate holes. Place reverse gate in position and insert pivot pins; align bolt hole in pin with bolt hole in deflector. Install pivot pin retaining

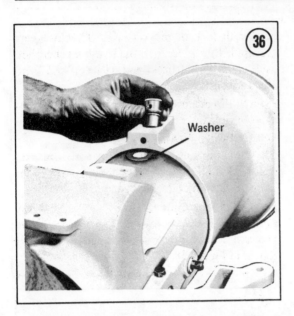

2. Using feeler gauge, measure clearance of all impeller blades (see **Figure 37**). When blade with least clearance is located, compare with Table 1. If clearance is beyond 0.010 in., shims (2 per set) must be added.

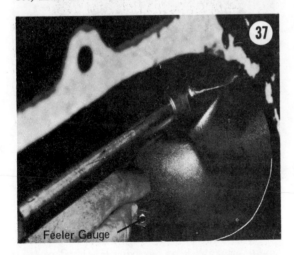

3. Loosen bearing cap. Insert screwdriver through inspection opening and aft of seal spring retaining pin. Pry entire impeller and shaft bearing assembly forward until impeller seats on wear plate (see **Figure 38**).

4. Insert shims, 2 at a time, of same thickness (one on either side) between existing shims and suction piece, until space is filled.

NOTE: *Shims must be between bearing retaining ring and suction piece.*

### CAUTION
*Make certain number and thickness of bearings on each side are identical to avoid cracking bearing cap.*

5. Tighten bearing cap and remeasure smallest clearance. Make certain clearance is within tolerance (0.001 to 0.010 in.). Also make certain impeller does not seat against wear plate at any point.

**Steering Deflector Adjustment**

With most steering systems there will be about 1½ turns of the wheel "lock-to-lock."

1. To insure that deflector reaches its full travel in both directions, disconnect steering cable from tiller arm and center deflector (**Figure 39**).

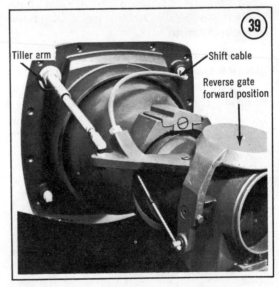

2. Locate center position of steering wheel and adjust steering tube (see Step 3) so that cable will engage tiller arm while both wheel and deflector are in their center positions.

3. To move tube, loosen jam nut on outside and loosen steering cable from tube.

    a. For further travel of deflector to port (left) screw in tube.

    b. For further travel of deflector to starboard (right) screw out tube.

4. Tighten steering cable to tube. Tighten inside jam nut by hand. Hold tube with wrench and tighten outside jam nut only enough to prevent any leakage.

### Reverse Gate Adjustment

The engine couples to the jet drive directly, so that the jet operates as long as the engine runs. The shift cable moves only the reverse gate to provide either forward or reverse thrust. Neutral is achieved by providing equal and opposite forward and reverse thrust.

When the shift lever is fully forward, the bottom edge of the reverse gate should clear the top edge of the deflector opening. See Figure 39.

When the shift lever is fully in reverse, the reverse gate should be firmly against the deflector. See **Figure 40**.

Adjust the length of the shift cable at the reverse gate end.

### Trim Adjustment

The unique design of the Jacuzzi Jet Drive gives it the ability to trim the attitude of the boat. Trim by changing the angle of the deflector up or down. The desired position is locked in by a set screw in the trim cap just above the trim head (see **Figure 41**).

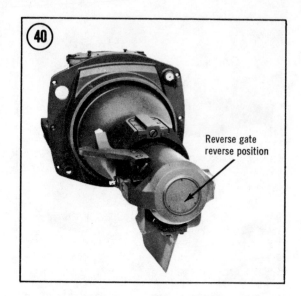

Reverse gate reverse position

1. Loosen setscrew.

2. Turn the trim screw counterclockwise until it hits the upper stop.

3. To trim the deflector parallel to the boat bottom, turn the trim screw 5 complete turns from the full up position. Each turn and a half moves the deflector one degree.

4. Any further adjustment of the trim must be made after the boat has been launched or from past experience with a particular hull design.

5. Tighten setscrew.

# INDEX

11